# 15 Minutes of Fame

# 15 Minutes of Fame

## Becoming a Star in the
## YouTube Revolution

Frederick Levy

ALPHA

A member of Penguin Group (USA) Inc.

## ALPHA BOOKS

Published by the Penguin Group

Penguin Group (USA) Inc., 375 Hudson Street, New York, New York 10014, USA

Penguin Group (Canada), 90 Eglinton Avenue East, Suite 700, Toronto, Ontario M4P 2Y3, Canada (a division of Pearson Penguin Canada Inc.)

Penguin Books Ltd., 80 Strand, London WC2R 0RL, England

Penguin Ireland, 25 St. Stephen's Green, Dublin 2, Ireland (a division of Penguin Books Ltd.)

Penguin Group (Australia), 250 Camberwell Road, Camberwell, Victoria 3124, Australia (a division of Pearson Australia Group Pty. Ltd.)

Penguin Books India Pvt. Ltd., 11 Community Centre, Panchsheel Park, New Delhi—110 017, India

Penguin Group (NZ), 67 Apollo Drive, Rosedale, North Shore, Auckland 1311, New Zealand (a division of Pearson New Zealand Ltd.)

Penguin Books (South Africa) (Pty.) Ltd., 24 Sturdee Avenue, Rosebank, Johannesburg 2196, South Africa

Penguin Books Ltd., Registered Offices: 80 Strand, London WC2R 0RL, England

International Standard Book Number: 978-1-59257-765-1
Library of Congress Catalog Card Number: 2007941351

10   09   08      8   7   6   5   4   3   2   1

Interpretation of the printing code: The rightmost number of the first series of numbers is the year of the book's printing; the rightmost number of the second series of numbers is the number of the book's printing. For example, a printing code of 08-1 shows that the first printing occurred in 2008.

*Printed in the United States of America*

**Note:** This publication contains the opinions and ideas of its author. It is intended to provide helpful and informative material on the subject matter covered. It is sold with the understanding that the author and publisher are not engaged in rendering professional services in the book. If the reader requires personal assistance or advice, a competent professional should be consulted.

The author and publisher specifically disclaim any responsibility for any liability, loss, or risk, personal or otherwise, which is incurred as a consequence, directly or indirectly, of the use and application of any of the contents of this book.

**Trademarks:** All terms mentioned in this book that are known to be or are suspected of being trademarks or service marks have been appropriately capitalized. Alpha Books and Penguin Group (USA) Inc. cannot attest to the accuracy of this information. Use of a term in this book should not be regarded as affecting the validity of any trademark or service mark.

Most Alpha books are available at special quantity discounts for bulk purchases for sales promotions, premiums, fund-raising, or educational use. Special books, or book excerpts, can also be created to fit specific needs.

For details, write: Special Markets, Alpha Books, 375 Hudson Street, New York, NY 10014.

**Publisher:** Marie Butler-Knight
**Editorial Director:** Mike Sanders
**Senior Managing Editor:** Billy Fields
**Acquisitions Editor/Development Editor:** Michele Wells
**Production Editor:** Megan Douglass

**Copy Editor:** Jan Zoya
**Cover/Book Designer:** Rebecca Harmon
**Indexer:** Angie Bess
**Proofreader:** John Etchison

# Contents

# Acknowledgments

Wow. Another book. It's been a few years since my last one. My agent, Andree Abecassis, was probably thinking I'd lost interest in writing. Thanks to her, I've done it again. But it never would have happened if she hadn't done her thing. Thanks, Andree.

I'd also like to thank the following people for their help with this project: my editor, Michele Wells; the technical editor, Damon Brown; the production editor, Megan Douglass; the copy editor, Jan Zoya; for their editorial assistance: Rebecca "Tay" Taylor and Caitlin Jane Berry; and for his help with research: Matt Marini.

Thanks to the next generation of YouTube celebrities who let me interview them for this project: Luke Barats (BaratsandBereta), Joe Bereta (BaratsandBereta), Jay Brannan, Ysabella Brave, Michael Buckley (WhatTheBuck), Matt Chin, David Choi, David Colditz (DaveDays), Ryan Divine (Maldroid), Myles Dyer (Blade376), Emmalina, Millie Garfield (MyMomsBlog), Ben Going (boh3m3), Koichiben, James Kotecki (EmergencyCheese), Cherry Lee (TheBathroomGirl), Matthew Lush (GayGod), Remy Munasifi (GoRemy), Kevin Nalty (Nalts), Clive Newstead (Nuodai), Stevie Ryan, Justin Sandercoe, Matt Sloan (BlameSociety-Films), Charles Trippy, Valentina (ValsArtDiary), Aaron Yonda (BlameSocietyFilms), and Tay Zonday.

I'd also like to thank the following people for letting me interview them: Kevin Flynn, Kip Kedersha, Bernie Spektor, and Matt Sugarman. And the following people for their help in securing photo releases: Tamera Alexander, Valerie Arismendez, Sandie Black (memechannel), Baron S. Cameron, Tim Carter, Lance Cassidy, Tyler N. Cavell, Michelle Cox, Angela Wilson Gyetvan, Mary Hodder, Stephanie Ichinose, James Immekus, Luke Johnson, Noah Kalina, Judson Laipply, Taryn Langer, Kay Luo, Jessica Murphy, Vlasta Pokladnikova, Bill Porfido, Jeremy Stoppelman, and Kerry Vance.

A special thank-you to my partner at Management 101: Bryan Leder. Also thanks to Jay Johnson, all my amazing clients who are the reason I do what I do, Andy Putschoegl (because he told me he was thanked in all of my other books), my poker buddies, my friends, and my family.

at the Buck?!

Godzilla Here

# chapter 1

# Beginnings

The story of YouTube co-founders Chad Hurley, Steven Chen, and Jawed Karim might seem like the ultimate rags-to-riches fairytale, a computer geek version of Cinderella. In only two years, YouTube has become the number-one online video site, selling to corporate giant Google for $1.65 billion in stock in 2006, and supporting over 50,000 visitors in the month of June 2007. It has morphed from an unsuccessful dating site to a thriving website, delivering user-generated questions for candidates at the 2007 Presidential Debates.

The founders themselves do not even seem to particularly fit the role of billion-dollar CEOs. As one YouTube user commented after viewing Hurley and Chen's video announcement of the Google sale, "Apparently when you become a billionaire, you become a perpetually smirking idiot. God, I hope that happens to me some day." Despite outward appearances, however, YouTube's founders did not simply stumble across a glass slipper. A closer look reveals a story of entrepreneurial savvy, revolutionary ideas concerning new media and technology, and dedication to an identity that resonates with the young, emerging generation of consumers and artists.

But where did this cultural phenomenon originate? The truth is, we may never really know how it all began. Even among the co-founders, apocryphal accounts abound as to the genesis of the site and its subsequent boom. Nonetheless, no one can dispute the site's humble beginnings or rapid growth. Whether intentional or not, Hurley, Chen, and Karim have filled a need and created a vehicle of progress that might very well take media culture of the twenty-first century to the next level.

In this chapter, I will look at the roots of YouTube, from the evolution of *viral video* to the lives of YouTube's founders and the original conception and invention of the site that would become a cultural phenomenon.

YouTube founders Chad Hurley and Steven Chen announce the site's acquisition by Google in their own YouTube video.

In only two years, YouTube has become the number-one online video site

# **Viral** Video

The twenty-first century has been a turbulent time of change for technology. Devices have grown smaller and the user base has grown larger, causing modern media to start a shift from a top-down system to a bottom-up culture. The evolution of viral video has had no small part in these changes. As David Moore, who works for viral video site GetDemocracy.com, told the BBC News, "Everyone is able to, say, create a local news channel, or to publish video of their family reunion online easily. And more and more people are watching this kind of video online and taking their eyes away from the TV screen and moving toward the computer screen." By placing the uploading, sharing, editing, and content creation into the hands of the general public, viral video has kick-started massive change in modern media.

*Webster's New Millennium English Dictionary* defines viral video as "a video clip or recording, especially sent via email and which gains widespread popularity through sharing." Nowadays, viral video is rampant. It has become a part of everyday life and an art form, a way of entering film festivals and providing hours of distraction for errant college students. It has also become a major problem for businesses. According to Lance Ulanoff from *PC Magazine*, "They're finding employees just watching videos. They can't help themselves."

But how did media culture get to the point of turning out stars like Brooke Brodack, who landed a development deal with Carson Daly Productions, or films like "Evolution," winner of the Grand Prix Award at the Cannes Film Festival in 2007? How did viral video become such a huge part of pop culture?

The precursors to viral video were mostly animated videos. Web developers first started producing basic Internet animation around 1994, sending out a series of consecutive GIF images over a live browser. GIF animation, or graphic interchange format, an eight-bit-per-pixel imaging format invented by CompuServe in 1987, was rudimentary and cumbersome, and used mostly for

"Viral Video"

Video content that gains popularity through email sharing, blogs, and other Internet websites is known as **viral video.**

Viral favorite "Evolution" won the Grand Prix Award at the Cannes Film Festival in 2007.

advertising on websites because it could be accepted by all Web browsers. Some independent GIFs, such as "The Hamster Dance," created by Canadian artist Deidre LaCarte in 1998, did gain public popularity. This basic form of online animated video would soon gain momentum as technology caught up with culture.

Progressing to a level beyond GIF images, many of the next wave of viral videos were created with Flash animation, a program introduced by Adobe in the 1990s, that allows video to stream within Web pages and browsers. Flash animation creates vector files, which are mathematically formatted to construct images out of computer graphics, as opposed to raster files, which create images out of a series of pixels. Vector file format gained popularity among many animation studios for its ability to transfer onto 35-millimeter film without compromising quality. It first appeared in cartoon shows such as "Ren and Stimpy" and quickly spread onto Internet cartoon sites, such as HomeStarRunner.com. Flash animation's popularity among professionals would only lead to further proliferation.

Flash animation videos soon turned into an early form of viral video, dubbed "Internet memes"—digital phenomena that spread rapidly throughout the Internet by organic sharing. After GIFs, such as "The Hamster Dance," Flash animation

videos flooded the Internet. Some of the more well-known Flash animations include "Peanut Butter Jelly Time," made by Kevin Flynn, and "The Spirit of Christmas," made by "South Park" co-creators Matt Parker and Trey Stone. Flash technology soon spread to video as well as animation, and soon, home videos were becoming the first wave of viral videos. Viewed just under a billion times, "Star Wars Kid," a video of a Canadian teenager pretending to be Darth Maul with a golf-ball retriever, became the most-watched video on the Internet after it was uploaded by the teen's classmates. Both accidental and intentional stars were born out of the viral video craze, from everywhere and anywhere.

Soon, home videos were becoming the first wave of viral videos.

Screen shot from the original "Hamster Dance" featuring GIF animation.

IT'S PEANUT BUTTER JELLY TIME!!!

"Peanut Butter Jelly Time" is one of the earliest examples of flash animation video.

## Viral Video and the Dark Side

It may be one of the most watched viral videos of all time, but the creator of "Star Wars Kid" is not amused by his video's popularity. In late 2002, a Canadian youth named Ghyslain Raza filmed himself imitating Darth Maul from the *Star Wars* movies by swinging around a golf ball retriever as if it were a lightsaber. His classmates found the tape and as a prank, uploaded it to the Internet. Before long, the file was viewed millions of times and parodies were crafted and uploaded to the Net.

Raza quickly became the butt of jokes at school (and around the world) and the object of incessant bullying. In July, 2003, his family filed a lawsuit against the families of his schoolmates. The case was ultimately settled out of court, but it has become legendary as the first publicized case of cyberbullying.

Spurring this proliferation along was the abundance of video-capturing technology. As camcorders became smaller and camera phones became more popular, more and more amateur filmmakers were in need of a platform and audience to showcase their work. As YouTube founder Chad Hurley himself wrote, "With easy and affordable access to cameras, editing software, and computing power, the playing field has been truly leveled. This growth will only increase, whether on mobile devices,

## Q&A

### PEANUT BUTTER JELLY TIME:

*An interview with Kevin Flynn*

FL:   What was the genesis of "Peanut Butter Jelly Time"?

KF:   The genesis wasn't exactly inspired by a divine entity. I basically got drunk one night and was listening to an old MP3 I had called "Peanut Butter Jelly Time," and just thought it'd be really funny if combined with a dancing banana. As you can tell, it may be the crudest animation ever done.

FL:   This video was created pre-YouTube. When did you create it and how/where did you post it to the Internet?

KF:   A friend and I put it on his personal website. … We actually didn't even know it was popular until he got a call from his ISP asking what the hell he was hosting on his site and why it got five million hits in two months.

FL:   How did this video become so popular?

KF:   It just "went viral." Friends pass it to friends who send out emails and so on. I really feel it makes absolutely no difference where a video is put online … if it's interesting enough, people will see it.

FL:   Did you ever imagine that it would spread the way that it did?

KF:   Absolutely not. We actually completely forgot about it. It really, really surprised us to hear that anyone found it funny, let alone millions and millions of people. Then NBC wanted to put it on *Ed*, and then of course it was on *Family Guy*. My favorite story I heard was some prison warden in Florida used to play it to let the prisoners know it was lunch time … because for lunch they served peanut butter [and] jelly sandwiches with a banana. I still live in fear to this day that somewhere out there is an ex-con who was driven mad by the song who's hunting me down to shank me.

FL:   Some might call you the father of viral video. How do you feel about that title?

KF:   I think it's a pretty silly thing to call me. I just created a stupid

among our broadly expanding international audience, or anywhere that people enjoy an online video experience." As devices and software became more available and affordable, viral video was becoming a tidal wave in popular culture.

But the videos were still hard to share and download. Not everyone had a high-speed connection. These problems were nasty stumbling blocks to moving viral video into the mainstream. Then YouTube came along.

> "With easy and affordable access to cameras, editing software, and computing power, the playing field has been truly leveled."
>
> —Chad Hurley

movie that got popular. If I'm the father of viral video, it's the result of a drunken one-night stand.

FL:   There have been many remakes of the video, parodies, etc. Which are your favorites?

KF:   To be perfectly honest, I haven't really seen many. I actually hate the damn song now; it drives me nuts. I think that no matter what else I accomplish in my life, I'll be haunted by a heavily pixilated dancing banana.

FL:   Have you made money from this video?

KF:   Not a cent, aside from the t-shirt sales. Those came only after the whole *Family Guy* thing and they found out that they actually needed me to sign off on the t-shirts in order for them to produce them. I didn't make

much, and used most of it to fund my startup.

FL:   What's next for viral video?

KF:   What I really hope is next is some way of tracing and keeping track of who the real authors are. I mean, if you were to go on YouTube now and search for "Peanut Butter Jelly Time" you'd find a couple thousand results—not a single one was uploaded by me. What's going to end up happening if this continues is the authors who put a lot of effort, time, and money in making really neat videos (much higher quality than my own) are just going to give up. Not only are they not getting any money, more importantly they aren't getting any credit. So what we're left with is a bunch of uninteresting people talking into their webcam giving

their thoughts on politics or the war or something.

FL:   What do you think is the future of media and what role does the Internet and online video-sharing sites play?

KF:   The Internet is the future of media. You really can't separate the two.

--:   7

# Founders:
## The Early Years

Be nice to the guys in your high school's computer club—they may be worth over a billion and a half dollars one day. From the very start, YouTube co-founders Chad Hurley, Steven Chen, and Jawed Karim, the crown princes of Internet video sharing, all had brains and a nose for a good idea.

Now millionaires and some of the most popular guys on the planet, they have yet to lose touch with who they were at the beginning. Of Hurley and Chen's Google announcement, *The New York Times* wrote, "It was refreshing to see two executives act a bit more like real people than stiff businessmen. But there was something slightly disconcerting about watching two men who just made hundreds of millions of dollars each act like teenagers." And yet, this youthful, smart-aleck spirit is what drives the identity of YouTube, and its origins can be found even in the early lives of the three founders.

## Chad Hurley

From an early age, Chad Hurley has tried to find business in art. Raised in Bidsboro, Pennsylvania, Hurley's first business venture was attempting to peddle his own paintings from his front lawn. Though he might now admit that a lemonade stand would have been more profitable, no one can deny his early entrepreneurial spirit.

Hurley grew up a child of many interests, but he always had a proclivity for art, particularly watercolor and sculpture. He was a middle child, born in between an older sister, Heather, and a younger brother, Brent. His father, Donald, is a financial consultant, and his mother, JoAnn, is a math teacher and a teacher in the gifted program at Twin Valley High School, where Hurley graduated in 1995.

It was in high school that Hurley's artistic aptitude began to meld with his interest in technol-

ogy and business. He joined the Technology Student Association and, as a freshman, won third place in a national electronics competition for building an amplifier. Hurley was also a champion cross-country runner throughout high school and college, winning two PIAA State titles with his high school team in 1992 and 1994. The interests he developed in high school would follow him into college.

Hurley began attending Indiana University of Pennsylvania in 1995. He originally majored in computer science, but ultimately switched to graphic design and printmaking. As his father told *Time* magazine, "Computer science, that was too technical, too mechanical for Chad. He wanted to be on the creative side." His education in graphic design led him to further interest in Web design, animation, and Internet gaming. Staying true to his enterprising spirit as well, he sold

knives for a pyramid-marketing scheme to make money during the summers. But selling knives was not Hurley's long-term professional goal, and upon graduating, the young graphic designer began job hunting.

Luckily, Hurley already had an idea of where he wanted to be. After reading an article in *Wired* magazine about PayPal, a new development company gaining momentum on the dotcom bubble, Hurley sent out his resumé, requesting an interview. Within a week, PayPal flew Hurley out to California and asked him to showcase his design skills by creating a company logo on the spot. Hurley was offered the job as the company's first designer. The logo he created remains in place as PayPal's logo today. It was there, in the PayPal offices, that Hurley was united with Steven Chen and Jawed Karim, and the YouTube journey began.

## Steven Chen

Steven Chen might be the ultimate computer brain, but not even that could prepare him for the unexpected success of YouTube. When he was six, Chen's mother reportedly took him to a fortuneteller, who predicted that Chen would never become rich. Boy, did he prove that palm reader wrong.

Born in Taipei, Taiwan, in 1979, Chen's family immigrated to the United States when he was eight. After attending John Hersey High School in Illinois for a few years, Chen enrolled in the Illinois Mathematics and Science Academy, a charter boarding school. Like the other students at IMSA, Chen underwent an intensely competitive curriculum of math and computer sci-ence. The coed school required students to take on college-level courses and adopt a nose-to-the-grindstone work ethic. Chen stood out for his slightly mischievous ability to find the quickest path to any solution, a risky approach that would later play a pivotal role in Chen's life and career.

After attending the University of Illinois at Champaign-Urbana for three years, where he majored in computer science, Chen left prematurely to take a job at PayPal, despite anxious warnings from his family. According to his younger brother, Ricky, "[His family] told him it was risky; he just had a few months left. But he was determined to give it a shot."

The computer science department of the University of Illinois at Champaign-Urbana was a hot recruiting ground for PayPal employees, especially those with an educational background such as Chen's. PayPal co-founder Max Levchin, now the founder of the Internet venture Slide, is a U of I alumnus, as are a number of other original employees of PayPal. As Levchin said in an interview with *Time* magazine, "IMSA plus University of Illinois is generally a very winning formula. The kind of people IMSA attracts are the kind of people very prone to choose their own path." In 1999, Chen was hired as one of PayPal's first engineers.

## Jawed Karim

Also coming to PayPal from University of Illinois' computer science department was YouTube's third, and lesser known, founder, Jawed Karim. Karim, also born in 1979, was born in Merseburg, East Germany, but moved to West Germany at the age of one. In 1992, Karim and his parents moved to St. Paul, Minnesota, where Karim graduated from Central High School in 1997. Karim was brought up in a household based on learning and discovering new ideas. His father, Naimul, is a Bangladeshi researcher and chemist for 3M, a technology company, and his mother, Christine, works as a research assistant professor of biochemistry at the University of Minnesota. As she says when talking about her son's aptitude for technology and interest in education, "To develop new things and be aware of new things, this is our life." Karim carried this mindset with him at the University of Illinois at Champaign-Urbana.

Karim admits to basing part of his interest in U of I on the success of one of its other computer science alumni. "It wasn't like I wanted to be the next Marc Andreessen, but it would be cool to be in the same place," he told *The New York Times*. (Andreessen, who graduated in 1993, went on to become a co-founder of the popular Web browser Netscape.) In his commencement speech at his alma mater in 2007, Karim remembered, "I figured, why would I go anywhere else, if the

## Jawed Karim (continued)

people who invented the first Web browser are in my own backyard?" Karim knew that he was meant to follow in their footsteps. "It was a no-brainer. At that moment I knew. I wanted to join the innovators."

Joining the innovators might have been easier said than done. After applying to U of I, Karim was initially rejected from the computer science department and was instead assigned to ceramics engineering. Not looking for a future in pottery, Karim wrote to the university begging them to reconsider his application, promising to "be a highly motivated, dedicated, and ambitious student." The university had a change of heart and invited him into the computer science department, where he upheld his promise until his junior year.

In 2000, Karim dropped his classes to join the small arsenal of PayPal's young computer engineers. "At PayPal, I felt once again that I was following in the footsteps of the Illinois innovators. The experience taught me the importance of being true to yourself." However, Karim stayed true to his earlier promise, even after joining PayPal, and continued his studies via online classes at the University of Santa Clara, eventually obtaining his Bachelor's degree in computer science in 2004.

> YouTube's very own tin man, scarecrow, and lion ... journey down the yellow brick road toward success.

And so it was that by the year 2000, the three brainchildren behind YouTube would meet in the San Mateo offices of PayPal. The artist-entrepreneur, the quick-thinking computer nerd, and the ambitious student—YouTube's very own tin man, scarecrow, and lion—would begin their journey down the yellow brick road toward success.

## Pay Pals

For the young and future founders, their work together at PayPal would provide an important catalyst for the relationships, experience, and ideas that would eventually germinate into YouTube. Founded in 1998, PayPal started off trying to develop a way for PDA users to send payments to each other. Ultimately, the company invented a quick and easy method for people and businesses to make and receive payments online in real-time, in a secure, global setting.

After only four years as an independent company, PayPal was bought by eBay, one of its long-running competitors, for $1.54 billion, turning its tight-knit handful of employees rich over night. Hurley bought a Tag Heuer watch, which he still wears today, while Chen splurged on an apartment in San Francisco. Hurley and Karim left the company soon after the sale, while Chen stayed on until 2005. Those initial years at PayPal, albeit short-lived, would later prove invaluable to YouTube's founders.

Worth millions of dollars each, Hurley, Chen, and Karim still attribute many of the lessons they learned to their time at PayPal. Karim remembers, "It was a great opportunity to see up-close how a group of talented people could overcome seemingly insurmountable challenges." It is true that PayPal had its rough times staying above water. In its early years the site was plagued by hackers and competitors, which led to the loss of millions of dollars every month. Employees bonded over long hours and late nights, drinking too much coffee and learning to remain positive. Most of PayPal's employees were in their 20s and 30s, and many came from similar backgrounds, most notably from the University of Illinois and from Stanford University, where PayPal co-founder Peter Thiel co-founded the *Stanford Review* in 1987. As Max Levchin told *The New York Times*, "We all became each other's social life. Because of that, we formed deep connections." The experiences and relationships nurtured at PayPal would help the YouTube co-founders in the future.

Though Silicon Valley is known to be a small network community, the alumni of PayPal have remained extremely close, both as friends and as business partners. Meeting regularly at social functions, many Internet start-ups have been born from the ashes of PayPal's legacy. Reid Hoffman, former PayPal vice president, started LinkedIn, a business social networking site that was funded in part by former PayPal chief executive Peter Thiel. Max Levchin started Slide, a site that makes it easy for users to view slide shows, much like YouTube does with videos. David Sacks, former chief operating officer at PayPal, founded Room 9 Entertainment, the movie production company that grossed $24 million at the box office on its first film, *Thank You for Smoking*, which YouTube founder Chad Hurley worked on for a time, even designing the company's logo, and which was funded in part by Peter Thiel, Max Levchin, and Elon Musk, another

PayPal founder. The conception for Yelp, a site that lets users review local businesses and services, such as restaurants, doctors, and plumbers, originated through conversations at the celebration of Levchin's twenty-ninth birthday party. Most on the guest list were ex-PayPal employees.

The origins of YouTube follow a similar tale. YouTube was already in its first humble months of production when co-founder Karim showed the site to Keith Rabois, a former PayPal executive who now works with Hoffman at LinkedIn, at a backyard barbeque in the summer on 2005. Rabois, in turn, showed the site to former PayPal chief financial officer Roelof Botha, now a partner at the venture capital firm Sequoia Capital, who ultimately convinced Sequoia to invest in YouTube for $8.5 million. With Sequoia, Hurley, Chen, and Karim would find another mentor—National Semiconductor founder Pierre Lamond. Lamond was instrumental in giving the founders advice via daily email, especially when YouTube site growth would start to curve off. "They would tell me, 'We're running out of storage capacity,'" says Lamond, who would encourage them to purchase more and more space to accommodate the growing site.

This pattern of new ideas finding management advice and financing within the PayPal family rings true to what *The New York Times* reporter Miguel Helft observed in 2006, "The effectiveness of the PayPal network stems, in part, from the fact that it includes all the elements to put together a start-up: talented engineers and entrepreneurs with innovative ideas and a love of the start-up life; experienced managers who can turn ideas into businesses; and financiers, who have used their PayPal money to become angel investors." Rabois and Hoffman even helped YouTube find office space, making room for them at LinkedIn's Palo Alto offices. These lasting relationships from PayPal gave YouTube the leg up it needed to rise to success.

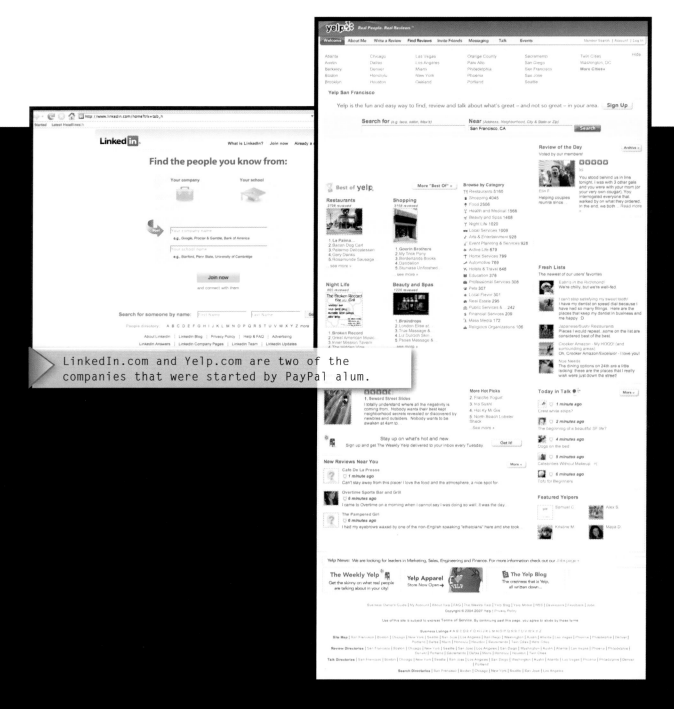

LinkedIn.com and Yelp.com are two of the companies that were started by PayPal alum.

# The Initial Stages

An idea that is as colossal as You-Tube is not created overnight. It comes into existence as a slow, unfolding process, unfortunately leaving lots of room for variation on the story of its birth. Over the few years since its popularity landslide, the site's founders have often been asked the question of how it all began, but even Hurley and Chen, the public faces of YouTube, have yet to develop a stock story to answer this question. No matter what story they decide on, the truth is that You-Tube was born out of a need in modern media culture. A faster, more interconnected world demanded a way for every person, big or small, to upload and share video easily, quickly, and with as many other people as possible. It was this very need that Hurley, Chen, and Karim picked up on and, using their highly experienced knowledge of the technology and their start-up business savvy, they provided exactly what the public was seeking.

While still at PayPal, Hurley, Chen, and Karim would discuss ideas for other start-ups. After the sale of PayPal to eBay, Hurley departed the company looking for something to assuage his ever-present artistic side. He designed messenger bags and worked on Room 9 Entertainment's film *Thank You for Smoking*. Karim looked forward to going back to school. Chen stayed the longest at PayPal, helping to launch the company's expansion into China. He then did a brief stint as an employee at Facebook. By 2005, however, all three were about to become knee-deep in the biggest idea any of them had ever had.

The initial idea of a video-sharing website is attributed to Karim, though this has been slightly disputed. Karim has made a number of attempts to remind the public that, despite the fact that he left YouTube to attend Stanford without ever becoming a full-time employee and holds a lesser percentage of YouTube's stock than Hurley and Chen, the idea was originally his, no matter what stories the other two spin for the press. Chen remarked rather scathingly to a *New York Times* reporter, "Chad and I are pretty modest, and Jawed has tried to seize every opportunity to take credit."

No matter what angst-ridden tensions now belie the relationships among the three founders, all admit that the original idea to start a video-sharing site was in fact Karim's. Karim claims that the idea came from two events in 2004: Janet Jackson's half-time show at Super Bowl XXXVIII and the Indian Ocean Tsunami. "It was the first natural disaster ever captured on cell-phone video cameras, and the video clips quickly flooded the Internet," Karim said. "But there was no good way to find these video clips. They were scattered all over the Web. There was also no good way to share them." The same problem arose from video clips of Janet Jackson baring herself to audiences of football fans. Karim posed his raw idea to Hurley and Chen, setting a spark that would evolve into an inextinguishable flame.

YouTube was born out of a need in modern media culture.

With Karim's idea in the back of their minds, Hurley and Chen claim to have attended a dinner party in San Francisco in early 2005. At the party, many digital photos were taken along with extensive video footage. But the friends soon discovered that, like Janet Jackson or the Asian Tsunami clips, there was no good way to share this footage. Video files were too large to send over emails and in order to download video, users were forced to download media players, often a different media player for each download. Karim's observation of the public need for video sharing and Hurley and Chen's personal, frustrating experience led the three friends to come together with a goal of setting up a public, Web-based, video-sharing site.

> "It was the first time that someone had designed a website where anyone could upload content that everyone else could view."
>
> —Jawed Karim

# Tune In-Hook Up

Of course, no idea is perfect in its infancy. Originally, the founders sought to create a dating site where users could upload video of themselves searching for the perfect mate and enjoying long walks on the beach. The concept was based on another dating site at the time, HOTorNOT.com. On HOTorNOT.com, users could each upload pictures and information about themselves and then be rated 1 through 10 on their attractiveness by other users searching for that special someone. Not particularly classy, no, but as Karim states, "It was the first time that someone had designed a website where anyone could upload content that everyone else could view. That was a new concept because up until that point, it was always the people who owned the website who would provide the content."

The goal became to create a video version of HOTorNOT.com and gain an edge on the thousands of other dating sites populating the Internet.

And thus, the wildly unpopular dating site, Tune In–Hook Up, was hatched. Hurley, Chen, and Karim began work on the new site on Valentine's Day of 2005. "That's another thing about being a computer science major," jokes Karim. "Valentine's Day is just another day, so why not start a new website?" The site officially became operational on April 23, hosted on a single server that rented for $100 a month. Despite the potential of the idea and the high hopes of the founders, Tune In–Hook Up floundered in its initial stages. "In the beginning, we found that very few people came to our website," says Karim. "The product was so primitive that you couldn't even choose which videos you wanted to watch. Instead, the website picked for you—randomly. And because there were so few videos, they were the same ones over and over again."

Not only did Tune In–Hook Up have a few kinks to work out, it had a larger problem: without users, they had no videos. In footage shot by Karim of the three founders working on the site in Hurley's garage, Chen laments the fact that only 50 or 60 videos had been up-loaded onto the site—and "not that many videos I'd want to watch," he adds. "Videos like these," Hurley quips to the camera, referring to Karim's footage. The three continued to meet in Hurley and Karim's garages and at Max's Opera Café near Stanford, trying to come up with ideas to save their site. Hurley, Chen, and Karim knew they would have to come up with a solution, fast.

Their first few ideas still did not seem to get them anywhere. Desperate, Hurley, Chen, and Karim started uploading ran-dom videos onto the site just to fill space. Karim remembers putting up footage of 747 airplanes taking off and landing. "Dating? Airplanes? Who wants to date airplanes? The whole thing just didn't make sense," he says. The three even turned to the popular ad-posting site, Craigslist. They offered women in Las Vegas and Los Angeles $20 to upload videos of themselves, but the founders solicited zero replies. The three began to think that their heavyweight idea just might not fly.

# A Life of its Own

But Hurley, Chen, and Karim's technology provided a much-needed platform to Internet surfers everywhere, and ultimately the Web media community made it their own. In addition to looking for material for their site, the founders had continued to work out the kinks in the programming. Karim and Chen used Adobe's Flash development language to create a way for users to stream video clips within their browser instead of having to download media players. Hurley worked on the site's interface, developing a system so that users could easily share their videos and *tag* clips with ratings and descriptions. Us-ing his artistic flair, Hurley also designed the site's new name and logo. As he said in an interview, "I'm the marketing guy, UI guy, designer guy. We combined forces to create a highly techni-cal, highly advanced architecture with an extremely easy-to-use interface." All three founders also programmed the site to enable users to post clips directly onto their own Web pages, a feature that would prove instrumental in conjunction with the growth of the new profile site, MySpace. With the technology working more smoothly, YouTube began to take on a life of its own, con-ducted by the users themselves.

Tags are words used to classify, and later identify, videos.

[YouTube] has always been about the idea of creating and developing something that would change the world.

In the end, Hurley, Chen, and Karim say that all they had to do was sit back and watch. After discovering the advantages of the new site's technology, users began uploading videos of all sorts, not just dating videos. The founders started seeing home videos of vacations, pet tricks, and an array of other subjects. After a month of languishing in Internet no-man's-land, YouTube appeared, renovated and open to everyone, in June 2005. By the time Sequoia Capital invested its initial $3.5 million in the site, YouTube was already moving eight terabytes of the community's data per day, the "equivalent of moving one Blockbuster store a day over the Internet," according to Hurley.

The eventual response of You-Tube's users forced the company to expand to 21 employees and move out from the garage. Their new offices were above a pizzeria in San Mateo, California, complete with sparse Ikea furniture and a rubber chicken hanging from the rafters—a start-up haven. Hurley became the company's CEO, and Chen took on the title of Chief Technology Officer. Karim opted to carry on only as an advisor to the site and instead enroll in Stanford University's computer science Master's program. The ephemeral ideas of three budding computer nerds had become a company with a bright future. The YouTube users themselves helped Hurley,

Chen, and Karim mold a site that was on its way to changing media culture forever.

Jawed Karim quoted Larry Ellison, the founder of Oracle Corporation, in his Commencement address to the University of Illinois at Champaign-Urbana as saying: "I don't know of any place or any time where there aren't great possibilities." There is no surprise as to why this statement stuck in Karim's mind. The idea of YouTube came from many different places—from the historical progress of viral video, from the ambition and interest of each of the founders, and from experiences shared by everyone along the way. For Hurley, Chen, and Karim, it has never been about those millions of dollars. For them, it has always been about the idea of creating and developing something that would change the world.

All three founders, whether it was Hurley and his artistic mind, Chen with his need to solve problems at high speed and high risk, or Karim and his continuous striving to learn and develop knowledge, have always been committed to the idea of YouTube—the need it fills and the problem it solves—rather than business models and stocks. "What we're really committed to is providing the best experience, and we're not really thinking about what we're worth," says Chen. "We're just viewing this as solving a really hard problem and that's how to distribute video in an entertaining way. So as we move forward, we're going to stay committed to that."

Though it has been a wild ride, YouTube and the success of the men behind it were no fluke in Web history—the story is one of long hours, hard work, revolutionary ideas, and brilliant minds. "We started this to solve a personal problem," says Hurley. "Now we're creating a new way to reach audiences." Hurley, Chen, and Karim's lives will never be the same, nor will modern media culture, but through it all, their own roots and the original spirit of YouTube will hopefully never be forgotten, even as YouTube continues to explode and rock the foundations of modern media and technology. And while these three men have become the unwilling stars of Silicon Valley, they hadn't any idea of the media stars their site would one day create.

# chapter 2

# Jumping on the
# Bandwidth Wagon
## and Going Mainstream

Although it seems like YouTube rocketed to superstardom overnight, a variety of factors aided in its exponential growth. First there were both methodical and strategic initiatives from within the company that fostered a sense of community online and drew potential partners to the party. At the same time, consumers were spreading YouTube virally across the globe in ways that couldn't have been predicted. YouTube simply provided the forum for them to do that.

During the summer of 2006, YouTube was one of the fastest-growing websites on the World Wide Web and was ranked as the fifth most popular website on Alexa, a site that provides information on Web traffic to other websites, far outpacing even the growth of MySpace. According to a July 16, 2006 survey, 100 million clips are viewed daily on YouTube, with an additional 65,000 new videos uploaded every 24 hours. The site has almost 20 million visitors each month, according to Nielsen/NetRatings, where around 44 percent are female, 56 percent male, and the 12-to-17-year-old age group is dominant. YouTube's preeminence in the online video market is staggering.

On October 9, 2006, it was announced that the company would be purchased by Google for $1.65 billion in stock. The deal to acquire YouTube closed on November 13, and was Google's second-largest purchase of all time. Currently staffed by 67 employees, the company was named *Time* magazine's "Invention of the Year" for 2006. Even political

candidates are jumping on the bandwidth wagon. Candidates for the 2008 U.S. presidential election have been using YouTube as an outlet for advertising their candidacy.

Hillary Clinton addresses her online viewers.

Barack Obama discusses his presidential campaign.

Rudy Giuliani talks about his plan for 2008.

# If You Build It,
## They Will Come

From the get-go, YouTube's mission was and always has been to meet the needs of its users.

The timing was perfect. At the time of YouTube's conception, Silicon Valley venture capital firms were specifically looking to back websites that facilitated global community. The notion of a website where users at opposite ends of the world could share the details of their everyday lives, from styling tips and recipes to personal diaries and dog-training tricks, was unheard of. Essentially, they wanted to create a place for anyone and everyone.

This place was being called "the Next Net," and it was defined by the capacity for someone to instantaneously access millions of Web users through computers, PDAs, or cell phones. The idea was that users could collaborate on a project, chat about a mutual interest, or solve personal problems with fellow users dispersed around the world. Physical boundaries for community were being eliminated.

YouTube's office was still above the pizzeria in San Mateo, California, with only a piece of paper taped to the door serving as a sign. Yet they were firmly harnessing the ever-growing trend of the Next Net. In a matter of 14 months, the company had gone from being virtually unknown to becoming one of the most popular and linked-to sites on the Internet. YouTube received a second round of funding from Sequoia Capital just five months after the site had gone live. In April 2006, the number of videos viewed online had risen to three million per day.

But it wasn't all right-place, right-time. There was another important factor that inevitably led to YouTube's wild popularity. From the get-go, YouTube's mission was and always has been to meet the needs of its users. The creators were firmly dedicated to creating a community of their own.

In her 2006 *Washington Post* article, Sara Kehaulani Goo concurred that ultimately it was the fact that YouTube placed the power in its users' hands, and that was what led to its mass appeal. Goo wrote, "YouTube's do-it-yourself popularity, fueled by word of mouth, catapulted the site past its bigger competitors in months. That success is drawing the attention of mainstream media."

But how did they do this? By always keeping people—not dollar signs—in mind. First, YouTube created an extremely friendly interface, making it easy to navigate and thereby meeting the needs of a broad spectrum of users, from those who barely know where to find the computer's on-button to those who've got experience writing software pro-grams. With their user-friendly interface, YouTube appealed to the widest possible audience and even catered to those who otherwise might be turned off by the Internet. If you had a way of capturing video and had a high-speed connection, YouTube was there, ready to use, and virtually impossible to resist.

## An Irresistible Interface

*Slate* columnist Paul Boutin wrote, "There are two design requirements meant for the masses. First you need to automate all the techie parts so that people can just press Play. To watch television online, I shouldn't have to install extra video software and figure out my bandwidth setting ... and sign up with the player's maker." He stated that YouTube handles the technological component so that it doesn't feel as if, in order to upload or watch a video clip, you're "launching a mission to Mars." Other notable strengths were the fact that the sign-up is free, it doesn't give you pop-ups or error messages, and there's no software to install or settings to adjust.

And YouTube, true to its democratic roots, is far from being elitist or exclusive. It will serve as host to anyone's website, and happily personalizes it by listing age, gender, interests, and other statistics. It gives the user a strong sense of immediacy and connectivity in streaming videos, rather than downloading them. YouTube made its site further interactive, reinforcing the sense of community, by launching the "spin-off and response video," so that people could respond however they like to a video they see and create a video thread that creates a certain kind of internal growth and furthers community all on its own.

In the same *Slate* article, Boutin commented that YouTube's hearty popularity is due to the fact that it's not only easy to use, but it also doesn't tell users what to do and treats them with utmost respect. "Web moguls shouldn't presume to foresee what 100 million people will want to do with their site. I'm one of the many who stopped using Google's Orkut social network because its hardwired page designs made everyone look like they were there to find a date and/or a job." YouTube also lets their users decide what clips are appropriate or inappropriate for the site. Users themselves are responsible for flagging items that may raise eyebrows a little too high.

But YouTube did not stop there. They were constantly discovering new and innovative ways to meet the needs of their Web users and to make accessing YouTube easier and more widespread. In May 2006, for example, they launched a service that enabled users to upload clips from their PDAs or cell phones, giving their users much more mobility. Users could now be conveniently unplugged from their webcams and computers.

In a May 2006 *C/Net* article, Steve Chen said, "Most user clips are taken with Web and digital video cameras ... the new service will likely produce greater numbers of spontaneous and candid clips," and that, "the good thing about it is that you don't have to go home to YouTube anymore .... People may not carry their digital cameras with them when they go out. But everyone carries their cell phone .... I'm interested in seeing what kind of content this will produce." Members could create a mobile profile on the site, and YouTube created an email address that they could send the videos to.

Members were able to then simply film clips with their cell phone, email them to YouTube, and post them under their profile.

When asked in a *Financial Times* 2006 interview about what the "YouTube phenomenon" was all about, cofounder Chad Hurley answered, "I think it's empowering people with a video solution. That's why Steve (Chen) and I started the company, to help people deal with video online, (based on) our own personal experiences and frustration of trying to share these clips with each other. So we looked at the problems here:

'How do we remove the barriers for people? How do you not require any type of software, and allow everyone to participate in the process?' Other video sites in the past were kind of making decisions on what was entertaining to the community. We also removed that barrier by allowing everyone to participate and add content. It's really the users of the community that decide what's entertaining to them, so that will rise to the top." Indeed, by making their users their number-one priority, YouTube created user loyalty, which has paid off in spades.

# Professional
## Content Providers

True to the founders' credo, early users of YouTube felt welcome. People, rather than a billion-dollar profit, were at the forefront of YouTube's plans. Despite temptation, YouTube consistently refused advertising aside from rolling banners, and resisted placing ads before videos.

Hurley and Chen had taken a huge risk. They had used their own credit cards to bankroll the cost of storing and sending out clips, despite persuasion to sell the "unskippable" ads that their rivals allowed. Having already built a fan base, they gambled on the possibility that the steadily falling cost of bandwidth would boost them past their ad-laden competitors and enable them to use alternative forms of promotion that were more elaborate and better suited to their site.

In a May 2006 CNNMoney.com interview, Steve Chen said, "If we wanted to, we could instantly turn this into $10 million in revenue per month by running pre-rolls (short video ads) on the videos. But at the same time, we're going to make sure that whatever revenue model we've built is going to be something that's accepted by users."

Chad Hurley added, "We're building relationships with studios, networks, and labels because they're looking for ways to reach new audiences, and we have a great platform to make that happen." But they hadn't yet hired a salesperson due to the fact that they wanted to "develop something that works for our community first."

Steve Chen was quick to point out in an April 2006 FT.com interview that YouTube was still creating a community around video that would cater to potential content providers. "This is a really good way for people to meet an audience. Traditional media companies have a way to reach new consumers." How could they not? They needed to make money somehow. They were simply in the process of creating a new model where everyone comes out a winner.

It seems that YouTube was on the mark regarding not bombarding their users with advertising. One YouTube user told the *Washington Post*, "If I want to watch commercials, I can watch TV … I would hope they are keeping to entertainment. People would be more put off by seeing a commercial."

So YouTube continued to reject interruptive video ads. Hurley told *Adweek*, "We think there are better ways for people to engage with brands than forcing them to watch a commercial before seeing content …. You could ask anyone on the Net if they enjoy that experience, and they'd probably say no."

It wasn't easy. But part of YouTube's challenge was to find a way in which they could build a working and efficient business model, while keeping their users happy and not dissuading them from using the site by including intrusive ads.

> It seems that YouTube was on the mark regarding not bombarding their users with advertising.

# Let's Make a Deal

Some say a good thing can't last forever. And in June 2005, advertising came to YouTube. But it wasn't a decision that was made lightly. Having previously, and continually, ignored advertisers' desires to insert pre-roll ads on YouTube, the creators couldn't put off the inevitable any longer.

When they did post their first ads, Chen and Hurley even went so far as to apologize to their users, saying that they needed money to fix the office sink. YouTube turned to Disney, allowing them to buy up every banner slot available in order to promote the *Pirates of the Caribbean* sequel.

Shortly after, Hurley and Chen went to New York City to meet with Digitas, one of the country's leading digital marketing agencies. They listened carefully to every—and any—idea possible regarding how to create a profitable business model with community still at the forefront and integrity intact. In August 2006, YouTube created "brand channels" and launched full-force into video ads. In a way, it was a win-win situation for the community. Users had access to a company's promotional material, but at the same time they could choose to go to a Channel or not. Various companies (or those who were entrepreneurially inclined) could control their own material, and, in addition, they had the potential for greater interaction with the mass public. Paris Hilton, for example, created her own Channel and posted an original broadcast where she promoted her new album produced by Warner Bros.

## The MTV Generation

Other deals followed, and the list of official partners grew. In March 2006, MTV came on board as an official partner. Although there was no money exchanged, MTV was to "seed" YouTube with clips as a part of an MTV marketing strategy. By using the term "official partner," MTV and YouTube were securing the fact that the content was coming directly from MTV firsthand.

The next month YouTube partnered with the Weinstein Company and screened the first eight minutes of the movie *Lucky Number Slevin*. The YouTube press released stated that this screening marked "the first time that the opening of a feature film (would) be released specifically for the YouTube audience." Gary Farber, Executive Vice President of the Weinstein Company, stated that, "deciding to partner with YouTube was a no-brainer—what better way to help fuel the film's positive buzz than by partnering with the number-one word-of-mouth website out there today?" The promotion was a success.

Clips of *Lucky Number Slevin* were viewed roughly 60,000 times in one week—about equal to the amount of times the two-minute trailer was viewed online in one month.

Trailers for other Weinstein Company Films, such as *Clerks II* and *Scary Movie IV*, had also been posted on YouTube, and to equally great effect. Ian Schafer, CEO of Deep Focus Films, an entertainment marketing and promotions agency, said, "Prior to YouTube, there was no other way to premiere the first few minutes of a movie in a viral way. With help from the YouTube community, *Scary Movie IV* had a record-breaking box-office release. With the upcoming release of *Clerks II* and with *Lucky Number Slevin* in theaters nationwide, we are excited to continue to find cool new ways to bring our movies to market."

Warner Music Group and YouTube created a partnership in September 2006. YouTube would distribute the library of videos from Warner Music, as well as behind-the-scenes footage and exclusive interviews. And YouTube users were granted permission to incorporate music from the Warner Music catalog in their personal videos and upload it onto the site. The two companies agreed to share in the revenue from ads YouTube placed alongside Warner material. Chad Hurley noted, "Partnering with Warner Music Group is one of the most significant milestones for our company and our community, and shifts the paradigm in this new media movement. By providing a new distribution opportunity, we are paving the way for media companies to harness the vast financial potential of user-generated content on YouTube."

And the deals continued to roll in. Many companies got in line to partner with YouTube after seeing the success of the early pairings. While more and more companies approached the site to seek ways to work together, another Web-based corporation had an idea percolating on an entirely different plane.

# Google

People were talking. Rumors were circulating. And in October 2006, something many had been anticipating finally happened. Google bought YouTube for $1.65 billion in stock. The two companies were to remain independent from one another. Eric Schmidt, Chief Executive of Google, stated, "The YouTube team has built an exciting and powerful media platform that complements Google's mission to organize the world's information and make it universally accessible and useful." He also said that the two companies were "… natural partners to offer a media entertainment service to users, content owners, and advertisers."

Furthermore, an October 2006 *CNNMoney.com* story reported, "For Google, the purchase of YouTube gives the company the ability to tap into the potentially lucrative online video and social networking markets. Some analysts have criticized Google for relying too much on advertising tied to keyword searches. The combination of Google and YouTube could further strengthen Google's dominance in online advertising, giving it an edge over rivals."

Some say that YouTube was likely courted by other companies such as Yahoo, Microsoft, and Newscorp, but Google was the one to snap them up—and at a hefty price, at that. It raised some eyebrows and brought up many questions. Why did they pay so much, and why in stock? Would it be worth it?

Martin Pyykkonen, an analyst at Global Crown Capital, stated that Google's purchase of YouTube had to do with Google strategically placing themselves against Yahoo!. Rumor had it that they were looking seriously at purchasing Facebook (a social networking site that allows users to communicate and exchange information with their friends). Clayton Moran, an analyst with Stanford Group, stated that Google was paying such a high price for YouTube in order to be more competitive with MySpace. At the time, MySpace was ranked second in online video market share. Moran said, "My sense is that Google is paying a full price, considering that YouTube is still unproven in regards to its revenue potential. But considering the success of MySpace, it was clearly worthwhile for Google to take this step." Some say another reason Google paid such a high price was due to the fact that YouTube could help to expand Google's text-based search platform into video.

There were many benefits to YouTube. Why a stock deal? David Drummond, Google's General Counsel, explained that by paying in stock, the deal was essentially tax-free. For one thing, $1.65 billion can buy you a lot of bandwidth (not to mention houses, cars, and yachts). YouTube would also benefit from an improved search experience. The Google press release stated that "… the acquisition combines one of the largest and fastest-growing online video entertainment communities with Google's expertise in organizing information and creating new models for advertising on the Internet." Chad Hurley stated, "By joining forces with Google, we can benefit from its global reach and technology leadership to deliver a more comprehensive entertainment experience for our users and to create new opportunities for our partners."

When people caught wind of the Google–YouTube deal, shares of Google rose 2 percent on Friday and then an additional 2 percent on the NASDAQ on Monday, climbing higher yet in after-hours trading. Furthermore, from October 2006 (the time of the acquisition) up until now, the Google stock has steadily risen to over $500 per share. YouTube traffic also rose drastically after Google acquired the site. They received 50 percent more traffic than all video sites combined. It seems to have been a win-win all around.

## **More** Deals

Together, Google and YouTube continued to create distribution deals with content providers. Universal Music Group and CBS, which wanted to offer short-form video programming, were two of the first notable partnerships under the new regime. Verizon Wireless became the first cell-phone company to enable people to watch videos from their mobile phones—charging customers an extra $15 per month to access the most popular videos on YouTube.

The deals YouTube was making were suddenly endless: Nokia, Vodafone, Chelsea digital media, Wind Up Records, the Spanish broadcaster Cuatro, Germany's Kinowelt Films, Apple's new iPhone, Nike, the NHL and NBA, as well as E! Networks—just to name a few.

# **New Channels,**
## New Users

One of YouTube's most significant achievements was creating a forum for politicians.

These new partnerships provided different ways for people to use the site. For example, YouTube launched, with Cingular Wireless as a sponsor (and supervised by Chop Shop Music), a contest for undiscovered musicians: bands could submit a video of their performance and potentially be rocketed to stardom themselves. (See "Maldroid," in Chapter 6, to keep up with the contest winners!)

Ford Models launched a Channel and gave contestants of the "Ford Models of the World" contest cameras whereby the models videotaped themselves and broadcasted their experiences. Even the Sundance Film Festival caught wind of the potential publicity opportunities and launched a Channel. They posted profiles of film competitors, video clips from prior festivals, and other exclusive, related content. YouTube also launched its first sketch comedy contest: a three-round competition in which comedians were pitted against each other for nine weeks, the goal being to "build and sustain an audience for episodic comedic series." The contest was backed by Sierra Mist.

One of YouTube's most significant achievements was creating a forum for politicians. Not only did former British Prime Minister Tony Blair launch a Labour Party Channel on YouTube in order to connect directly to voters, but major 2008 presidential candidates are now showcasing their own videos on YouTube on their own Channels, and encouraging users to post their own replies. Vishesh Kumar of *Street* magazine said, "YouTube's political venture provides a blueprint for the type of unique content that can make it continue to stand out. Its powerful brand—combined with its enormous contributor base and community—allow it access to content that neither the big media studios nor those looking for mercenary contributors can match."

# **Politico** Tube

Back in his 2006 campaign, someone captured on video Virginia Republican Senator George Allen making a controversial comment to a young campaign aide working for his opponent. It was placed on YouTube and promptly became a hit. People thought that Allen would be re-elected, but he lost his seat to Democratic opponent James Webb. It is said that the YouTube posting caused Allen's defeat. A similar video posted on YouTube is thought to be responsible for Senator Conrad Burns's defeat that same year. Is it possible that YouTube essentially caused the Senate to swing to the Democrats?

They're considered "gotcha" moments—unauthorized campaign videos posted on YouTube, or debate questions put forth by YouTube users—and they have the power to affect the political environment. For Allen, the YouTube video was said to have cost him his chance of making it to the White House. Regarding this incident, CNN Political Editor Mark Preston stated, "If not for YouTube, Allen would most likely be one of the front-runners today for the GOP presidential nomination."

Regarding YouTube's presence during the Democratic debate in South Carolina, Steve Grove, head of news and politics at YouTube, told CNN, "Time was, if you wanted to engage in a primary debate process, you had to be in New Hampshire, or in Iowa," and now, due to YouTube, the questions can come from anyone in the world, and be on any topic. Dan Rather said, "Candidates do hate, genuinely hate, audience participation, because they like to control the environment ... tell candidates people will ask them questions via a YouTube video and they get the shivers."

Senator John McCain had a "YouTube moment" that was picked up and watched by the mainstream media. Democratic hopeful Joe Biden had one, as well. Apparently McCain was chatting with a crowd in South Carolina and said, "Remember that old Beach Boys song, 'Bomb Iran'? Bomb, bomb, bomb ..." The conversation was captured on video, uploaded onto YouTube, and picked up by the mainstream media. Joe Biden was caught on video, saying, "You cannot go to 7-Eleven or a Dunkin' Donuts unless you have a slight Indian accent. I'm not joking." This clip was also posted on YouTube, causing Biden to have to explain himself afterward. It is said, however, that this statement was taken out of context.

There are also clips of old debates on YouTube that come back to haunt presidential hopefuls and force honesty. Many politicians seem to have changed their position on various issues, but YouTubers won't let them, or the world, forget their previous stance. By posting archival video footage from previous debates, the earlier positions quickly resurface for all the world to see.

On the flipside, YouTube can be harnessed by political campaigners. Back in April 2007, YouTube spotlighted one political candidate per week. Each candidate was allowed to ask anything he or she wanted to the public via a YouTube video. Viewers answered the call and spoke back. One video that created a huge buzz was called "I Got a Crush ... on Obama." It featured an attractive young lady seductively singing about her love for the presidential candidate. The woman was actually lip-syncing and the video was the idea of ad exec Ben Relles.

"I Got a Crush … on Obama" by Obama Girl.

YouTube is most definitely empowering citizens, if not forcing candidates to think twice before they speak in public. The Democratic debate, indeed, was groundbreaking. The YouTube videos added a personal and creative flair to the questions. Whether seeing the viewers changed the way the questions were answered (or even affected the candidates' opinions) is another question entirely that perhaps we'll never know, but we certainly know one thing: YouTube does have an effect on shaping and changing society.

Steve Grove, head of news and politics for YouTube, said, "This program is absolutely unique to YouTube. The candidates are very excited about coming on a platform that has millions of eyeballs across the world. They recognize the power in that."

One of the most significant influences YouTube has had thus far was the presidential debate in which candidates were asked questions by the public via YouTube videos in 2007. The *LA Times* wrote, "If not a revolution, (the debate) was at least a significant development in a process that has grown more open to voter input and less driven by political professionals and Washington pundits." One Massachusetts voter stated, "The American citizen is now star of the show …." It seems this viewer's words aren't just true for the presidential debates, but rather true of the YouTube phenomenon as a whole.

# Just the Facts

Less than a year earlier, the YouTube founders were bankrolling costs on their own credit cards. Now their site had become a vehicle for huge corporations and American politics! Clearly YouTube was experiencing enormous growth.

In March 2006, YouTube was serving 30 million videos per day and uploading 30,000 new files per day. Five million unique users were said to be visiting the site each day. By May 2006, YouTube had captured 43 percent of all visits to video search sites, and in three months had seen its share of visits increase by 160 percent.

YouTube had nearly *doubled* its traffic since April (only one month earlier) reaching 12.6 million visitors. Surges in growth are not unfamiliar to YouTube. For example, during the week of July 9, 2006, traffic apparently rose 75 percent when World Cup footage was shown. It drew 12.8 million visitors compared to 7.3 million unique viewers the previous week.

For 2006, in general, Neilsen/Netratings had reported that YouTube's traffic had quadrupled in the first six months of the year. It also stated that, statistically, the site was skewed toward the younger male audience; younger males apparently were 20 percent more likely to visit than women. As well, people between the ages of 12 and 17 were one and a half times more likely than average to visit the site. Now, do you remember that in March 2006, YouTube was serving 30 million videos per day? Well, by July 2006, YouTube was serving *100 million* videos per day.

As of September 2008, YouTube is still standing strong. Traffic continues to move upward even after Viacom ordered the removal of thousands of clips (see Chap-

ter 3, "SueTube"). YouTube's average weekly traffic has steadily increased by 7 percent per week since the beginning of the year. Interestingly, however, the ages of viewers are changing slightly. In 2006, 59.7 percent of viewers were under the age of 34. That figure has since dropped to 43.8 percent. Perhaps this is due to the widening variety of content available to older audiences?

By late June 2007, YouTube's site audience was 50 percent larger than *all rivals combined,* and the visits to its site are up 70 percent since May 2007. By contrast, visits to the next 64 largest sites rose only 8 percent during the same five-month period. Ellen Lee of the San Francisco Chronicle predicts that by the year 2010, user-generated video sites such as YouTube are expected to make more than $850 million per year in revenue.

YouTube has also garnered some nice awards and recognition. In May 2006, YouTube was named one of *Red Herring* magazine's top private North American entertainment and media companies for 2006. It was also listed in *PC World* as one of the best 100 products of 2006, as *Entertainment Weekly's* Entertainer of the Year, and *Time's* Best Invention of the Year in 2006, to name a few.

> By July 2006, YouTube was serving *100 million* videos per day.

# YouTube Takes on a Life of Its Own ... Virally

Some of the factors that caused YouTube to grow so enormous didn't have anything to do with YouTube at all. Remember, YouTube had provided the *means*. It was the users who took their cue and ran—boosting YouTube's success in a manner that could not have been foreseen or planned. Indeed, from the get-go, Chad Hurley had stated that YouTube was all about "democratizing the entertainment experience." *Time* magazine named "You" its Person of the Year in 2006, due to the fact that YouTube's democracy was (and is still) "seizing the reins of the global media."

Seize it, they did: both professionally created content as well as everyday user-generated amateur content. Sometimes the clips that rose to viral popularity were seemingly random and out of the blue. One example was the now-ubiquitous *Saturday Night Live* skit "Lazy Sunday," which caused visits to YouTube to skyrocket. In December 2006 users uploaded "Lazy Sunday" onto YouTube and the skit proved so popular that visits to the site shot up 873 percent. Some, in fact, attribute this very video to bringing YouTube into the mainstream.

## The Rise of Homemade Videos

The Back Dormitory Boys lip sync to Backstreet Boys' "I Want It That Way."

Equally unexpected was the way homemade content made the viral rounds. The Back Dormitory Boys (two Asian students lip-syncing to the Backstreet Boys), the now-infamous LonelyGirl15, and Judson Laipolly's "The Evolution of Dance" (which was viewed 23 million times) have infiltrated popular culture. With as much talk about YouTube as a site for professional content, the user-generated videos have been massively popular, if not even more so than professionally produced content. Michael Geist, in a *BBC News* article, thinks it is because "user-generated content was previously all but unavailable to the general public—with the forgettable exception of television shows such as *America's Funniest Home Videos*—the best of user-generated video today attracts large audiences and competes with anything being offered on the major networks."

Homemade clips have become all the rage. Take, for example, people dressing up in chicken suits and doing daring (although some not-so-smart) stunts, video "mash-ups" (whereby content is re-spliced and edited), home-made music videos, "how-tos" of various kinds, local tours of previously forgotten home-towns, and, yes, inevitably some material unsuitable to those of a younger audience.

YouTube has turned the short, homemade video into an art form in and of itself, something to be created and collected. And don't forget the actual recordings of real, unstaged life—at least,

unstaged as far as we can tell. In the now-famous clip "Bus Un-cle," Elvis Ho of Hong Kong was sitting on a bus minding his own business when he asked Roger Chan, the man sitting in front of him, to talk on his cell phone more quietly. Elvis Ho was then berated by the man for several minutes. The whole incident was captured on a cell phone camera and uploaded to YouTube. The candid video became a sensa-tion, and some of the enraged man's verbiage (like the now-hilarious catchphrase "I've got pressure!") has even become part of our vernacular.

> "[U]ser-generated videos have been massively popular ... even more so than profes-sionally produced content."
> —Michael Geist

## The Celebrity Next Door

YouTube has also helped to launch a new kind of celebrity. David Lehre, for example, was a college student from a small town in Michigan. After creat-ing and starring in a short film, "MySpace: The Movie," he up-loaded it to YouTube, where it became a viral hit. Now he has a talent agent and a deal with Fox. Millions of viewers have taken it upon themselves to attempt the very same strategy to launch

their own careers. Everyone from musicians to video animators is waiting to be discovered on the information superhighway.

Later in this book, I'll give you some tips to help you make videos that stand out and get recognized. In creating your own success, it is important to study the achievements of others to an-alyze why what they did works. Soon, you could be a YouTube celebrity in your own right.

## Blasts from the Past

YouTube also caters to an older, more nostalgic and sophisticated audience. The possibility of seeing rare archival clips of all varieties has made YouTube irresistible to those who have a penchant for the past. For example, one can find George Clinton in 1969 in a television show called *Say Brother,* as well as a rare Bob Dylan documentary, and virtually any live performance of a beloved band. Through the new, YouTube has revived the old. You could spend weeks sifting through the random clips users have uploaded, lost in memories ….

YouTube has also managed to revive a contemporary, but failed, TV show. When the series *Nobody's Watching* wasn't picked up by NBC, the creators were so passionate about having it seen that they uploaded it onto YouTube and brought it back to life via the YouTube audience. Users are now downloading it more than 300,000 times in one day, and it now has an ever-growing fan base.

## Reality Tube

Entertainment isn't the only thing that's taking YouTube by storm. More weighty issues are getting exposure, after having spread across the globe via YouTube. Not more than a year after YouTube was up and running, people were using the site to post videos of the Israel-Hezbollah conflict, uploading very real, and unmediated, footage of destruction and propaganda as well as homemade documentaries.

One 27-year-old man named Mohammed placed a video on YouTube that became one of the most popular in the week of its posting. In Beirut, Mohammed had taped bombs exploding in the night sky, and had uploaded it to YouTube in an attempt to show viewers, firsthand, the gritty horror of the situation. He was just one of thousands who recognized the opportunity YouTube provided as a forum for those who were being under- and misrepresented.

The U.S. Military also recognized the opportunity to educate Americans (and the world) on its operations in Iraq. It launched a Channel on YouTube, offering viewers a "boots-to-the-ground" experience and perspective on what is going on in Iraq. While it's not a completely unbiased view of the war (because unlike some soldiers' direct uploads, this Channel is undeniably backed by the Pentagon), it does lend some insight into our current situation overseas.

YouTube has also provided a way for people to express and share their grief. After the tragedy of the shootings at Virginia Tech on April 16, 2007, users deluged YouTube with tributes to the students and faculty who were killed. Remarkably, these clips weren't made solely by the people who were involved and who were personally affected; rather, they were created by people from all across the country who felt the need to provide some form of support system.

It's clear to see that YouTube's unbelievable growth has much to do with Hurley and Chen's ability to understand, and act upon, the personal needs of their users, while also gracefully (and uniquely) meeting the needs of the content providers who want to take advantage of the huge audience. They did all this with a hefty dash of daring in order to make sure that what they stood for (providing a democratic environment) remained consistent and true—no easy feat, considering the pressure involved on all sides.

A little idea, wanting to provide a simple way to share videos, has truly taken on a life of its own. This type of growth could never have been predicted. YouTube has been wildly successful in growing and building a community—one surely beyond the creators' wildest imaginations.

What the Buck?!

Godzilla Here

# chapter 3

# SueTube

One of the things I love to search for on You-Tube is clips of hard-to-find vintage television. Remember *The Brady Bunch Variety Hour?* How about the short-lived *Brady Bunch* sequels, *The Brady Brides* and *The Bradys?* You can find clips of all these shows uploaded on YouTube.

Interested in the comedy of today? Want to see that funny *Saturday Night Live* sketch from two weeks ago? How about footage from one of your favorite movies that was just released on DVD? Chances are good you'll find it online, as well.

We've all watched content like this on one online video-sharing site or another. But did you know that not all of this content was uploaded legally? Don't get me wrong. Some of it is. As you read in the last chapter, sites like YouTube have licensing agreements with many professional content providers. Yet there is still a proliferation of unlicensed content invading these sites. And protecting the

rights of the copyright holders hasn't always been easy.

Since YouTube's inception, major media corporations have kept a wary eye on the upstart company due to the number of copyrighted clips that Web-savvy (and Web-happy) YouTube users upload onto the site without the owners' permission. Copyright infringement in its most basic terms is the unauthorized use of material covered by copyright law in a manner that violates the original owner's exclusive rights to the work. In an age where the government is cracking down on piracy, the Internet is no longer safe.

YouTube has had some difficulty with those parties who claim that the video-sharing site has infringed on copyrighted materials. They insist that YouTube benefits financially from content that does not belong to them. As you'll see, it's not so cut and dried.

## "Lazy Sunday"

It aired on December 17, 2005: the two-and-a-half minute skit entitled "Lazy Sunday" with *Saturday Night Live* cast members Chris Parnell and Andy Samberg comically rapping about their cupcake-eating journey to the Sunday matinee of *The Chronicles of Narnia*. The skit was so popular that after it aired on the late-night show, multiple

copies of the video were promptly uploaded onto YouTube. One version was downloaded over five million times.

With their antennae raised, NBC, the network that produces and airs the show, contacted YouTube and asked them to remove "Lazy Sunday" from their site. They also asked that they remove the

In an attempt to strengthen its policy against potential copyright infringement, YouTube instated a 10-minute maximum length on videos.

more than 500 other clips, both entertainment and Olympics-related, that were posted by Web users on the site without NBC's permission. YouTube didn't argue. They removed "Lazy Sunday" from their site, and politely stated in their blog, "We know how popular that video is, but YouTube respects the rights of copyright holders."

NBC then posted the clip of "Lazy Sunday" on their own website, NBC.com. However, Web users grumbled about the incompatibility of the video with non-Windows computers. In addition, users were not thrilled that they now had to sit through commercials in order to view the clip. But they didn't have to grumble for long.

Keeping the sketch off YouTube proved harder than originally thought. A YouTube user promptly reposted "Lazy Sunday," hiding it amongst other user-generated sequels and parodies, and consequently making it difficult for YouTube to find and remove the clip. In an attempt to strengthen its policy against potential copyright infringement, YouTube instated a 10-minute maximum length on videos.

If you can't beat 'em, join 'em. Soon after, NBC announced a strategic partnership with YouTube and set up an official NBC Channel on the site where it showed

promotional clips for shows such as *The Office* and *Heroes*. After each *Saturday Night Live* episode, NBC uploaded several authorized *SNL* clips simultaneously on NBC's YouTube Channel and on NBC.com.

Less than a year later, *Saturday Night Live* made active use of YouTube's capabilities. After the FCC censored a version of a televised skit featuring Justin Timberlake and Andy Samberg titled "Dick in a Box," NBC presented the unedited "director's cut" on the Internet. In less than a week, the uncensored version of the video had been viewed by over two million viewers on YouTube alone (not counting the other Internet sites where it was available).

Despite its Web popularity (and *SNL*'s producers' support of YouTube-based publicity), NBC eventually decided to pull the plug once again. In October 2007, they scoured YouTube for their videos and requested they remove all NBC content from their site. NBC Universal then announced that they were teaming up with News Corp. to introduce a competitor to YouTube called Hulu.com (see Chapter 8 for more information), creating a new Web venture that allows the two companies to be in charge of distributing their own copyrighted shows across some of the Web's most heavily trafficked sites, including AOL, Yahoo!, MSN, and MySpace.

# Viacom

After Viacom and the British Broadcasting Corporation (BBC) asked YouTube to stop unauthorized postings of copyrighted video, due to "160,000 free video clips viewed at least 1.5 billion times," Viacom filed a lawsuit on March 13, 2007. This came after a similar suit by Robert Tur, who first sued YouTube in 2005 for using film footage of the L.A. riots. Seeking $1 billion in damages, Viacom also asked for YouTube to stop the practice of making available materials that did not rightfully belong to them. Viacom stated that YouTube "willfully" infringed copyrights from varying shows on its networks, such as MTV, VH-1, Nickelodeon, and Comedy Central.

Both Google and YouTube countered that they fall under the "safe harbor" provision of the Digital Millennium Copyright Act (DMCA) that tries to find a happy medium between "promoting the growth and development of electronic commerce and protecting intellectual property rights." YouTube also argued that they have been more than conscientious toward copyright holders, going far beyond the DMCA law. Not only do they

provide an automated take-down tool to anyone who asks, but they also have set a 10-minute limit on videos that play. If a user breaks the rules three times, YouTube cancels that user's account. In addition, YouTube argued that they were now using anti-piracy software, a "hashing" feature that helps to prevent re-uploading when detecting similar or the same material, and the use of something called "acoustic fingerprints" whereby auditory-signature technology is used to spot a low-quality duplicate of a licensed music video or copyrighted TV clip.

But how successful were they at that point at truly keeping pirated materials off-line? According to an online tracking firm, fewer than one in ten videos on YouTube were uploaded without the permission of copyright holders, and "pirated clips that were pulled off YouTube attracted only 6 percent of (total) viewers."

But Viacom countered that YouTube was only counting videos that were removed as unauthorized content, and that many others, such as duplicates, slipped between the cracks. They

also claimed that the study was flawed in other manners. Viacom stated, "YouTube's site is designed in ways that make it impossible for rights holders to locate all of their copyrighted content, so even a robust take-down notice program will miss significant amounts of material."

Soon thereafter, the English Premiere League (the British football organization) launched legal action against YouTube. The Premiere League stated that YouTube had "knowingly misappropriated" the organization's property by "encouraging footage to be viewed on its site" in order to raise YouTube's profile. The stakes for the Premiere League were high. Its commercial value had been climbing over the years, and protecting their rights had become of greatest importance. To give you an idea, for the combined TV, radio, and Internet rights to show both live games and highlights over the next three years, the league had received 2.7 billion pounds sterling, or approximately $5.5 billion U.S. dollars.

# Followed Suit

"… [there were] going to be bumps along the way, but we're trying to make an effort to make the new model work for everyone."
—Chad Hurley

In May 2007, NBC Universal joined Viacom as a co-plaintiff in the case, arguing that "YouTube.com encourages massive copyright infringement in its video-sharing website in order to generate a great deal of public attention, and boost site traffic as well as advertising sales," and that "many of NBCU's most valuable copyrighted works have been copied, performed, and disseminated without authorization by YouTube and other similarly operated websites. NBCU has a strong interest in preserving the strength and viability of all of its legal rights and remedies in response to such conduct."

France's top soccer league and national tennis organization, the *Federation Française de Tennis and Ligue de Football Professionnel* (the group that puts on the French Open) followed suit. Michel Grach, the league's media director, stated, "YouTube hinders our efforts to develop and promote the sport of tennis in the interest of amateur and professional players and fans throughout France in the world through a variety of media, including our own innovative websites."

Cherry Lane Music Publishing, an independent publisher that manages more than 65,000 copyrights (including publishing rights to music from Elvis, Quincy Jones, and the Black Eyed Peas), also joined the party. In June 2007, Cherry Lane was quoted as saying that they have been meticulous thus far in the protection of their clients' copyrights. A spokesperson for the company said, "(Cherry Lane) has a long history of finding outlets for the music catalogues we manage, and in doing so have struck innovative partnerships with dozens of entertainment companies and have licensed songs for all media, including websites. We want to be able to continue these important efforts on behalf of our songwriters and composers, so that they get the full benefit of their hard work, without being held hostage by YouTube's infringement."

# The Other Side

From the get-go, Chad Hurley insisted he was trying to improve the site for users while "working to find arrangements that (would) satisfy Hollywood." He said that there were "going to be bumps along the way, but we're trying to make an effort to make the new model work for everyone."

In fact, back in 2006, Hurley had signed a deal with Warner Music that he thought could potentially model how he worked with all of Hollywood and other music companies in the future. YouTube also was in the process of developing technology that would, for example, identify if an uploaded video belonged to Warner, and, subsequently, when the site played the video, it would share some of the revenue, generated from advertising, with Warner.

## Partial List of Companies with YouTube Licensing Deals

| | |
|---|---|
| BBC | NBA |
| BBC World News | Playboy |
| CBS | Reuters Video |
| CelebTV | Saily Mirror |
| EA | Showtime |
| Ford Models | The Sun Newspaper |
| Fox News Blast | Universal Music Group |
| G4TV | Warner Bros. Records |
| National Geographic | |

Hurley also argued that YouTube was much more than users simply uploading the copyrighted videos of others. Many professionals, such as the team that created LonelyGirl15 (see Chapter 6, "The Pioneers") were creating material for YouTube. This continues to be the case today.

From the beginning, it seemed that Hollywood executives were interested in finding ways to create a cooperative synergy with YouTube, but they just weren't sure how to do it. A 2006 *New York Times* article stated that companies "are happy to use YouTube as a free place to distribute movie trailers and TV clips, but users prefer the very best bits of hit shows." It seemed that executives wanted to find a way to have YouTube promote their programs, but didn't want to give away the crown jewels.

Hurley also rejected the idea of inserting commercials before video segments. He stated that YouTube was developing new, more "engaging advertising formats that will lure people to watch commercials that interest them." He also argued that YouTube's bargaining power with Hollywood would increase as YouTube gained popularity.

More recently, on behalf of YouTube, Google chief executive Eric Schmidt stated, "Viacom is a company built from lawsuits; look at their history." He was referring to the fact that Viacom had hired Philippe Dauman (Viacom's previous general counsel of 20 years) to be their CEO, as well as Viacom's high-profile anti-trust suit against Time Warner in 1989, while they claimed that Time Warner's HBO pay cable movies service attempted to put Viacom's Showtime out of business by a process of intimidation. The suit was ultimately settled out of court in 1992, in which Time Warner paid $75 million and agreed to purchase a cable system (above market price) and agreed to distribute Showtime more broadly on the Time Warner cable TV system.

The case of Viacom against YouTube has yet to be resolved. Indeed, due to the lawsuit, much is at stake for YouTube, as well as billions of dollars in advertising revenue for YouTube and Google. Much is at stake for everyone, in fact. The outcome of the case shall affect millions of Web users and companies, paving the trail for the future. That said, there have always been companies like Warner Music who have been willing to deal with YouTube more amicably and to work *with* them in licensing deals that benefit them both.

# **Deal or** No Deal?

"[A]bout 15 percent of You-Tube's 100 most popular clips are videos edited to music tracks."

When the music video for Acon's hip-hop single "Smack That" was uploaded to YouTube and viewed over half a million times, the site's administrators began to worry about potential lawsuits from the artists, record company, or songwriters, so they promptly began negotiating licensing deals with Vivendi (who owns the label that released the song). Agreements with other TV and music companies followed soon after.

However, getting the necessary permissions to license the songs and shows wasn't a snap. Sorting through the copyrights to music and music videos isn't such a straightforward matter. For instance, many of YouTube's agreements with record labels didn't include royalties for the music publishers who control the copyrights to the words and music.

This meant that YouTube had quite the undertaking when it came to vetting the different rights owners. They had to seek out studios, actors, music composers, and owners to get them to sign off on the permissions. If just one of these many people involved in making a music video (or just the song itself) didn't grant permission, YouTube risked yet another potential lawsuit.

This affects the average users uploading videos of themselves lip-syncing to their favorite tunes. These clips, in fact, pose the most complex problem. If it were simply the original music video that was uploaded, YouTube could get permission from the record label. However, with the lip-sync videos, they must obtain the permission of publishers who represent the songs' writers.

According to the *Wall Street Journal,* music publishing is a highly fragmented and compartmentalized industry where "hundreds of tiny players have various kinds of relationships with larger publishers." Each publisher needs to grant permission for, say, "Smack That" to appear alongside any imagery other than the official music video. This is no small thing. Apparently about 15 percent of You-Tube's 100 most popular clips are videos edited to music tracks. In most cases, publishers will likely be paid roughly 10 to 15 percent of "whatever share of advertising revenue is set aside for content owners."

Clips of TV shows pose similar problems when it comes to copyrights, due to the veritable mind-numbing network of rights owners. Apparently the detangling of rights and owners can take years. Would you believe it took more than two years for NBC Universal to clear the rights necessary to make the first two seasons of *Miami Vice* available on DVD?

In many ways, however, this is nothing new. These challenges have been foreshadowed by all the new entertainment channels that have sprung up over the years: DVDs, digital tracks on iTunes, satellite radio, cell-phone ring tones, and so on. Technology, in its explosion, has caused the slower cogs of business and law to scramble in order to catch up to the information age.

The sorting of rights will be no small task (roughly 60 percent of the most popular YouTube videos contain commercial music or video footage) but YouTube remains ever optimistic. They insist that the headache of combing through rights will be incentive for entertainment companies to "streamline their rights clearances," and that the system the company is building for managing commercial content should "eventually be able to automatically dole out ad revenue, sharing payments with

a multitude of rights holders for any given clip." As soon as rights issues are solved, the content will be spread further and faster than ever before.

Despite the apparent hassle of rights clearances, YouTube has signed a variety of licensing deals. In addition to Universal/ Vivendi, YouTube has a licensing deal with Sony BMG Entertainment that lets Sony artists' music and videos be included in original content posted on YouTube. A deal with CBS lets people view content such as news, sports, and primetime programming from the CBS brand channels. The deal also covers technology that enables CBS to find unauthorized content on YouTube and remove it—or choose to keep the content up and stream advertising next to it.

YouTube has also lined up a licensing deal with the National Basketball Association. The NBA has created a YouTube Channel that includes NBA content, but also encourages users to post their own video clips of personal on-the-court moves. The NBA

also retains the right to ask YouTube to take down any clips they deem copyrighted, or to apply to share in the company's advertising revenue. Apparently they're following in the steps of the National Hockey League, which has a similar deal with YouTube. More and more companies are recognizing this opportunity and have signed deals with the site.

Eventually the BBC decided to part ways with Viacom, and became the first international broadcaster to sign on with YouTube in a partnership that helps bring the BBC to a worldwide audience. Apparently, through YouTube, the BBC also hopes to attract Web users and viewers to its own Web-based service. The BBC has created BBC brand channels on the YouTube site. And while they do not actively hunt down clips, they retain the right to swap clips that are of poor quality, request the takedown of clips that infringe on the copyright of others, or that have been edited in some way that potentially damages the BBC "brand."

# **Pornography** on YouTube

Copyright infringement isn't the only challenge YouTube has had to face. While YouTube allows anyone the opportunity to post videos online, there are limits

to what is deemed acceptable content. For those users who create their own amateur X-rated videos, YouTube may not be the right place to share them.

But it didn't take long for people to figure out all the creative ways to exploit YouTube as a forum for another sort of ... er ... self-expression. And just as it's been

There is also the argument that YouTube *shouldn't* patrol too heavy-handedly lest it become big-brotheresque and squelch people's freedoms.

impossible for YouTube to constantly sift through and remove videos that are copyrighted, it has been equally challenging for YouTube to locate and eliminate clips of an explicit nature. What's more, that which may be considered explicit by some may not be thought controversial by others. And does YouTube really want to be in the censorship business?

Users can flag a video of questionable content and, if deemed inappropriate, YouTube can remove it from the site. And although the YouTube user agreement "forbids" users to upload videos that are "unlawful, obscene, defamatory, libelous, threatening, pornographic, harassing, hateful, racially or ethnically offensive, or encourages conduct that would be considered a criminal offense, give rise to civil liability, violate any law, or is otherwise inappropriate," people still find a way to get their exhibitionist videos on the site.

There has been some public outcry that YouTube's ability to patrol their site for pornography is clumsy and ineffectual; yet on the other hand, there is also the argument that YouTube *shouldn't* patrol too heavy-handedly lest it become big-brotheresque and squelch people's freedoms. According to YouTube's policy, "YouTube will remove all Content and User Submissions if properly notified …. YouTube also reserves

the right to decide whether Content or a User Submission is appropriate and complies with these Terms of Service for violations other than copyright infringement and violations of intellectual property law, such as, but not limited to, pornography, obscene, or defamatory material."

Ineffectual at keeping these videos off their site or not, YouTube was (and is) clearly not interested in being a site known for adult entertainment. Other Internet opportunists recognized this fact and YouTube spin-offs began, such as PornoTube and XTube.com (see Chapter 8).

Indeed, due to pornography on its site, YouTube did attract the government's eye. The United States government subjects websites that host pornographic content to decency rules with the intent to protect those underage from being seen in that content and also sheltering those minors from seeing the content. YouTube now dissuades users under the age of 13 from going to the site at all! Minors ages 13 to 17 are encouraged to use the site only if they have permission from a parent or guardian. In fact, any time a video with questionable content is requested, YouTube directs the user to a simple age verification page.

If potential filmmakers want to share certain content with friends and family, they should. But they should consider marking those videos private so that only their friends can see them. In fact, YouTube has great instructions on how to mark your own videos as private. (To learn how to mark your videos "private," see Chapter 5.)

If you're a user who stumbles across a video that you find offensive, you can always flag it.

Just click the link on the video page to flag it as inappropriate to report it to YouTube. The system administrators will then review the content, and if they agree that it is inappropriate material for their site, the video will be removed.

YouTube has taken significant steps to alleviate this problem. There is little else they can do.

Dissuading viewers from posting such content, dissuading younger children from gaining access to the site, policing the site as best they can, and allowing others (the public) to police the site themselves and flag videos they deem inappropriate, seems like a plan that covers all the bases.

# **Happy** Slapping

YouTube has also been used as a conduit for displaying a strange and dark fad known as *happy slapping*. Happy slapping is the phenomenon whereby an accomplice, using a camera phone or other recording device, records an assault of an unsuspecting victim. The assault can be as small as someone being slapped (as the name suggests), or it can be as drastic as someone being beaten. Usually the perpetrators are young, and the other defining feature is that the attacker usually makes the assault look like play (hence the "happy" in "happy slapping").

There was one case in Scotland whereby someone used a cell phone to record and subsequently post footage of a 15-year-old boy punching the rector of a high school. The image was distributed among other students, and as a result, the police had trouble

tracing the student who recorded the incident. The incident came after a veritable rise in happy slappings in Scotland. One article in the Scottish press said, "Such behavior is sadly an unwelcome by-product of advances in technology, which, coupled with almost unlimited access to Internet video outlets, has opened up unprecedented opportunities for attention-seekers to get themselves noticed. It far exceeds the thrill of spraying their names on the wall of the local underpass."

As a result of this and other related incidents, there has been a call to arms requesting more control of content by websites such as YouTube. Some have even suggested that YouTube encourages criminal behavior. However, there is a fine line between what is acceptable and what is not. Making such determinations is dangerous territory to explore.

"Happy Slapping"

**Happy slapping** is the phenomenon whereby an accomplice, using a camera phone or other recording device, records an assault of an unsuspecting victim.

Other cases of happy slapping posted on YouTube make the previous incident seem positively tame. In 2006, seven videos from New Zealand were posted to YouTube involving teens and recorded with cell-phone cameras. In one video, two students, surrounded by a large circle of boys, knock another boy unconscious. The boy subsequently went into convulsions. Rather sickeningly, viewers went so far as to rate the clip (four and a half stars out of five). The video, however, was promptly removed (as was another clip of two girls fighting). A third clip involved three students standing around while one boy is punched in the face. When a teacher stops the fight, the teacher is criticized for doing just so on camera.

Huge public uproar followed after the posting of a video in which a man was involved in an argument. In the video, he is punched, and when he runs away he is followed, knocked to the ground, and repeatedly kicked in the head until unconscious. Oddly, for the short time users could view this video, they were simply forewarned, "This video may contain content that is inappropriate for some users" and quickly forwarded to YouTube's age verification page. Now, in addition to removing such videos as quickly as possible, YouTube also states on its website, "Real violence is not allowed. If your video shows someone getting hurt, attacked, or humiliated, don't post it."

Be careful of what you do and how you behave in public. We've really gone camera-crazy, and every day you could wind up on an episode of *Candid Camera* or *Punk'd*. There was a case in Canada whereby two 13-year-old girls provoked their teacher, who was unknowingly being videotaped, until he yelled at one of them. It was, once again, posted on YouTube. Apparently the girls were suspended and the school board decided to side with the teacher, who subsequently went away on stress leave.

Additionally, Michael Richards (from *Seinfeld* fame), was taped in a stand-up comedy routine, "spewing racial epithets" when audience members heckled his performance. The tape, on YouTube, was viewed more than 470,000 times. Richards acknowledged his actions and subsequently apologized publicly.

# The YouTube Effect

Not all is doom and gloom. There is a positive side of the story, whereby the ubiquity of YouTube can affect change, and change for the better. YouTube has the ability to put more power into the hands of the masses when it comes to politics and issues of human rights.

The "YouTube effect" is dubbed as being "the phenomenon whereby video clips, often produced by individuals acting on their own, are rapidly disseminated through the world" and with subsequent wide-ranging impact. Not always posted for entertainment, indeed, many videos include posts by terrorists, human rights advocacy groups, and even U.S. soldiers in Iraq.

One example was the video of Tibetan refugees being shot on a high mountain pass in the Himalayas. It was posted on YouTube, and though the Chinese government swore the shootings were in self-defense, the eye of the camera and the recording showed, clearly, otherwise. The result was that the U.S. ambassador to China was able to complain, protesting China's treatment of refugees.

Not only that, but oftentimes there is a synergy between television and the Internet that creates even wider impact. Videos posted on the Web are "re-aired" on mainstream TV networks, or images on TV are captured and disseminated on the Web, causing an informational reverberation around the globe.

Governments are keeping a wary eye on this trend. On the one hand, there is power in the hands of the people, which is good. But the degree of control that a government has could be very dangerous. It's hard to know for sure what to believe and what is being planted in order to sway public opinion.

In fact, the U.S. military has now ordered that its soldiers not post videos that have not been screened, and (scarily) the Iranian government restricts connection speeds to "limit its people's access to video streaming." Yet, this does little to stop its proliferation. It seems that there already is a filter in place with bloggers who watch and fact-check the video content—perhaps far more effective than one massive fact-checking entity.

Despite all the outcry, despite all the controversy the young company has caused, it does seem that YouTube wants to do, and has always wanted to do, the right thing. Indeed, it's doubtful that it could have been better handled; after all, YouTube began as three young guys who saw an opportunity in the wild west of the Internet. They likely could not have foreseen the impact that their site would have on Web users and the entertainment industry in general, let alone the fact that they would affect the entire world through, say, exposing human rights issues. YouTube provides the forum—it is people, like you and me, who are proliferating the content, questionable or not. But as always, it's much easier to shoot the messenger ....

They likely could not have foreseen the impact that their site would have on Web users and the entertainment industry in general.

# chapter 4

# YouTube for Virgins

**W**arning! When reading this chapter, proceed with extreme caution. Exploring YouTube may be responsible for the loss of many valuable hours in your day. Of course, using YouTube is not a bad thing. In fact, you will probably find much enjoyment from viewing videos online. But this hobby can be highly addictive.

There are several reasons you may lose track of time while perusing this site. First off, there are hundreds of thousands of videos to browse. They cover a vast number of subjects and are posted by users from around the world. Every page is filled with *hyperlinks* connecting you to even more fascinating *podcasts*

and *webisodes*. It is just so easy to click link after link until you have completely lost track of time.

This chapter helps you explore YouTube in a logical and easy-to-follow manner. Read straight through, you will be given a basic map and game plan for using this site. But if you are like me, and like to just explore on your own, you can always reference the topics in this chapter on an as-needed basis to find solutions to some of your unanswered questions.

Don't say I didn't warn you. If you are ready for adventure, type the following address into your browser: www.youtube.com.

**Hyperlink, Podcast, Webisode**

**Hyperlinks** are used to connect to different Web pages on the Internet. Simply click on the hyperlinked text or object, often notated by an alternative color, and a new Web page will appear. In this book, hyperlinks will be indicated in bold print.

Audio broadcast delivered to users over the World Wide Web are known as **podcasts.** Think of them as radio for your computer.

**Webisodes** are episodes of an entertainment program produced primarily for distribution on the Internet.

# Creating an Account

While it is not necessary to create an account in order to explore YouTube and enjoy most of the site's features, it is required for certain advanced functions and for uploading video. Because it is a relatively painless process and it is also free to become a member, I will walk you through the steps.

## Blogs Versus Vlogs

**Blogs** are online written journals that users update periodically for their friends or anyone else to read. Sometimes they feature photos, viral video, and even hyperlinks to other pages.

**Vlogs** add a camera into the equation. Journals are now visual, and users can speak their thoughts into the lens for their friends or anyone else to view.

"Logging In"

If you've already got a You-Tube account, but you're using this particular computer for the first time, you may have to log in manually. From the YouTube homepage you can click **Log In** on the upper right-hand corner of the screen. Enter your user-name and password when prompted. You are now ready to begin.

At the very top of the homepage, you will see a series of menu options. Start by clicking on **Sign Up.** A simple form will appear for you to fill out. All questions are straightforward, and the information you enter will assist in creating a username and password so that you may access the full services of the site. The only question that may confuse you is **Account Type.**

There are various types of accounts you can select. If you plan to simply use the site to discover new streaming content, then a *standard* account will be adequate. If you plan to upload videos that you create, choose

a *director* account. If you are a *musician* or *comedian*, there are accounts specific to you. Finally, a *guru* account is for people who consider themselves to be an expert in a particular field, and plan to share video blogs about their subject of expertise. You can always change the type of account you have, so don't stress over your selection. In fact, you can pretty much post or view anything you like from any of these accounts, so feel free to make one master account, or multiple accounts if you prefer to keep your various interests separate.

After successfully completing the signup form, you will be directed to a new page thanking you for joining YouTube. A confirmation email will also be sent to the email address you entered. You must click on the link inside the email to start using the service. Once this is done, you will automatically be logged in to the website.

# Setting Up My Account

You may set up your account at any time, but it is not necessary to do so prior to surfing the website and discovering all that it has to offer. If you want to jump right into watching videos, skip ahead to the next section. When

you are ready to set up your account and choose preferences for using advanced features, you can revisit this part of the chapter and read it through at your leisure.

From the homepage, click on **My Account.** From here you will see an overview of all of your YouTube settings. The first box you will see has statistics on your YouTube activities. It lists information such as the number of videos you have uploaded, the number of videos you have watched, and the number of times users have viewed your videos. You may also notice that your username is hyperlinked in this section. If you click on it, you will be taken to your personal user page, or *Channel*.

Beneath the user statistics, your account is divided into several sections that you can manage. They include *Videos*, *Channel Settings*, *Account Settings*, *Inbox*, *Subscriptions & Subscribers*, *Friends & Contacts*, and *Groups*. Each of these sections is explained below. Also, this list is always available under the "More" heading in the upper right-hand corner of the Account screen.

An individual YouTube user's homepage is called a **Channel.**

# Videos

In this section, you can manage and keep track of your videos. It is divided into three categories: **My Videos, Favorite Videos,** and **Playlists. My Videos** contains all of the videos you have personally uploaded to the site. **Favorite Videos** encompasses the best videos you have seen while browsing the site. In order to save a video to this list, you must tag it as a favorite.

*Playlists* can be assembled to play videos in a particular order, to categorize them by subject, and to easily share them with friends. Playlists can be both public for all to see, and private for only your friends to see. This section also has a button to **Upload New Video.**

Users may create **Playlists** to arrange their videos in a specific order or to share them easily with other users.

# Channel Settings

On YouTube, your own personal Web page is called a Channel. To set up your Channel and control how other users see your page, go to Channel Settings. **Channel Info** lets you title and describe your Channel. It also enables you to select several preferences such as a Channel Icon, Channel Comments, Who can Comment, Channel Bulletins, and Channel Type. **Channel Design** lets you select a visual theme for your Channel with various layouts and colors to choose from.

**Organize Videos** lets you arrange the order of your first nine videos. **Personal Info** gives you an opportunity to tell users a little about yourself. Remember, anyone can gain access to this information, so only post what you want others to see. **Location Info** lets you post where you grew up and where you currently reside. Finally, **Channel URL** is the Web address where people can find you on YouTube.

## Account Settings

This is the real administrative part of the site where you are able to make changes to your account preferences. You can change your **Password,** choose **Email Options,** fill out **Personal Info;** set up your **Video Posting Settings, Mobile Upload Profiles,** and **Developer Profile;** enable **Active Sharing;** and terminate your relationship with YouTube by clicking **Close Account.**

**Email Options** enable you to receive a personal email when certain events occur, such as someone subscribing to your Channel or posting a comment or video response to one of your video logs, or *vlogs*. **Video Posting Settings** makes it easy to post videos directly to an existing *blog*. Creating a

**Mobile Profile** lets you upload videos directly from the camera on your cellular phone. A **Developer Profile** is for software developers, giving them the ability to integrate YouTube Videos into the applications they are creating.

**Active Sharing** lets other users know what videos you are watching by adding them to your Channel and by putting your username on the video pages as you watch them. For anyone with privacy concerns, be sure to turn **Active Sharing off.** On the other hand, trendsetters may choose to keep this function enabled at all times.

## Inbox

With YouTube, you get your own mailbox from which you can send and receive **General Messages, Video Comments,** and view **Received Videos.** This is the place where you will receive **Friend Invites,** as well.

Imagine posting a vlog online and receiving an email from a complete stranger about something you said. Now, imagine getting a video response where you can actually see the passion and emotion behind their words. Just be careful what you say!

## Subscriptions & Subscribers

When we subscribe to a magazine, a new issue is delivered to us on a regular basis. Subscriptions on YouTube work the same way. When you subscribe to a particular Channel, you will be notified each time that user uploads a new video. You can also subscribe to a user's favorites, or to particular tags.

This is the area of YouTube where you can manage your subscriptions. You can also manage those users who subscribe to your personal Channel. This may not seem necessary when you're starting out, but once your Channel becomes popular,

"Subscriptions"

To ensure that you don't miss certain videos, you can subscribe to various Channels, user favorites, or tags. When a new item that matches your subscription list is uploaded to YouTube, it will appear in your Subscription center.

you'll need some tools to keep track of your fan base. Conversely, once you begin adding Channel Subscriptions, you'll need some way of organizing your media.

## Friends & Contacts

In this section you can manage your friends and contacts. You can sort fellow YouTube users into various groups including **Friends, Family,** and **All Contacts** if you just want to view a complete list. You can even create a new category by clicking **Create New List.**

Find out if your friends are already using this website with a simple **Search.** You can also ask non–YouTube pals to try out the site by clicking **Invite Friends to Join YouTube.** Finally, you can prevent users from contacting you at all by categorizing them as **Blocked Users.**

## Groups

The final area you can control from this page is Groups. Groups are used by people with common interests. Here you can view and manage your YouTube groups.

You can also create new groups. Put together a group of retirees. How about a group of Harry Potter fans? Be creative and have fun! Creating and joining existing groups is one way that YouTube fosters community.

## Homepage

The YouTube homepage is generally where you begin your YouTube experience. Now that your account is set up, you are ready to begin exploring the site. If you are like me, you will find yourself jumping from video to video through a series of related hyperlinks. If you like to do things in a more orderly fashion, YouTube is also designed for easy accessibility through its four main components: *Videos, Categories, Channels,* and *Community.*

Click on the "YouTube" logo—in the upper left-hand corner—to go to the homepage. Before you access the four tabs at the top of your screen, you may notice that there are many **Featured** videos on the homepage. Generally, these are videos selected by the YouTube editorial staff that they think you will like. Sometimes this is the best way to discover new Channels. In addition to seeing the Featured videos on the homepage, you can also see the ones **Most Viewed, Most Discussed,** or the **Top Favorites.**

Once you start subscribing to various Channels, the newest video from each of your subscriptions will also appear on the homepage. This gives you easy access to see the latest and greatest from your favorite users. And when you start posting your own videos, your subscribers will see your newest video on their YouTube homepage when they log on.

# Videos

From personal vlogs and comedy skits to music videos ... there's truly something for everyone to enjoy.

There are so many types of videos online. In fact, the possibilities are endless. From personal vlogs and comedy skits to music videos and lost television episodes, there's truly something for everyone to enjoy.

At the top of the Video page you will find a search button, enabling you to browse videos by any keyword you enter. But you can also browse videos by a variety of attributes as well as by time and category. Try searching for videos based on your personal interests and see what comes up.

On the left-hand side of the main Video page, you will see the Browse menu. You can search videos the following ways: **Most Recent, Most Viewed, Top Rated, Most Discussed, Top Favorites, Most Linked, Recently Featured, Most Responded, Watch on Mobile.** You can browse videos that were posted **Today, This Week, This Month,** or from **All Time.** And videos are also divided into searchable categories including **Autos & Vehicles, Comedy, Entertainment, Film & Animation, Gadgets & Games, HowTo & DIY, Music, News & Politics, People & Blogs, Pets & Animals, Sports,** and **Travel & Places.**

So what are you waiting for? Starting watching some videos! When you click on any particular video, you will be directed to that video's page (see below). A square video display will play the video. You possess most of the same controls you have when you are watching a DVD, for instance, so you can pause, rewind, adjust the volume, and even view the video full screen in all its glory.

The top right corner of the screen gives you statistics about the video you are watching. It lets you know when it was added to YouTube and who added it, and it gives you an option to subscribe to this user's Channel. It also lists the video's title, description, and category. Finally, tags are clickable, giving you easy access to similarly themed videos, and URL and embedded codes are available if you want to post the video somewhere else, like your personal Web page. Directly below this box, you can choose to click directly to browse **Related Videos,** see **More from this user,** or select user-created **Playlists,** which are Playlists from other users that include this video.

Directly beneath the video display, you have several more options. Using a five-star system, you can **Rate This Video.** If you really like a video, you can **Save to Favorites** for easy access on your personal Channel. Favorites can be divided into Playlists, or folders, if you want to organize your videos into various categories. On my Channel, I have playlists for music videos, helpful videos for using YouTube, and third-party videos about me. Alternatively, you can share the video with your online friends by clicking **Add to Groups.** If you want to share the video with a friend who does not have a YouTube account, you can email the person a link by clicking **Share Video.** If you want to post it to your blog, simply click **Post Video.** If, by chance, you come across content that is inappropriate or offensive, there is even a button to **Flag as Inappropriate.**

Below these clickable options are additional statistics about the video including: number of views, number of comments, and number of times users added the video to their favorites list. You can also see the number of honors the video has received, as well as the URLs of the sites that have linked to the video.

A typical video page featuring one of the author's videos.

The lower left-hand section of this page is the Comments & Responses section. Responses take the form of a video. Comments are text-based. You can watch other users' video responses and read their text comments, or you can post your own video response or text comment for others to see. Who knew that watching videos could be such a truly interactive experience?

# Frederick's
# Favorite Videos

Below are my top-10 favorite YouTube videos.

#1

"*Evolution of Dance*"—Judson Laipply

Standup comedian Judson Laipply takes us through 40 years of dance in this hilarious six-minute clip. Starting with famous moves from the '60s, he grooves onstage to classics like Elvis Presley's "Hound Dog" and Chubby Checker's "The Twist." He then visits the '70s and the disco era, dancing to tunes like the Bee Gees' "Stayin' Alive" and the Village People's "YMCA." The '80s are represented by such classics as "Mr. Roboto" by Styx and a few tunes by Michael Jackson. He brings it into the '90s with "Tubthumping" by Jambawamba, and ends the sketch dancing to "Bye, bye, bye" from N'Sync. The music changes every 20 seconds, as do Laipply's moves. For a complete song list, visit Judson's website at www.evolutionofdance.com.

#2

"*The Luke Johnson Phone Experiment*"—
Luke Johnson

Luke Johnson decided to run a little experiment on YouTube. He wondered what would happen if he posted his phone number in a video and invited people to call him. More than 1.75 million hits and 130,000 calls later, the experiment is still going strong. With appearances on *The Rachael Ray Show,* BBC, CNN, and NPR, Johnson has certainly gotten his fair share of attention. What I love about this inventive idea is that it really shows the strong community features of YouTube. And with calls from as far away as China, it also shows how small the world really is and how tightly the Internet connects us together.

#3

"*RMCS—The Guide on How to Become Big on YouTube*"—Matt Chin

Matt Chin is a comedian from Toronto, Canada. In addition to hosting his own talk show online, he makes very funny videos. This one shows viewers in a tongue-and-cheek way how to become a YouTube star. The advice is solid, but it parodies so many online videos that you can't help but laugh out loud. For anyone who has an interest in becoming big on YouTube, and for those who are simply fascinated by those who have become big on YouTube, this video is a must-see!

#4

> "Numa Numa"—Gary Brolsma

This is one of the earliest viral videos to hit the Net, and also one of the fastest to spread. If its creator was ever reluctant to claim ownership, his tune has certainly changed. He's got a second, professionally produced video called "New Numa—The Return of Gary Brolsma!" and a third on the way. When a young Gary decided to film himself lip-syncing to a funky song by the boy band Ozone, he never imagined that the video would touch so many people and have such a lasting impact. Because it still holds up today against the plethora of online videos, it definitely makes my favorites list.

#5

> "Noah takes a photo of himself every day for 6 years."—Noah Kalina

The title really says it all. But when you watch the ongoing collection of still photos in rapid succession while listening to the hauntingly beautiful score by Carly Comando, you've got a true work of art. Kalina says this is just the

beginning. Since releasing this video, he has continued to photograph himself on a daily basis and plans updates every few years for the rest of his life. I can only imagine the eventual impact this will have. To me, it speaks volumes about life, aging, and mortality.

#6

> "Mother's Day"—Barats and Bereta

Washington-based comedy duo Barats and Bereta have made some funny videos, but this one takes the cake. The two play brothers attempting to take a photo of themselves to send to their mother on Mother's Day. Of course, the brothers have their own ideas of how they should appear in the photo. Hilarity ensues. Maybe I love this video because it reminds me of my own brother and me. Maybe it's just comedy at its best.

#7

> "str8 outta compton"—Jay Brannan

Jay Brannan is one of the most talented undiscovered musicians on YouTube. He's got an amazing voice, deep and meaningful lyrics, and

# Frederick's Favorite Videos (continued)

a folk rock sound that's destined for greatness. While I love his original material, this cover of Nina Gordon's cover of "Straight Outta Compton" by NWA is just classic. And his rap in the middle is brilliantly funny.

*#8*

> *"Greatest Story Ever Told …*
> *Narrated by Many YouTubers!"—*
> Charles Trippy

This is another great online experiment, this time engineered by Charles Trippy. Trippy took the concept of one person starting off a story with a few words and letting the rest of the group finish it until it tells a continuous story. It's a game most of us played as children, but Trippy invited anyone on YouTube to contribute to the story, and he edited it all together in a very funny, yet somewhat cohesive, tale. It's extremely clever and makes a large statement about the community aspect of YouTube. If you search for the video title above, you'll find the completed story. But if you want to see Trippy's initial invitation to participate, search for his video "Continue this story … to create the greatest story ever told!"

*#9*

> *"Chips"—*Brookers

In this short film, our hero is haunted by a bag of chips. This piece is very well done, very funny, and like all of Brookers's videos, makes great use of its score to really build tension and suspense. How many of us can relate to being on a diet and being haunted by a bag of chips? I certainly can, and that's why this short is in my favorites.

*#10*

> *"'You Tube' (A Love Song)—*
> *Original Song—Acoustic Version"—*
> David Choi

David Choi is an extremely talented songwriter who periodically posts his original songs to YouTube. This one is brilliant, with lyrics like "YouTube, you can comment all over me" and "I'll log in and out to please you," the song does a great job of capturing the true culture of YouTube. On top of that, it's a catchy tune. Personally, I think the owners of YouTube should purchase this song and use it in all their advertisements.

# Categories

The Category tab enables you to go directly to the searchable categories discussed above. However, there are a few added bonuses on this page. Mainly, you get the benefit of the hard-working YouTube editorial staff that constantly searches the site for the best videos to showcase.

Not only does YouTube offer their "Pick of the Day," but they also highlight featured Channels and a featured video within each category. Having your video as one of the featured videos is a goal that most YouTube directors share. All in all, this page offers a great sampling of videos to get started with.

# Channels

As I stated earlier, Channels are user-generated pages. Here you can browse videos by categories such as **Comedians, Directors, Gurus, Musicians, Partners,** and **Sponsors.** You can view them in order of **Most Subscribed** or **Most Viewed.** You can also view them by time period including **This Week, This Month,** and **All Time.** You can click on the name of the Channel to go to that Channel's homepage, or you can click on the featured Recent Video to go directly to that video's page and screen it.

Every user has a Channel once he or she sets up an account. What you do with your Channel is up to you. Much of the information you input earlier when you were setting up your account will already be integrated into your Channel. You can always go back and revise what you wrote. If you would like to see your own personal Channel's homepage, just click your hyperlinked username from the main YouTube homepage. A screen shot of my personal Channel is shown here.

As you can see in the screen shot, or on your own Channel online, the left side of your Channel provides viewers all of your personal details such as your name, viewing statistics, Channel statistics,

Author's YouTube Channel.

Channel description, location, interests and hobbies, website address, and so on. Below your personal details sits a box with options on how others can communicate with you: **Send Message, Add Comment, Share Channel,** and **Add Friend** (which on *your* personal page will say **Remove Friend**). There will also be a hyperlink for your direct Channel URL. Below that is another box listing your Subscriptions. And finally, at the bottom of the left column are Bulletins that anyone can post for all who view your Channel to see.

The right half of your Channel is where most of your media resides. Typically at the top will be your main video that generally consists of your most recent upload. Below that is the remainder of your uploaded videos. That is followed by a display of your Favorite Videos. Then you will see a list of your Subscribers—those users who have signed up to receive new videos from your Channel. After Subscribers, you will see a list of your Friends. And finally, at the bottom of the right column, there is a box containing Comments.

It could go either way here. It may or may not be something you click on (as indicated by underlined text) depending on how many Favorites you have and the layout of our personal Channel.

Of course, every user's Channel is set up a bit differently. After all, when setting up your account, you may recall that there were several different options for Channel Design offered under Channel Settings. Some Channels will have more sections, while others will have fewer; still others may have all of the same options that you have on your Channel, albeit arranged in a completely different sequence. In any case, you are now familiar with the general setup, and are prepared to navigate any Channels that come your way.

# Community

A community is a group that shares common interests. The community page puts you in contact with other users who have similar interests. Here you can join Groups and enter Contests.

Groups and Contests each have their own Channels. On these Channels, you can meet and network with fellow Group members, see Contest entries from other users, and even enter a contest yourself. Be sure to check out the contests, as some of the prizes are truly out of this world.

The community page puts you in contact with other users who have similar interests.

# **Lost** Virginity

Congratulations! You are no longer a virgin to YouTube. By now you have some semblance of how to navigate the website. I suggest you put this book down for a few hours, log on to the site, and have fun!

When you tire of browsing videos (can you ever *really* tire of browsing videos?!), and you cannot contain your urge to post a video response to a vlog, or make a comedy short to share with the World Wide Web, meet me in Chapter 5 where we will discuss the keys to making successful videos. We'll talk about what you need to make a video, and how to make your video stand out above the rest. We'll also break down the process of uploading these videos to YouTube.

What the Buck?!

Godzilla Here

# Making the Video

Y ou've watched hundreds, if not thousands, of videos online. Maybe they inspired you to make your own video and upload it to YouTube. Finally there's a forum where you can be heard. Perhaps you think you can make better videos than the ones that currently exist. Or maybe, just maybe, you think this is the beginning of your ticket to stardom. Whatever the case may be, this chapter will help you craft a video that stands out from the rest.

Whether you're a novice or an expert, I'll walk you through the steps and tell you what you need to make and upload a video to YouTube. I'll explain technical details like the equipment you'll need to film your video and the settings that are ideal to save your masterpiece. I'll also give you tips to help make your vlog or short film stand out from the throngs of others in cyberspace.

Finally, as I write this chapter, I'll also be making my own video and uploading it to my personal YouTube Channel (www.YouTube.com/FrederickLevy). Be sure to log on to YouTube to check out "Welcome to my Vlog" to see how it comes out. Maybe you'll even leave me a comment—or better yet, because you'll soon know how to make one, a video response.

Tim Carter demonstrates how to make a video in his DIY YouTube video, "How to Make a Video."

# Equipment

Many books have been written about filmmaking, and there's a plethora of equipment available for rent or purchase for all levels of filmmaker. As our reason for making videos is to share them online, our discussion will focus on equipment that is sufficient for this purpose.

Because online streams are generally viewed in a small box that is no more than 3 inches tall and 3 inches wide, highest-quality footage is simply not needed. What this means to you is that you don't have to spend thousands of dollars to purchase equipment to begin making online videos. The total setup may end up costing only a few hundred dollars. Of course, any time you add bells and whistles, the price will go up. But you can worry about options such as effects and titles programs later.

This section will give you the basics for what you need to do to get up and running. With a few simple items, you can get started and make your first video. If your newfound hobby turns into a career ambition, you can always upgrade later.

# Camera

The type of video you want to make may determine the type of camera you will need. For simple vlogs or other videos where you will be somewhat static, such as sitting in front of your computer, a webcam will suffice. If you envision greater movement or on-location shooting, most low-level consumer video cameras will do the job.

The webcam you purchase will be determined in part by the type of computer you own. One of the more popular webcams for Mac is iSight. However, they stopped making these and most other Mac-compatible webcams, since most new Mac computers come with a camera built in. If your Mac didn't come with its own camera, you can always try finding an iSight cam on eBay.

PC users have several more options at their disposal. It really comes down to which features are most important to you and how much money you want to pay for a webcam. Several brands from different manufacturers exist, but the most popular models seem to come from Logitech. Microsoft and Creative provide additional webcam options.

Before purchasing a webcam, there are several factors you should consider. Standard resolution for video is 640×480 pixels, and that is perfectly fine for the purpose of streaming content online. While some webcams come with higher-resolution options, be careful, because using higher settings could put an unnecessary drain on your processor.

The frames-per-second (fps) rate determines how fast a webcam captures and moves video. Standard speed for full motion is about 30 fps. The smaller the fps, the choppier your video images will appear.

Be sure to consider features such as pan, tilt, and zoom capabilities. The ability to manually focus might be important to certain users, as well. Some webcams might even come equipped with a remote control to activate these features, while others are executed manually.

Most computers come with a built-in microphone. But if your computer doesn't have one, make sure your webcam has one built in. If not, you'll have to purchase one separately for a nominal fee; otherwise, you'll only be able to make silent movies that probably won't translate very well if you're making a vlog. Most webcams also come with their own software. Many editing programs also come with software that enables you to

## For More Information

Creative: www.creative.com

Logitech: www.logitech.com

Microsoft: www.microsoft.com/en/us/default.aspx

make videos with your webcam. For me, QuickTime Pro does the trick.

If you're planning to make less static, more complex videos that require a lot of movement and on-location shooting, a webcam may not be adequate. Instead, consider a low-level, consumer-grade camcorder. It can do everything a webcam can do, and more.

For the purpose of making videos to edit on your computer and stream online, there are three camcorder formats you should consider. Digital8 or Digital Video (DV) both record onto special tapes. MICROMV lets you record directly to MPEG2 files, which is the format you ultimately need your footage in. Rather than tape, some camcorders allow you to record directly to DVD. Others come equipped with their own hard drive.

Like the webcams, camcorders also come in all shapes and sizes. Prices range from as little as $250 to as high as $1,000, some even higher. Camcorders may come with various features that will also determine the price.

Features may include any or all of the following. Flip-out LCD monitors are nice because you can see your picture on the screen. It sure beats looking through the eye hole. You also

can watch the footage instantaneously that's already been shot on the screen.

An image stabilizer helps steady the camera and warrants against shaky hands. While it's best to use a tripod for the smoothest shots, an image stabilizer will assist when you can't use a tripod for whatever reason.

Autofocus might be a great feature for amateurs—the camera does all the technical work itself. But for the more seasoned videographers, they'll want a model that they can focus on their own.

Zoom is a great feature if you want to get in very close to your subject. A built-in light and built-in microphone may eliminate the need for a lot of external equipment while you're shooting. Look for cameras with audio input jacks so you can add an optional external microphone for premium sound quality.

You'll also need a way to connect your camcorder to your computer. There are basically

three ways to do this. The most common way is through firewire, which really is the standard in transferring digital video from your camcorder to your computer. If you're using an analog device (most likely an old video camera that records directly to VHS, 8mm, or Hi-8 tapes), you'll need a device to convert the analog data into a digital format. There are plenty of devices in the marketplace, but if you're going to go out and purchase a converter, you may as well spend the money on an updated digital camcorder with firewire. Finally, many cameras come with USB. While that's great for transferring digital photos, it is not compatible for transferring video files.

All the major electronics manufacturers make camcorders. Check out Sony, Panasonic, Canon, Hitachi, and Samsung to compare various models, features, and prices. Once you decide what's best for you, grab your camera and get ready to shoot.

## Every Which Way but Off

Filmmakers utilize a variety of shots to bring their movies to life. A **pan** is a horizontal camera move from right to left, or left to right. A **tilt** is a vertical camera move up or down. In both the pan and tilt, the camera remains fixed on its axis. A **zoom** is a rapid movement either toward or away from the subject being photographed. This affect can be achieved by either using a zoom lens or moving the camera on a dolly (a track on the ground allowing the camera to move easily and fluidly).

# Editing Software

Once you've made a few videos, I'm sure you'll want to experiment and try putting them together with additional footage. Maybe you refer to your sister and want to insert her picture on the screen when you mention her name. Perhaps you saw something very funny that you captured with your phone's video camera and you want to first talk about the incident, and then show it. In both cases you will need the assistance of a good editing program.

There are so many choices available for both Mac and PC platforms. They range in price from free (freeware) to thousands of dollars. They offer various features for every editor from the amateur to the professional.

I use Final Cut Pro. It's only available on the Mac. This program is used mainly by professionals, but it's easy enough to learn the basics and edit footage together. Of course, there are many features this program contains that I haven't a clue how to use. And for someone just starting out, there are several cheaper alternatives.

Other top-of-the-line programs include Adobe Premiere (although Adobe Premiere Elements is a consumer-level program that will be sufficient for amateurs) and Avid Express, both of which are available to Mac and PC users, and Sony Vegas Movie Studios and Canopus Edius Pro, which are only available on PC.

The best consumer-grade editing programs include the following: for PC, Pinnacle Studio, Adobe Premiere Elements, Windows Movie Maker, Canopus Let's Edit 2, PowerDirector, ShowBiz DVD, Video Studio, Easy Media Creator, and Ulead VideoStudio are best. For the Mac, iMovie is your best option. And Avid Free DV works on both platforms.

## For More Information

Adobe Premiere: www.adobe.com/products/premiere

Avid Express: www.avid.com

Avid Free DVD: www.avid.com/products/freedv/index.asp

Canopus Let's Edit 2: www.planetdv.net/Content/By_Manufacturer/Grass_Valley/Video_Editing_Cards/Canopus_Let39s_Edit_2.asp

Easy Media Creator: www.roxio.com/enu/products/creator/suite/overview.html

Final Cut Pro: www.apple.com/finalcutstudio/finalcutpro

iMovie: www.apple.com/support/imovie

Pinnacle Studios: www.pinnaclesys.com/PublicSite/us/Home

PowerDirector: www.powerdirectorsoftware.com

ShowBiz DVD: www.arcsoft.com/products/showbiz

Sony Vegas Movie Studio: www.sonycreativesoftware.com/products/product.asp?pid=447

Ulead VideoStudio: www.ulead.com/vs

Windows Movie Maker: www.microsoft.com/windowsxp/downloads/updates/moviemaker2.mspx

Editing can be one of the more difficult skills to master. If you're serious about making videos, you may want to consider taking a software-specific editing class at a local community college. Or contact the software companies directly as many of them offer their own training seminars throughout the year. With or without training, editing your videos will help take them to the next level in terms of professional look.

I wanted to mention one other note about editing software. Like the software that comes with webcams, editing software often comes with the ability to capture and make your own videos. If this is a concern for you, be sure to read the features carefully. Look for software that will capture a live feed and not just pre-recorded footage.

## Other Considerations

There are several other pieces of equipment you should consider. The more toys you have at your disposal, the more sophisticated and professional your video will appear.

Lighting is integral when you make a video. If there's not enough light or if there's too much light, you won't be able to see what's on screen. While you could rent or purchase a studio-grade professional lighting kit, for most of your needs, lamps and natural light will suffice. And because you can see yourself on screen while you're recording a video, you'll know if you've got too much, or not enough, light. Repositioning the camera or computer, pulling down or raising a shade, or redirecting the lamps and overhead track lighting are all ways to help make the picture perfect.

Webcams come with a holder so they can be attached to the computer and not bounce around. If you're filming away from your computer, be sure to use a tripod. Tripods will help steady the camera, while enabling the filmmaker to pan and tilt in a steady motion. And while handheld may be a nice effect to use occasionally, shooting your entire film that way may cause your viewers to get nauseous. *The Blair Witch Project*, anyone?

Your computer or webcam will come with a built-in microphone, but that may not be enough to suit your purposes if you plan to film away from the

### Who Needs Software?

YouTube has its own software you can use to make videos right on their website. Follow the directions below to upload a video to YouTube. (See Uploading to YouTube, later in this chapter.) Once you fill out all the requested information, instead of choosing **Upload a Video,** choose **Use Quick Capture.** Quick Capture is a program that will let you make videos and automatically upload them to YouTube instantaneously.

It's extremely easy to use. If your camera is plugged in, the system should automatically recognize it. If not, YouTube gives you an option to find your camera. Once it does, you'll see your image onscreen. Just hit record when you want to begin, and click end when you are done. YouTube will process the video, and in no time at all, you'll be able to see it on your homepage.

hardware. Two other types of microphones are available for purchase. You can use a boom microphone, which is held above the actors, out of camera range, to pick up their sound. Or you can mic your subjects separately with their own personal cordless or lavalier mics.

Finally, there are many software programs you can purchase to add all sorts of bells and whistles to your videos. Software like After Effect will let you add cool digital effects to your video. Programs like Live Type for Mac will help create cool credit sequences. Most of the editing programs mentioned earlier will have some effects and title abilities, but if you want to take your work to the next level, know that there are plenty of options out there.

# My First Vlog

Several years ago blogging became all the rage. Online diaries were filled with essays and photos for all the world to see. Blogs made media stars out of Perez Hilton, Jeff Jarvis, and countless others. They continue to be an exciting faction of the World Wide Web.

A few years later, as high-speed connections became more common, and webcams became part of the average user's operating equipment, a new sensation took form. Blogging on camera, or vlogging, became the new way to communicate with the masses online. Vloggers like Paul Robinett (a.k.a. Renetto) and James Kotecki are the new voices (and faces) of the Internet.

The great thing about YouTube is that anyone can start a vlog. In fact, as I began writing this book, I started my own vlog. It's the simplest type of video to make, but don't let that fool you. Make sure you're engaging to the camera and that you have something to say. If not, you may find that you're vlogging to no one but yourself.

The author introduces us to his YouTube Channel with a video titled "Welcome to my Vlog."

Make sure you're engaging to the camera and that you have something to say.

# Music Videos

Maybe you have nothing to say. Or maybe you just don't know what to say. For those users with musical talent, consider making a music video instead.

A lot of users sing covers of popular songs. Esmée Denters, Mia Rose, and Ysabella Brave are some of my personal favorites. Esmée even landed a recording contract when record execs heard her beautiful voice online. (See Chapter 6, "Fame.") Who needs *American Idol?*

YouTube is also a great forum for undiscovered singer/songwriters. Jay Brannan, David Choi, and Tay Zonday have all entertained users while making a name for themselves with their original material. Still working on a song, but you're not sure if it's ready? Post it on YouTube and you'll get immediate feedback from the public. How's that for instant focus group!

If you have no musical ability, but still want to make a video with music, why not lip sync? From the Back Dormitory Boys to Danny Diamond, lip-sync videos have become quite popular online. They're fun, they're silly, and they're great for sharing.

Ysabella Brave belts out a cover of The Doors' "Love Me Two Times."

# Do It Yourself

Do It Yourself, or DIY, videos are a great way to learn about a particular subject or skill. As a viewer, I love watching them because they're both educational and entertaining. Learn to play guitar with online lessons by Justin Sandercoe. Start speaking Yiddish after you watch videos by Millie Garfield. Or let Tim Carter from AskaBuilder show you how to build a new kitchen cabinet. The possibilities are endless.

Maybe you have a skill or expertise that you're willing to discuss with fellow users. Why not make a series of videos sharing your knowledge? Remember to keep them short and make them fun and entertaining. Maybe it will help expand business opportunities.

As an expert on the entertainment industry, I plan to make a series of vlogs talking about various aspects of show business while answering questions from users who write in. Topics may include getting started in a show business career, how to write a query letter, and how to put together an acting resumé. Tune in to my Channel to learn more.

Justin Sandercoe shows finger positions as he teaches users to play "Yesterday" by The Beatles in his video "039 Yesterday for Solo Guitar pt1 (pro Guitar Lesson)."

# Comedy

YouTube is also a haven for great comedy. Do you like to make people laugh? Are you a comic genius waiting to happen? Can you create funny characters that people will tune in every week to see?

Some of the earliest viral videos were comedic in nature. A short clip that can make someone giggle is contagious. Whether it's animated, shot on location, or created in front of your webcam, YouTube provides a forum for your work.

I'm not the funniest person in the world, but I love watching funny videos online. Whether they're *SNL* clips sponsored by NBC, or original comedy sketches from the likes of Barats and Bereta or Blame Society Films, they keep me rolling on the floor. If you've got what it takes, this could be your niche.

Blame Society Productions brings you a very sick and twisted, but funny, Halloween comedy short, "The Life and Death of a Pumpkin."

# Short Films

Short films tend to be slightly more complex. But if you're an aspiring filmmaker, YouTube could offer you the guaranteed distribution you've been longing for. What better way to showcase your work than in front of the massive audience using this site?

There are three types of shorts you could make. Narrative films tell a story. Documentary films document real life. And experimental films, well … that's where you put everything else.

In my book *Short Films 101: How to Make a Short Film and Launch Your Filmmaking Career*, I detail the secrets to making successful short films. I'll share some of these secrets here, and also point out some of the key differences between making shorts for, say, the festival circuit as opposed to making them for the Internet.

First and foremost, keep them short. Seems obvious, but many filmmakers shoot films that are 30 minutes or longer! In a way, I love that the time limit on YouTube is 10 minutes. It forces directors to limit their work to fit within the time constraints. What I tell aspiring directors is, if they can't show someone they can direct in five minutes, a longer film won't aid their cause. If you watched the Fox TV show *On the Lot*, you know that short films can indeed be short (in the case of the show, two and a half to three minutes) and still pack a powerful punch.

Speaking of punch, make sure your short has one. Follow the old "joke formula." Set up your story and then pay off the gag. Then throw in an unexpected twist to end with a punch. Your film need not be a comedy to use this simple guideline. This formula will work in any genre.

Finally, if you're making short films for the distinct purpose of posting them online, you can shoot them with your consumer-grade digital camcorder. In my book, I'm insistent on shooting with film (after all, a major movie studio isn't going to hire you to make a $20 million full-length video). But because the short will be viewed in a small window on your screen, you really don't need top quality and a high-resolution picture for it to be effective. These features just won't transfer on the Net.

One last thought about YouTube shorts: keep them coming back. A great way to retain your viewers is to turn a successful short film concept into a series of webisodes. Each week, or each month, post a new video in the series. Just look to the success of LonleyGirl15, Chad Vader, or

Ask a Ninja to see how effective a well-made Web series can be.

Bree tests Daniel on the type of caveman he would have been in a LonelyGirl15 episode titled "Daniel the Neanderthal."

# Let's Get Creative

If you're still trying to find your niche in the video-making webisphere, don't fret. Try out several different options until you find the one that's best for you. In the meantime, continue to browse other users' videos to search for new ideas and inspiration.

Maybe you'll play a game like Luke Johnson and his phone experiment or Baron S. Cameron's "The YouTube Match Game." How about entering a contest, or better yet, creating your own? Charles Trippy started the YouTube Staring Contest and The Video Scavenger Hunt, among others.

Maybe you like filming random things that strike you as funny or compelling. Silly animal behavior, strange road signs, or classic cars all might be interesting to you as well as other users. Film them and post them online.

Try to be as creative as possible. If you're the first to the table with an idea, you become the innovator. Innovative videos get noticed and featured on YouTube. Put on your thinking cap and start coming up with ideas for new videos.

Baron S. Cameron's "The YouTube Match Game" takes the format of the old game show and gives it an international YouTube spin with contestants and celebrity guests comprised of various YouTube users.

If you're the first to the table with an idea, you become the innovator.

# Uploading to YouTube

You've made your video. You've edited it into a visual masterpiece. Now you're ready to upload it to YouTube for all the world to see.

First thing you need to check is the video's format. YouTube accepts content in the following formats: .WMV, .AVI, .MOV, and .MPG. However, the video also should be saved using the following recommended settings: MPEG4 format, 320×240 resolution, MP3 audio, and 20 fps (frames per second). You may recall that earlier in the chapter

I mentioned that 640x480 pixels was the standard resolution for video, but because of the size of the YouTube screen, their requirements are lower.

If you're good to go, log on to YouTube and hit the **Upload** button from the main page. You'll see the first of two video upload screens. You'll need to type in information about the video you made.

The title is what you name the piece. Make it catchy or descriptive. I called my first vlog, "Welcome to my Vlog." Not entirely

original, but it got the point across.

Next is your description. This is the matter that users can read to the right side of the video as it plays on the video page. Include a description of the video, additional notes or comments about your video, or contact information if you want fans to be able to contact you directly.

The Tags are vital to your success on YouTube. Add as many keywords as you can so that users can find your video when searching in general. Don't be afraid

## Troubleshooting

Seems easy enough, but it took me a few times to upload my first video to YouTube. Because I made my vlog using QuickTime, it automatically saved as a .MOV file. Being on the list of acceptable formats, I simply clicked the upload button and added the name of my file. While it uploaded to YouTube right away, the system had problems processing my video and it would not run on the site.

I decided to check my settings to make sure I had the optimum settings YouTube suggests. Lo and behold, I did not. Under preferences, I noticed that I was not recording using MPEG4 format, so I changed my selection to make that my default option in the future. Then, I chose to export my .MOV video I had made to the MPEG4 format. By clicking the Options button, I could select image size, audio type (AAC-LC worked as a compatible option to MP3), and frame rate. I was good to go.

Once the file converted, I returned to YouTube and followed the upload protocol yet again. Within a few minutes my video had uploaded. Within 20 minutes, it had processed. The video was ready for my friends and other users to watch.

It is quite possible that the video will take longer to process. Variables such as file size, connection speed, and site traffic will all affect how quickly your video will appear. If several hours have gone by and your video still hasn't appeared, check the YouTube help menus, which are an excellent resource for troubleshooting. All my troubleshooting needs and questions were addressed and answered right there on the website. They really do make it so anyone can figure it out.

to put in too many words—the more choices, the better. Also, choose a video category for your clip (such as Comedy, Entertainment, or Sports).

Next come the broadcast options. You can make your video public and share it with the world. Or you can make your video private and only share it with your friends.

Date and Map options let you put the date you made the video into the system. The map lets you show users the exact location you recorded the video using technology from Google Maps.

Finally, in sharing options you can control who is allowed to leave comments and post video responses, whether or not your video can be rated, and whether or not it can be embedded in other websites.

Once you've finished selecting your various options, click on **Upload A Video** to upload an existing video to the site, or **Use Quick Capture** if you want to make a fresh new video on the spot. If you're uploading an existing video, you will be able to browse your computer to locate the file. Once you find it, click **Upload Video** and your work is done. It will take a few minutes to process. Just monitor for problems. If the file is the correct size and your settings are good, the video should be up in no time at all.

# For Your Eyes Only

What if you make a video that you want to post, but you're not quite ready for the entire world to see? Maybe you want to run it by a few close friends before sharing it with the World Wide Web. On YouTube, you can mark your videos private so they are only visible to your friends. Here's how to do it.

From the main YouTube page, click on **My Account** in the top right corner of the screen. From the next screen, click on **My Videos.** A list of all of your videos will be displayed. Choose the video you wish to make private by clicking **Edit Video Info.** Under the Broadcast Options, click **Choose Options** and check "Private." Your various contact lists will appear. You can choose to allow members of an entire list to view the video, or you can choose to allow only select members of that list to view the video. Finally, click **Update Video Info** at the bottom on the screen to institute your changes. Your video will now only be available for viewing by your friends.

hat the Buck?!

Godzilla Here

# chapter 6

# The Pioneers

First *Time* magazine named YouTube the 2006 Invention of the Year; that doesn't come as too much of a surprise given the rapid rise to popularity the site has experienced. But then *Time* named "You" (as in **YOU**Tube) the 2006 Person of the Year. In their own words, their reason was, "For seizing the reins of the global media, for founding and framing the new digital democracy, for working for nothing and beating the pros at their own game, *Time*'s Person of the Year for 2006 is you."

In the beginning, I don't think it was anyone's intention to go to YouTube seeking fame. I think people were drawn in for the fun opportunity of making and sharing videos with other users. But then certain member Channels started taking off and got quite popular. While *Time* focused the spotlight on the users of digital media as a whole, the light was shining even brighter on certain members of the YouTube community.

In this chapter and the next, we'll explore some early success stories, meet 25 YouTube celebrities who are on the cusp of popping, and review some pointers on how you can use YouTube to strategically launch your own career. What you make of these opportunities is strictly up to you, but your 15 minutes start now ....

# Early Rising Stars

We've seen it happen before our very eyes. A virtual unknown posts videos on YouTube, and suddenly becomes a star in the mainstream media. Television roles, recording contracts, and other fantasies that are intangible to most of us are quickly becoming normal rewards for quality talent on the Net.

Were these early innovators just lucky to stumble into once-in-a-lifetime opportunities, or was this their plan all along? Is viral video the wave of the future for promoting your band or brand? Its effectiveness has already been proven repeatedly. Will the novelty wear off, or is this the new way in?

Following, we'll look at five early YouTube celebrities who have managed to launch show business careers from their living rooms. Later, we'll meet the next generation of YouTube stars. If their dreams are your dreams, maybe this is the big break you've been looking for. Forget *American Idol*—now you can launch your career on YouTube.

Television roles, recording contracts, and other fantasies that are intangible to most of us are quickly becoming normal rewards for quality talent on the Net.

## Terra Naomi

Terra Naomi's original "Say It's Possible" YouTube video.

Born in Saratoga Springs, New York, Terra Naomi and her two brothers grew up on a farm before moving to Cleveland for six years and eventually settling in upstate New York. Her mother, a social worker, and father, a plastic surgeon, encouraged her musical pursuits growing up. Ever the overachiever and perfectionist, she played piano and French horn, and performed in many high school singing groups, even spending her summers attending Belvoir Terrace Fine and Performing Arts Camp in Massachusetts and Interlochen Performing Arts Camp in Michigan. It was at Interlochen where Naomi was scouted by an opera coach to study with him at the University of Michigan.

Naomi found her rebellious streak during her college years. Twenty-year-old Naomi was still studying classical music when she became addicted to heroin. "Needless to say, college was a blur, but I did learn one thing: I did not want to be a classical musician," writes Naomi on her Web page. Despite cutting most of her classes and sleeping through the rest of her college experience, Naomi graduated with honors and decided that music, though not classical music, was what she wanted to do with her life.

After returning home and getting clean, Naomi moved to New York City. She peddled her songs at The Bitter End, The Sidewalk Café, the Living Room, and many other East Village dive bars, while pursuing the noble profession of many an up-and-coming star: waitressing. "The waitressing went well," Naomi writes, "with the exception of a few spills here and there and one unfortunate incident involving a plate of chicken curry and a designer handbag." After a few years, Naomi self-booked her first national tour, where she met and was offered a job by producer Paul Fox, who produced such artists as Edwin McCain, Phish, and Sixpence None the Richer. She was off to L.A., where she would finally find her much-awaited success.

Of course, this is where Naomi's story of rockstardom takes a pleasantly unexpected twist. During the summer of 2006, while still working for Fox, Naomi decided to do what she titled her "Virtual Summer Tour." "My usual summer tours included lots of driving, crappy hotels, and terribly high gas bills. The tour from my apartment in Hollywood seemed like a fun alternative." It would also prove to be a lucrative one. Naomi began posting videos on YouTube. Her single "Say It's Possible," her most popular video, generated over 2.5 million hits. She signed a recording contract with Island Records, and her CD sold out before it ever hit stores—twice. She is the number-one Most Subscribed Musician on YouTube, followed by P.Diddy at number two. Naomi has played to sold-out concert halls all over America and in the U.K. Her songs have been featured on network television shows and in the feature film soundtrack for *Sherrybaby*, starring Maggie Gyllanhaal. Most recently, she played in the London leg of the Live Earth Concert Series in the summer of 2007.

About her unusual rise to fame, she says, "I have been featured in numerous news publications in articles dealing with the new world of online promotion and music distribution. It is indeed a changing industry and I am thrilled to be one of the success stories."

# LisaNova

Screen capture from her controversial video "LisaNova does YOUTUBE!!!!"

If there is one person who proves that viral video stars can really stick it to studios and networks, that person is Lisa Donovan. Donovan grew up in Scarsdale, New York, and attended the University of Colorado at Boulder. Interested in becoming an actress, she moved to California upon graduation to try her luck. Like many an aspiring youth in the City of Angels, Donovan was unsuccessful in her preliminary rounds of auditions and could not manage to land an agent. But that didn't stop her.

With no acting jobs in sight, Donovan instead learned all she could about the corporate side of filmmaking. She worked for production agencies and learned how to shoot and edit video. Soon, she asserted her independence by taking her new knowledge and starting her own production company with her boyfriend Dan Zappin (a.k.a. Danny Diamond). Zappin Productions was formed and specializes in producing viral videos. Producing more than 30 of her own short films, Donovan posted a few of them on YouTube for fun under the username LisaNova. Her first, "Introducing LisaNova" appeared on June 7, 2006.

Donovan never expected how a few three-minute videos on YouTube would change her life. "In no way did I think this was going to be like a career-changing thing," she told *The New York Times*. Nevertheless, collectively, her videos have attracted over 8.6 million viewers. Her most popular film, "Teenie Weenie Raw Flesh," a parody of Britney Spears, became the number-one most-viewed video on YouTube, followed closely by her latest short, "LisaNova does YOUTUBE!!!!," posted on July 10, 2007, which gained more than two million hits in one month. As of July 2007, Donovan was listed as the seventh most-subscribed YouTube Channel, with over 660,000 members. Donovan had clearly made it in the eyes of the public, but she still hadn't cracked the Hollywood system.

All that was about to change. A year and a half after her first video aired on YouTube, Donovan was offered a spot on Fox's *MadTV*. Ironically, Donovan had auditioned for *MadTV* when she first came to California, but she hadn't made the cut. However, Nicole Garcia, the show's casting director, rethought that decision after seeing LisaNova in action on YouTube. Specializing in a variety of impersonations, Donovan seemed a shoo-in for sketch comedy. But Donovan did more than just obtain a role on the show. *MadTV* contracted Donovan to shoot her self-produced shorts for the show. Cast members came to Donovan's L.A. apartment, shooting with a camcorder and by the light of bare bulbs. "I think our audience likes that grittiness, that guerrilla look," says executive producer Dick Blasucci.

What Donovan likes most is staying in control of her own art. Shooting films for YouTube is still her favorite platform. She says, "Here it's impulsive. I have an idea, I call two people, and we shoot it. You can't do that on a show. I like being in control of it, and I want to continue to do that." As long as she continues to turn heads and get attention with her viral comedy clips, it seems that LisaNova will remain in control.

## Esmée Denters

Esmée Denters sings "Unwritten" by Natasha Bedingfield.

Until she discovered YouTube, only Esmée Denters' showerhead knew what an amazing voice she had. Growing up in a small town in Holland, Denters remembers her father instilling in her and her sister a love for music. "I fell so in love with singing that sometimes my own mother would go crazy from me singing too much!" writes Denters on her MySpace page. Denters was studying to become a social worker when she saw other people posting videos of themselves singing on YouTube. She decided to join the trend and post videos of her own. In August 2006, with the help of her sister's webcam, the 18-year-old posted a number of videos of herself singing covers to her favorite artists: Alicia Keys, Goo Goo Dolls, and Destiny's Child, among others.

One of the millions of voices on the YouTube airwaves, Denters seemed to hit just the right note. By June 2007, Denters' videos had been viewed over 21 million times, making her the eleventh most-watched YouTube star of all time. Denters was touched and overwhelmed by the support she found in fellow YouTubers and became inspired to begin writing her own songs and travel to America to record her music. Her life was a fantasy-come-true, and it was about to get even better.

Many teenage girls might claim that Justin Timberlake has changed their lives, but only Esmée Denters can state it as fact. On June 5, 2007, the day after Denters posted a video of a spur-of-the-moment recording session in London where she sang Timberlake's "What Goes Around," with Timberlake himself singing backup and accompanying her on piano, Denters announced that she was the first official artist signed on Timberlake's new record label, Tennman Records. On June 16, she performed for her first live audience, opening for Timberlake's concert in Amsterdam, and then again in Antwerp. In July, Denters went on tour with Timberlake, opening for his FutureSex/LoveSounds tour in six venues.

In the midst of her sudden burst of fame, Denters still remembers exactly how she got to be where she is. "Words can't describe how amazing it is. I am so excited! It is something I have always dreamed of doing. I have to thank YouTube and its viewers for giving me the opportunity to show the world my voice."

By June 2007, Denters' videos had been viewed over twenty-one million times ...

# LonelyGirl15

Jessica Rose as lonelygirl15.

It is impossible to tell the story of YouTube without at least mentioning lonelygirl15. Bree Avery, a.k.a. lonelygirl15, first appeared on YouTube on June 16, 2006. She was a 16-year-old girl with an innocent sense of humor, overbearingly religious parents, and a withdrawn best friend, Daniel, who would video-blog from her bedroom about the trials and tribulations of her life. Bree had a MySpace page, her videos responded to users' comments, and she was developing a massive Internet following. Until, of course, everyone found out that Bree Avery did not, in fact, exist.

Investigations into the genuine nature of lonelygirl15's identity began as viewers started questioning the progressively more complicated storyline her vlogs began to take. In August 2006, *Los Angeles Times* reporter Richard Rushfield wrote an article exposing lonelygirl15 as a produced and scripted series. Bree Avery was actually a 19-year-old actress named Jessica Rose. Born in Maryland and raised in New Zealand, Rose graduated from the New York Film Academy in Universal City, California, and discovered the audition for the part of lonelygirl15 on craigslist.org. The show's producers were revealed to be screenwriter and filmmaker Ramesh Flinders and Miles Beckett, who had previously studied to be doctors before turning to film. By the end of September, the entirety of the hoax had been revealed.

The exposure of lonelygirl15, the charmingly naïve teen whom audiences had come to love, as a fake generated turbulent reaction from fans; however, it did not mean the end of the series by any means. Out of feelings of betrayal, the series only finished fourth in the "Best Series" category at the YouTube Video Awards in March 2007, but still, the lonelygirl15 series has generated over 81 million views and is now well into its second season. Its star, Jessica Rose, has moved on to star alongside Lindsey Lohan in *I Know Who Killed Me* and as a regular on ABC Family's new series *Greek*. The show has also gained publicity as being the first viral series to integrate product placement, working out deals with Hershey's and Neutrogena. Though many YouTubers placed a black mark on the series after its outing, lonelygirl15 continues to maintain a massive fan base, but more important, it paves the way as a viral frontier. Lonelygirl15 may not be real, but, in the universe of viral video, she is certainly a legend.

The show has also gained publicity as being the first viral series to integrate product placement ...

## Brooke Brodack, Brookers

Brooke Brodack made headlines when Carson Daly signed her to a development deal.

"I like to get extreme reactions," says Brooke Brodack to the *Boston Globe*. This seems fairly obvious considering the 21-year-old's massive success on YouTube. Hailing from Holden, Massachusetts, where she lives with her mother and sister, Melissa, Brodack was always the quietest sibling, according to her mother, which seems hard to believe after experiencing the madcap personality she exhibits in her YouTube videos. She describes herself in her YouTube profile as follows: "I am a moose I like to draw and paint I love film and I like to sketch. YOU ARE A mindless ZOMBIE!" This quirky, random sense of humor, one of the overarching traits of the YouTube community at large, is part of what makes Brodack one of the most legendary viral video stars to date.

In September of 2005, Brodack subscribed to YouTube, username "Brookers," and began her path toward becoming the site's first official success story. In her spare time between attending Worcester State College and working as a hostess at the local Ninety Nine restaurant, Brodack put together a number of zany short films using an outmoded eMachines computer, a camcorder, and Windows Media Player. Her premier video, "CRAZED NUMA FAN!!!!," featured Brodack and her sister lip-synching to "Dragostea din tei" by the group O-Zone and of course spoofing the original "Numa Numa" video by Gary Brolsma in which the chubby teen's funky dance launched an Internet sensation. The short gained more than a million and a half viewers right off the bat. More Brookers videos continued to hit the YouTube scene—music videos, monologues, spoof suspense dramas, and many, many more—all with the same nutty sense of humor that YouTubers seemed to crave.

Among Brodack's enchanted YouTube viewers was ex-VJ for MTV's *Total Request Live,* Carson Daly. Daly stumbled across Brodack's videos while surfing the Internet one night. "Something about her was extremely captivating, and I couldn't figure it out," said Daly. "I just wanted to reach out and see what I could do for her." Daly had the head of development for his production company, Ruth Caruso, get in contact with Brodack, which was actually harder than expected when Brodack deleted Caruso's first two emails. "I thought they were fake," Brodack remarks. "I get a lot of weird mail." Eventually, in June 2006, Carson Daly Productions and Brodack came together, and Brookers was offered an 18-month development deal to work on videos for television, Internet, and for download on mobile devices. Brodack became acclaimed as the first viral video-to-mainstream crossover star.

The fame has become a bit unexpectedly intense at times—sketchy vans circle around her house, people stare when she walks into the local Friendly's, not to mention she's appeared on *The Tyra Banks Show,* and recently finished producing a viral music video for The Barenaked Ladies—but Brooke Brodack has yet to lose that zany and brilliant personality that captured the attention of the user generation. "I make videos because I'm nuts," she writes on her YouTube profile. "But more normal than half you people, you and all your little hats!"

# What Set Them Apart

At first glance, YouTube's earliest success stories may not have anything in common. An edgy rocker, a pop princess, a comic oddity, a funny sexpot, and a lonely girl who's not even real ... they could be characters in a long-awaited sequel to *The Breakfast Club*. But like the characters in that classic John Hughes movie, outside appearances may be deceiving. On the inside, these YouTube sensations have a lot in common.

For one, they all have talent. It's obvious to their legions of fans. The number of subscribers they each have on YouTube speaks volumes.

They connect with their audience. The ability to make someone smile, laugh, or emote in any way at all is a special gift. Each of these ladies has shared that gift with their viewers.

And of course, they've all broken though to the mainstream be it in the form of record deals or TV appearances. And while mainstream ambitions continue to flourish, they've not turned their back on their online roots. I believe this to be an imperative factor to long-term success.

And while it's all still relatively new, they continue to succeed. Their fifteen minutes has come and gone, but they're still here and the clock continues to tick. I think we'll continue to hear from these unique voices for years to come.

# The Next Generation

Will YouTube continue to produce Internet stars? Will wannabes analyze past success stories and prepare a game plan to launch their own careers via viral video? Will the next Terra Naomi be a reader of this very book who took the advice outlined in these pages and laid it all out in front of her webcam?

In the next chapter, we'll meet twenty-five hopefuls who have already begun to experience their fifteen minutes of fame as a result of exposure on YouTube. I've chosen these people because I feel that they, like their talented predecessors, have what it takes to break through to the next level. Let's meet the new class.

# chapter 7

# Making It on YouTube

All the books I've written have been interview driven. This one is no exception. It's typically my favorite part of the writing process—getting to interview interesting people. But I'll admit, I was a little apprehensive coming into this project. My only experience with YouTube was browsing the occasional clip someone linked me to. I knew there were burgeoning YouTube "celebrities," but in my head, I filed them in the same drawer as your average reality-TV star. Honestly, until I started this project, I still thought LonelyGirl15 was a real person!

What I found on YouTube was a plethora of undiscovered (and some discovered) talent that really blew me away. I wasn't expecting much, but instead I found treasure, if not pure gold. I'm not saying that everyone on my list should have his or her own TV show or get a record deal with a major label (although I have no doubt that some of them will). Others will continue to exploit this medium as their stars rise and the viral craze continues to spread—and to replace aspects of modern media that we currently take for granted.

## Advice from 25 Up-and-Coming YouTube Stars

I chose these interview subjects in a similar way to how I choose the talent I represent. I used the following selection criteria: personality, talent, relate-ability, uniqueness, charisma, energy, and innovation. Some may be stronger in certain categories than others, but I'm fairly confident they all share these common traits. As I continue to scan the Web and consume more viral content, I'm sure my personal list will grow. Feel free to look at my subscriptions on my YouTube Channel to see who I think has what it takes

# Q&A

## Jay Brannan

Jay Brannan performs his song "American Idol."

*Jay Brannan is a New York–based actor and musician best known for his role as "Ceth" in John Cameron Mitchell's feature film* Shortbus. *Musically he may be best known for his song "Soda Shop," which was also featured in the movie. He plays acoustic guitar and kashakas (an African instrument used to make basic rhythms) in accompaniment as he sings his mellow brand of modern folk songs.*

**FL:** In your first YouTube video, "Body's a Temple," you almost seem reluctant to be making a video for YouTube. In fact, you say you're doing it because "YouTube rules the world." What brought you to YouTube initially? And if there was an initial reluc-

or insecurity. I just bought a new computer with a built-in camera and was making a video for the first time. I saw that other artists were beginning to use YouTube to introduce their music to new and broader audiences, and saw it for the invaluable resource that it is. I've always been an Internet/computer guy. I learned to read on a computer. Internet is my connection to the outside world. It's just the logical thing for me to go to as a creative outlet, for communication, and for promotional purposes.

**FL:** Has that initial opinion of YouTube changed since you started on the site?

**JB:** Nope. YouTube DOES rule the world! I really found that to be true when my video for "Soda Shop" was posted on the homepage. The exposure was massive. That video now has over a million views, and the comments and emails and subscriptions I started receiving were insane. It's truly amazing to me that YouTube's home-page has that much power. And the reaction from being featured also sparked the interest of some industry people, because they saw the potential for marketability and widespread interest. In the past, media and entertainment and communication were all controlled by certain "gatekeepers" who held the keys to what could be seen and heard by the masses. It's just not the case anymore

to obtain the approval of any executives or financiers.

**FL:** Oftentimes you'll qualify your videos and say something like, "It's gonna be horrible ...." And IMHO, it never is horrible. Where does this reaction come from?

**JB:** Um, that's just me being honest. I'm insecure, and my way of dealing with insecurities is to say them out loud. I know most of the world thinks the brave thing to do is to hide your fears and insecurities, repress them ... fake confidence or whatever. I disagree. I also like to set people's expectations really low, including my own. That way people are disappointed less often, and pleasantly surprised more often. I believe in the power of cynicism!

**FL:** In your song "American Idol," there's a line that goes, "American Idol, get the hell off my TV." I interpret that to mean that these contestants don't have any true talent. Please correct me if I'm wrong. A lot of people feel the same way about some of the stars of YouTube. Do you share this perception about certain YouTube stars?

**JB:** No, no, no, no. I think many of the contestants on *American Idol* are talented singers. And I really don't think it's my place to publicly judge the talent of others, which is such a subjective concept anyway, based on people's personal tastes. With that

opened a lot of doors for a lot of people, and I'm certainly very happy for them.

**FL:** Which YouTube users do you feel really are stars?

**JB:** I don't believe in the concept of "stars." I believe that YouTube is simply filled by videos from regular human beings trying to be heard. It's really the same with TV/movies/radio—all just regular people trying to make a living doing something they enjoy and, in some cases, be a part of something creative and/or meaningful.

**FL:** You mention in one of your videos that Terra Naomi is an inspiration. Why? And are there others from YouTube that inspire you as well?

**JB:** She was one of the first people I heard of that was really taking advantage of YouTube to expand her audience, and it seems to be part of what led to her signing a record deal with a major label. She achieved the impossible. It's kind of the American dream—a young American woman doing her thing on her own, and the impenetrable entertainment industry actually taking notice and helping her take it to the next level. I respect her for the achievement, as well as the inspiration she's provided to so many people who watched that happen.

**FL:** Please tell me how YouTube led to your iTunes deal.

**JB:** It didn't. I got on iTunes by signing up with an online dis-

tributor called CD Baby. Anyone can do it.

**FL:** In your latest video, "Please Don't Attack Me," you really open yourself up emotionally. What's it like to be that vulnerable for all the world to see on the World Wide Web? What made you do the video?

**JB:** Um, the vulnerability thing doesn't scare me. It's something I've been comfortable showing for a long time. I was a little nervous that people were going to accuse me of being melodramatic or disingenuous, or say that I was doing some sort of "acting" exercise. I truly was a little moved by seeing a song I wrote in a music video on television. It's just not the sort of thing that happens to me. And I want people to know that I'm a normal person ... "sub-normal," I might even say. Ha ha. I've spent most of my life paralyzed by depression and fear and substance abuse. So I want other people who can relate to those feelings of hopelessness to know that things really are possible. And they are possible for people like me who don't necessarily subscribe to the formulas and ideals forced upon us by others.

**FL:** Of all of your videos, which is your favorite?

**JB:** I don't really watch my own videos, but I guess if I had to pick, I would say "At First Sight." It's still simple, but the first time I tried something a little more creative ... just for fun. You might not be able to tell, but I put a lot

of effort into it. The song means a lot to me, too, because the experience it is written about is one I'm still not over.

**FL:** Do you have any favorite videos from other YouTube users?

**JB:** To be honest, I use YouTube mostly as a showcase for my own music and ideas. I don't browse content myself very often.

**FL:** Do you have a personal website?

**JB:** Several! Ha ha. www.myspace.com/jaybrannan, www.YouTube.com/jaybrannan, www.jaybrannan.com, and FaceBook (no direct link).

Jay Brannan performs "Soda Shop" from "Toilet Studios" … a.k.a. his bathroom.

# Q&A

## Emmalina

Emmalina busting some sexy moves in her video "Dancin'."

*Emmalina is a college girl living in Tasmania, Australia, who prefers to keep her real name private. Maybe this is due to the fact that shortly after becoming a You-Tube celebrity, her computer was hacked and some personal files were stolen. Early vlogs showed Emmalina dancing lasciviously in front of her webcam, making her an early Internet pinup favorite. These days her vlogs are more tame, but more popular than ever.*

**FL:** When did you first start vlogging?

**E:** March of 2006.

**FL:** Why did you start vlogging?

**E:** I read a newspaper article about a woman going by the name of "Nornna." She used to upload videos of herself engaged in random, mundane activities like cleaning, brushing her teeth, and going to work. She gained quite a large fan base (which now would be considered small given YouTube's growth) and I decided to get in contact with her because she seemed like an interesting character. She asked her viewers to make videos saying what they thought of her, and my video blogs began then.

**FL:** Why do you think you've developed such a large following?

**E:** Back in 2006 I was the number-four Most Subscribed of All-Time. Most of my videos consisted of me dancing and talking about somewhat taboo topics. Nowadays, I just talk about random topics regarding myself and my life, and I've fallen to number 39. I'd be a fool if I didn't recognize that my large following resulted from my "sexy" dancing. However, I still have a fan base who seem to like my down-to-earth, "real" nature and quirky humor.

**FL:** Have you ever met any of your fans? What were they like?

**E:** Not intentionally. I've exchanged a few words with a couple of people who like my videos when they've recognized me at Uni. They're very nice!

**FL:** When you started posting videos, you began by showing people yoga positions. But then you shifted gears and started vlogging. How come? Will we get to see more yoga in the future?

**E:** I actually began by dancing—the two yoga videos were just something fun that one of my viewers requested from me after I mentioned in passing that I do yoga. I stopped posting such videos, however, because they were easily taken out of context. I was dancing and doing yoga because they're things I love doing for fun and I wanted to share it; however, online people have different ideas. It becomes not so much for fun as it is for sex appeal.

I stopped doing it because I felt that it wasn't appropriate and now I just really enjoy vlogging; it makes you feel a lot closer to your audience as you get to initiate a form of conversation with them. I bring up a topic in a video, people comment with their responses, and I can reply to those comments.

**FL:** Why are there haters?

**E:** The anonymity of the Internet has always allowed people to run rampant with their views and opinions. The fact that some people are willing and confident enough to put their real identity online in their videos is obviously going to attract hateful, anonymous people. It fuels their fire; they have a real, live, talking person to attack anonymously and sometimes they get real, live reactions. Why haters hate, however, is a different matter entirely, and one I have no clue about.

**FL:** How important is fame?

**E:** Not at all. I received a fair amount of media attention in late 2006 and hated it. Articles were published even if I explicitly stated I didn't want them to be. It sounds weird, but that period was the most unpleasant of my entire YouTube experience.

**FL:** Did you come to YouTube to find fame?

**E:** Nope. I have no talent in filmmaking, acting, or producing. I try to keep the Internet as separate from real life as possible, and I pursue my real talents in real life. I came to YouTube just for a hobby, something to do in my spare time and maybe make a few good friends to chat to now and then.

**FL:** Do you think YouTube has the power to make someone famous and launch a career?

**E:** People like Esmée Denters [see Chapter 6] are proof that this is possible. I think it's rare, though, and I don't think it's a good idea to use YouTube to launch a career at this point. The site is already overflowing with people trying to get noticed as actresses and actors, and the chances of all of them getting famous are almost nil.

**FL:** What advice can you give to people who are new to vlogging?

**E:** Be prepared for negative, even hateful comments. Lots of them. Don't respond to them at all—just block the users who make them and forget about it. Everyone on YouTube gets a lot of hateful comments. You just have to think nothing of it, because those people don't even know you. Try to make

good-quality videos (e.g., good lighting, clear video, and clear sound). Edit out "um"s and "ah"s with a program like Windows Movie Maker, and try to be upbeat. Talk about things that the majority of your audience will be able to understand or relate to. Not that I really stick to that idea, ha ha.

A typical Emmalina vlog.

**FL:** Of all of your videos, which is your favorite?

**E:** I actually can't stand my own videos, heh.

**FL:** Do you have any favorite videos from other YouTube users?

**E:** I like all of drewtoothpaste's videos. He's great!

**FL:** Do you have a personal website?

**E:** I keep a blog at http://girldoll.livejournal.com.

"The anonymity of the Internet has always allowed people to run rampant with their views and opinions."
—Emmalina

# Q&A

## Matt Sloan and Aaron Yonda, Blame Society Productions

"Chad Vader—Dayshift Manager (episode 1)" started the popular Blame Society serial saga.

*This comedy duo from Madison, Wisconsin, has been making funny shorts together for years. Thanks to YouTube, they've garnered a national audience and representation in Hollywood. Best known for Web series such as "Chad Vader" and "McCourt's in Session," they produce stand-alone videos, as well.*

**FL:** You guys are the funniest duo to come from Wisconsin since Laverne & Shirley. When and how did you guys first meet?

**MS:** Aaron and I met doing improv here in Madison around 2000. He also had a public access show called "The Splu Urtaf Show," which I wanted to write for. We started writing and shooting videos and the rest is history.

**AY:** Matt came along at the perfect time because the guy I was working with on the public access show, Benson Gardner, had just decided that he would rather get married, make documentaries, and raise children. It turned out to be a really good thing because Matt and I have more complementary comedy stylings. Benson and I were like creamy peanut butter and crunchy peanut butter—combined we made a sandwich with way too much peanut butter. Matt and I are more like crunchy peanut butter and jam. Matt's raspberry jam.

**FL:** Had either of you made videos previously?

**MS:** I had a very short-lived public access show in college, but that's about it. My background is primarily in live theatre and improv.

**AY:** I started making videos back in high school. I worked at a TV station for a while in college and taught myself how to make videos.

**FL:** Where did the name Blame Society Films come from?

**MS:** It's Blame Society Productions, actually. Blame Society Films is the name of our YouTube channel because the other name wasn't available.

**AY:** It came from when I started making videos for public access in 1993. Society seemed like an appropriate thing to blame for our crazy nutball videos.

**FL:** When did you first start posting on YouTube? Why?

**MS:** Pretty much right after we created "Chad Vader." Someone else posted it, so we figured we'd better post our own version. Luckily our version got featured on the front page and became this worldwide sensation.

**AY:** It was around the same time that YouTube was becoming a household name, so the timing was superb.

**FL:** "Chad Vader" was nominated for best series in the first annual YouTube Awards. But it was beaten by "Ask a Ninja." How did that feel?

**MS:** Oh you know. It's an honor just to be nominated and all that. We didn't lose any sleep or anything. The "Ask a Ninja" guys are funny and they deserve it.

**AY:** It was definitely an honor.

**FL:** BUT—it was awarded the George Lucas Selects award for The Official Star Wars Fan Film Awards 2007 as chosen by George Lucas personally. How did that feel?

**MS:** Great. George mentioned our names in his press release and called Aaron "Aaron Yoda." I wish we could've been at the convention, but Mike McCafferty—one of our cast members who lives in L.A.—accepted the award for us.

**AY:** Just knowing George saw and liked "Chad Vader" is a huge thrill. I wish we could ask him what he liked about it most.

**FL:** How did you guys come up with the concept for "Chad Vader?"

**AY:** A friend of mine thought of the idea of Darth Vader working in a store for our public access show a long time ago, but we never did anything with it for a long time. Then Matt and I came up with the idea of making it Darth's brother Chad who's more of a weak-willed loser, and we thought of a bunch of other fun characters to surround him with, and then we got more excited about making it, and so we did.

**FL:** What do you think makes it such a big hit?

**MS:** It's a different spin on something that a lot of people are familiar with.

**AY:** It's more than just spoof— we're telling the story of a character people can really identify with. He's not Darth Vader; he's Chad, and he's just as confused about love and life as all of us are. Add to that some cool powers and a light saber and there you go. Chad's co-workers really add to the story, as well.

**FL:** How has YouTube helped your careers?

**MS:** Immensely. The exposure on YouTube has given us a huge audience and they've invited us to be part of their initial revenue-sharing program, which is pretty cool.

**AY:** It's given us the boost we needed to make a living creating videos, which is what we always wanted to do. It put us in the ideal position of being very much in demand.

**FL:** Did the William Morris Agency scout you on YouTube?

**MS:** We actually got involved with William Morris at the New York Television Festival in 2005. Our agent saw our pilot and wanted to represent us. We actually took some meetings with a few networks and pitched "Chad Vader" among some other ideas and got an enthusiastic response, which was part of the motivation for making it in the first place.

**FL:** Of all of your videos, which is your favorite?

"McCourt's in Session" is one of Matt Sloan's personal favorites.

**MS:** "McCourt's in Session." I get to play a crazy judge who yells at people and tells stories that make no sense (two of my favorite things). "Chad Vader" is pretty good, too. We also made this video called "What is Rolphing," which is pretty great.

**AY:** "Fun Rangers" is one of my favorites. It's wild and always unexpected. I like playing Chad Vader. It's funny how dressing up in Darth Vader's suit makes people on set suddenly respectful ....

**FL:** Do you have any favorite videos from other YouTube users?

**MS:** "Chocolate Rain" is pretty fun, in a minimalist sort of way. I like "The Vader Sessions." We like comedy videos, typically. Original stuff with thought put into it, and production and time. We're big fans of British comedy, like the *Mighty Boosh*. We also like the videos from Mediocre Films, Rob Schrab, JD Ryznar (who created "Yacht Rock"), and Ship of Fools Productions.

**AY:** "Dramatic Chipmunk" is cool.

**FL:** What advice can you offer to fellow viral videomakers to help them get noticed?

**MS:** Just keep doing what you love, rather than what you think people will want to see or what will "go viral." If you try to do that, you'll inevitably fail and probably won't have any fun. If you make what you think is funny or interesting or profound or whatever and stick to your instincts, your audience will find you, and even if they don't, you'll still be doing what motivates you and makes you happy, and there's definitely a sense of fulfillment in that.

**AY:** Make a lot of videos. Just keep making them and making them and you'll improve, and

## Matt Sloan and Aaron Yonda, Blame Society Productions (continued)

eventually, if you stick with it, you'll get some attention. Matt and I have made at least one short video a month since 2002 (one short video with a plot and characters, not a sit-in-front-of-the-webcam talky style video, which are easier to shoot). This honed our skills and built our audience until we finally made something that stuck, in the form of "Chad Vader."

**FL:** Do you believe that sites like YouTube can launch careers in Hollywood?

**MS:** I think that's already happened with us, so yes, I believe it's possible.

**FL:** What's next for Blame Society?

**MS:** We've just signed a production deal with SuperDeluxe.com and we're going to make a bunch

of videos for them. "Chad Vader season 2" is also in the works.

**AY:** We're going to branch out a little bit and start writing some movie treatments and pitch some TV shows. A book or two is in the works as well.

**FL:** Do you have a personal website?

**MS:** blamesociety.net.

# Q&A

## Justin Sandercoe

A shot from a typical Justin Sandercoe teaching video.

*Justin Sandercoe is a professional musician and music teacher. He plays in the Katie Melua Band and teaches at the Guitar Institute in London. He's also an accomplished songwriter and producer. He offers free guitar lessons through his YouTube videos.*

**FL:** How long have you been playing guitar? How long have you been teaching?

**JS:** I have been playing guitar for 27 years (age 33 now). I started teaching at the age of 12, just teaching other kids in the neighborhood to help me pay for my own lessons.

**FL:** When did you start making videos? When did you get the idea of making videos to teach guitar?

**JS:** My original guitar website has been running since 2000. I first started making videos to complement my website in December 2006. I had been watching stuff on YouTube and thought that it would be cool to add video to explain the things that are hard to explain using only text. I ran into my old friend Jed Wardley (who was a cameraman and who had just played me a video

he had made to help encourage disabled people to volunteer in the community) and after seeing that, I asked if he would be interested in filming some guitar stuff for YouTube, without thinking about potential money-making aspects; it was just to educate those who could not afford quality lessons.

**FL:** When did you first start posting on YouTube? Why?

**JS:** The very first videos we made were posted on YouTube and have been instrumental to the success of the site.

**FL:** There are several people who are now giving guitar lessons on YouTube. How do your videos compare to the others that are out there?

**JS:** I think I am offering the highest level of tuition available on YouTube and the Web in general. There are many other nonprofessional players out there offering advice, and many more trying to make a quick buck from it.

I really enjoy teaching and think I have a good knack for explaining things.

I earn my living as a pro player, but teaching is something that I love doing and have done since I can remember … I teach at one of the finest modern music schools in Europe, The Guitar Institute, and have written coursework for this and other music schools. I know I have a good head for organizing information and making it easy to digest. These skills are what I think people appreciate in my lessons. Plus, I would like to think that people like my "pay it forward" vibe—trying to be a good citizen in the global community and maybe bringing some awareness to world issues.

I don't want to slag off any other teachers on YouTube. There are some that can play okay but are not very good explainers, but they are lots of fun and get popular, and there are some that show teaching potential but screw it up by trying too hard to get cash or act like wankers.

**FL:** You've got two YouTube Channels. How come? What is the difference between them?

**JS:** I have two Channels, one for traditional lessons (scales and chords and techniques), and one for the more sticky legal area of songs. I am concerned that the songs channel may be shut down (as happened to another YouTube guitar teacher already), so I separated it from the traditional lessons.

**FL:** Is your concern about your Channel getting shut down due to the copyright issues? What is the concern? What are the boundaries of allowable use on YouTube?

**JS:** The allowable use of YouTube is not clearly defined. I am waiting for someone to have a go at me about it. The U.S. has a very strong "fair use" law, which I am very sure allows me to use copywritten songs for teaching in a nonprofit environment. But it has yet to be tested in court as far as I am aware. Though YouTube did pull down another teacher for copyright infringement, maybe because he was also selling that kind of material and making money from it, but I am not sure about that.

**FL:** Can someone really learn to play guitar by watching your videos? How well?

**JS:** If people follow my lessons, they can get very good indeed. I have met a few people around the world that have learnt from my site, some that are now doing their own concerts! But those guys were studying my site pre-video. I expect to see some good players coming out of my site over the next few years.

Of course, it does not take people right through to pro level; there is much that needs explaining in the flesh from a good teacher, and it takes many years of practice to get good. There is no "learn guitar in a weekend" course, like some of the bullshit ads that you can find on the Internet might hope you believe.

**FL:** Have any of your online students posted performance videos? How would you rate them? Any star YouTube students you can identify?

**JS:** There are quite a few that have posted video responses to my Solo Blues lessons, and some are quite good, and all are playing it well. No stars on YouTube yet, but some with loads of potential. One of my students is now a big star in Europe (Katie Melua). I now play in her band, though I first met her as my student many years ago now, and she learnt privately, not on YouTube.

**FL:** How have your YouTube videos helped your business?

**JS:** I have a very long waiting list for private students and I sell a lot of books and DVDs through the website, justinguitar.com.

Justin Sandercoe's "100th VID :) The Most Important Guitar Lesson Ever …".

**FL:** Of all of your videos, which is your favorite?

## Justin Sandercoe (continued)

**JS:** The hundredth video on YouTube in which I talk about transcribing and the "truth" about how to play guitar and also bring a heads-up about the genocide in Darfur. Lots of people took notice of that, and it felt good that other people cared about what I talked about, not just guitar lessons. I feel really honored that people dig what I do, and if that can be more than just teach guitar that would be super cool. [It] would be nice to make a difference.

**FL:** Do you have any favorite videos from other YouTube users?

**JS:** Yeah, loads! See the favorites on my channel—I guess my fave is the "George Carlin on Religion" video." I am an atheist and that vid just sums up the whole deal in a few minutes in a very true and funny way—that video can change lives. I love the Doll Face animation, there are many great clips of my favorite players, Jeff Beck, Joe Pass, and all the great songwriters too … and I love blogs, too, like Natalie at The Community Channel. She is too cool. :)

**FL:** Do you have a personal website?

**JS:** I do—www.justinguitar.com—currently the fifth highest-ranked guitar instructional site on the Web, between 6,000 and 10,000 visitors a day now, with millions of page views a month!

**FL:** Is there anything else you would like to add?

**JS:** I love YouTube; let's hope it doesn't get too corporate and censor too much. Keep it free as a forum for learning and discussion of politics and social structure. It's awesome. I am a big fan of the Internet.

# Q&A

## Ysabella Brave

Ysabella Brave as The PR Lady.

*Ysabella Brave is an American vocalist who makes videos of herself singing mostly covers of American classic hits. Her popularity on YouTube led to a record deal with Cordless Recordings, a division of Warner Music Group. In addition to her songs, she delights fans with sketches in which she plays an array of colorful characters.*

**FL:** Where did the name Ysabella Brave come from? Does "brave" have anything to do with being brave enough to put yourself out there on the Internet?

**YB:** Ysabella Brave is a nickname my father came up with long ago. My middle name is Ysabella, and my father considers me a brave person.

**FL:** When did you start singing? Have you had any formal training?

**YB:** I started singing about two years ago, somewhat accidentally. I sang poorly before this and had no interest in becoming a singer. On a lark when I was with some friends, I found I could sing well at that time. I have had no training of any kind. For now I'm just trying to sing all kinds of different things!

**FL:** What brought you to YouTube? What made you start posting your videos online?

**YB:** YouTube was a site I visited regularly to watch videos. When I realized I could sing, I thought I might share this with family and friends who were not nearby to see what their opinion was on it. Before long, I became quite popular on YouTube—that was very unexpected. The positive reaction from fans has really inspired me to keep going.

**FL:** I really love your characters (PR Lady, Supercool, Gossipgirl). Your acting is as amazing as your singing. Will we see more of it in the future?

**YB:** I hope to do more acting skits in the future—they're a lot of fun to make!

**FL:** There's a lot of debate as to whether you ever auditioned for *American Idol.* Did you? Do you think exposure on YouTube could help or hurt someone's chances of getting on that show?

**YB:** I made videos talking about my trip to *American Idol.* It was an unusual experience. I was told I had an "excellent voice but no thanks." I doubt that exposure on YouTube could affect anyone's chances one way or another for acceptance on *American Idol.*

**FL:** You don't ever come out and say it, but lots of people ask you about it. Have you ever found love through YouTube?

**YB:** I have never found love through YouTube, no. I do care for my subscribers. They are such nice people! But as far as romance, never found that on YouTube.

**FL:** You ask people to make donations if they enjoy your videos. Do people ever make donations? How much have you made? What's the average donation?

What's the single-largest donation someone has made?

**YB:** I put the PayPal button up on my site when subscribers kept asking if they could send me a gift of appreciation. I say if someone feels moved to send me something, feel free, and if not, that's fine. The amounts are usually small but sometimes people are quite generous.

**FL:** There's a whole he/she controversy with your songs. Some people want you to leave the original pronoun. Others want you to change it so it's gender specific for you, the singer. What's your personal opinion?

**YB:** There is an ongoing discussion amongst my viewers regarding he/she lyrics in songs and whether I should change them or not. I think this is because a lot of the songs I enjoy are traditionally sung by men. My personal view is to sing it where it's true for me. If I need to change the words to feel the song, I will. If I don't, I won't. There are plenty of songs that I enjoy where changing the pronoun would virtually alter the entire song, so I leave those alone.

**FL:** Of all of your videos, which is your favorite?

**YB:** My original song "James" took a lot of work to film and write the music and lyrics, then perform, so I value that one a great deal. Truly, it's hard to pick "favorites," because they are each so different and have such a unique story behind them.

**FL:** Do you have any favorite videos from other YouTube users?

**YB:** I love LisaNova's series, as well as HappySlip's. They both do skit-type comedy and I think they're phenomenally hilarious.

**FL:** Do you have a personal website?

**YB:** There's a really exciting site being built right now: stay tuned!

**FL:** Is there anything else you would like to add?

**YB:** I'd like to add that I'm very grateful I'm able to touch people in this way, even to make someone smile and their day lighter. I hope that the venue for my acting and singing can continue to grow so that as many people who want to enjoy what I do can.

Ysabella Brave sings her original song, "James."

## Matt Chin

Matt Chin chats up his sidekick, Ricky Thompson, on an episode of "My Show with Matt Chin."

*For as long as he can remember, this Canadian college student has always wanted to be a talk show host. So he built a set in his garage, and now he puts together a weekly talk show in the style of Carson and Letterman. He also makes very funny comedy shorts, which he posts to his YouTube Channel.*

**FL:** You look so young! How old are you?

**MC:** I'm 21 years old but I usually get people telling me I look 12, ha ha. I'm just going to use my youthful looks to my advantage.

**FL:** What is your day job? Do you go to school?

**MC:** My day job is the same as my hobby. So on top of my online show and shorts, I host, edit, and produce television shows for a digital cable channel here in Canada. I also host a top-rated weekly radio show on a small station. I just graduated from college in 2006. I studied radio, film, and television.

**FL:** I really love watching your talk show. You're a real likable host and very funny to watch. When did you first start doing the show and how did it come about?

**MC:** I first started doing my talk show in high school. I think I was about 16 years old when I first got the idea to do it. I had been a longtime fan of late-night talk shows. Ever since I was very young I loved watching David Letterman and all of the old *Tonight Shows* with Johnny Carson. Plus, with shows like *The Tom Green Show* being big at the time; that also inspired me. I figured the only way that I could get a chance to do something like that was if I made it happen on my own. So I just decided to start making a show even though I had no clue how to do it. I started by building a set in my basement, and then I started filming little skits in the classic late-night talk show style. I taught myself pretty much everything and learned as I went. Eventually I started getting the hang of it both technically and comedically, and it's developed into what it is today.

**FL:** You've also made so many funny videos. Which do you enjoy more, doing the show or the videos?

**MC:** I don't really view them as being very different. They're basically one and the same ... if I was making a talk show for television I'd be making it in my own style, by incorporating my funny videos and sketches into the late-night talk show environment. So by making all of these videos, it's like practice for my ultimate goal of getting that big network show.

**FL:** Who are some of the people you look up to in the entertainment industry?

**MC:** I look up to Johnny Carson, David Letterman, Conan O'Brien, and pretty much the whole late-night talk show scene. I even look back to the Jack Parr days. I'm fascinated by those shows. There's something about them that I love and I can't quite put my finger on why. It could be the live audience for instant reaction, the comedy bits, the interviews, the glamour of the whole show ... or it could just be the fact that these guys get to go out night after night and do something new, whether it be new jokes or new sketches or new guests. It's just awesome.

**FL:** When did you first start posting to YouTube? How was the response?

**MC:** I started posting on YouTube in 2006. The response was great. I had tons of people checking out my videos and loving them. It was really weird to get that kind of response because I wasn't used to getting much feedback, but when YouTube hit it really started exploding.

**FL:** How were you able to develop such a huge fan base?

**MC:** It wasn't something I was really conscious about. I just made my videos and posted them up, and then I think people just started passing them around because they really started getting popular. Then the YouTube editors started noticing my work and I was featured on the main page earlier this year. After that my Channel was featured, and then another video was selected as the pick of the day. Pretty soon I had 6,000 subscribers and was ranked the twenty-third most subscribed comedian on all of YouTube. Prior to YouTube I was running my own website (MyShowsCrazy.com) and that had a pretty good following, but when I started posting on YouTube it brought me into a whole new scene.

**FL:** What makes your show different than everything else out there on the Net?

**MC:** My show is different from everything else on the Net because I try to make a show that looks as professional as I can with no budget. Then there is the quality of the content—I really try and make my stuff funny for everyone rather than making something that only your friends laugh at. That's a huge problem I see out there right now ... all these people make these videos that they think are so funny, but to an outsider they're not. They just look like crappy digital camera videos and usually their camera work is so shabby that you can't even tell what's going on in the video. I basically try to make quality videos that are well written, well directed, well shot, and well edited. I pride myself in trying to do more than just sitting in my room talking on a webcam, even if it ends up costing me. It's just something I love doing and I think it shows.

**FL:** I recently saw a banner ad nominating you to take the Conan O'Brien spot on NBC once Jay Leno retires and Conan takes over for Jay. Would this be your dream job? If you could interview anyone on that first show, who would it be?

**MC:** Hosting a network late-night talk show is definitely my dream job and where I ultimately want to end up. I'd like to reinvent the talk show for this generation and I think I'm the guy to do it. I'm often asked the question about who I'd want my first guest to be and it always changes. I think anyone that has an interesting story [and] is willing to talk and joke around is going to be a good interview. I think George Clooney would be good to talk to—he's always great on talk shows and he has a good sense of humor.

**FL:** Recently your YouTube account was "suspended." What happened?

**MC:** Yeah, my account was shut down. Apparently, I violated the Terms of Use with some inappropriate content. I didn't think I had any inappropriate content, but I guess I did. Ha ha.

**FL:** Is there a possibility you will eventually return to the Tube?

**MC:** Yes, it is a possibility .... I have a new account, "mattchin28." However, we have just launched a brand-new MyShowsCrazy.com. It's now like our own personal community because people can sign up and create personal accounts, watch, rate, and comment all of our shows and videos right on our site. It's a place where fans of the show can come to one place to see everything and get updates.

**FL:** Do you think YouTube is a good venue for new talent to be discovered?

**MC:** YouTube is a great place for new talent to be discovered. Without YouTube I don't think I would be where I am today. It's really helped me get some notice, and for anyone that wants to showcase their talent it's the perfect place.

Matt Chin doles out advice to a young boy in his comedy short "The Advisor."

## Matt Chin (continued)

**FL:** Of all of your videos, which is your favorite?

**MC:** I like most of my videos for different reasons, but I have to say my favorite Random Shorts would have to be "The Guide on How to Become Big on You-Tube," "The Advisor," and "The Pee Break." My favorite "My Show" episode is harder to pick

because there are certain seg-ments I like, but I'd say Episodes 21 and 23 are good shows over-all.

**FL:** Do you have any favorite vid-eos from other YouTube users?

**MC:** Nothing in particular. I just surf around YouTube watching videos that look interesting.

**FL:** Is there anything else you would like to add?

**MC:** I also like directing, and make short films occasionally when I get time. I'd also like to get into acting in movies or tele-vision.

# Q&A

## David Choi

David Choi sings "'I Won't Smile'—Original Song—Acoustic Version."

*David Choi is a Los Angeles–based staff producer and song-writer for Warner Chappell Music Publishing. He's also not a bad performer, which he demon-strates frequently with a blend of original tunes and covers on his YouTube Channel. While he's more comfortable behind the*

*scenes, his YouTube videos have given him plenty of visibility.*

**FL:** How long have you been writing and playing music?

**DC:** I grew up being forced to play violin and piano, and sort of quit in the middle of high school. I started writing and recording when I was 16 years old and have been doing it ever since.

**FL:** When did you start posting videos to YouTube? Why?

**DC:** I started posting videos around January 2007. I posted a video out of boredom and to see how people would react.

**FL:** You work for a major music company as a songwriter. Who are some of the artists you write for?

**DC:** I write for all kinds of art-ists in different styles. I haven't had any cuts yet, but I'm getting close.

**FL:** Do you have ambitions to be a successful recording artist in your own right?

**DC:** Not really ... right now, I feel comfortable working behind the

scenes and posting videos ex-clusively on YouTube for my fans.

**FL:** Do you think YouTube can help make that dream possible?

**DC:** It has for a few people ... Esmee Denters and Mia Rose. Esmee signed to Justin Timber-lake's new label and Mia signed with Ryan Leslie at Next Selec-tion.

**FL:** Do you think YouTube is a good venue for new talent to be discovered?

**DC:** It's a great place to get dis-covered and it makes an A&R's job a lot easier when it comes to signing talent because they can see that a fan base is already built in ... most of the battle is already won.

**FL:** Why don't you ever smile in your videos?

**DC:** Because people want me to. :)

**FL:** You've got over 17,000 sub-scribers. How did you establish such a huge fan base?

**DC:** I'm not sure ... I know that getting featured with my YouTube song helped a lot, but that was only a short burst of subscribers. People keep subscribing for some reason … I'm guessing it's mostly word of mouth.

**FL:** Of all of your videos, which is your favorite?

**DC:** Honestly I don't like any of them, because I know I can do better, ha ha.

**FL:** Do you have any favorite videos from other YouTube users?

**DC:** There are quite a lot of videos I "favorite" so I can go back and watch them. Anything from comedy to science videos. As long as I enjoy watching them, I'll favorite.

**FL:** Do you have a personal website?

**DC:** www.myspace.com/ davidchoimusic.

**FL:** Is there anything else you would like to add?

**DC:** I'd like to add that the music industry is weird.

# Q&A

## Koichiben

A screen cap from Tofugu, Koichi's English language vlog.

*Koichi is a student living in Portland, Oregon. He has two YouTube Channels. Koichiben is a Japanese language Channel he created to teach Japanese people about American language, places, and culture. He started Tofugu to teach English speakers about Japanese culture.*

**FL:** When did you start your vlog? How did you come up with the idea?

**K:** I started the Koichiben Vlog Spring of 2007. I had to come up with an idea for an independent study project that involved practicing and learning Japanese. I had always wanted to try my hand at YouTube and blog writing, so I figured this was a good opportunity to accomplish both those things. I did a few vlogs in English on my Koichiben page and realized I shouldn't be catering to two audiences. It felt like bad branding. That's when I made an English vlog (Tofugu).

**FL:** When did you first think to bring Godzilla into the vlog?

**K:** I wanted to do a video that involved simple "gag" humor, so one bored night I decided to start a kind of running "story." I had a Godzilla mask, so I figured that was the way to go. I never expected it to be featured, and I'm really appreciative of the opportunity I got.

**FL:** How come Godzilla's vlogs are subtitled in English but your vlogs are only in Japanese (on the original Channel)?

**K:** The Godzilla videos were not about American culture, and were not necessarily directed toward Japanese people, so I felt that I should cater to a wider audience. The subtitles just allow more people to see it and understand it. I would put subtitles on everything, but I really want to keep Koichiben separate from Tofugu.

**FL:** Why did you start a second vlog in English? Other than the languages spoken, are there any other differences in the two vlogs?

**K:** For years I have always wanted to start a blog (in English). I figured that since I was writing a blog about American culture for Japanese people, I could try to do the opposite and teach non-Japanese about Japanese culture. It feels like a good balance of things.

## Koichiben (continued)

Koichi vlogs as Godzilla.

**FL:** What do Koichiben and Tofu-gu mean?

**K:** Koichiben: My middle name is Koichi, and ben means "dialect" in Japanese. For example, Osaka-Ben is "Osaka dialect." I added the word "dialect" to my name because I don't speak Japanese very well, so I say funny things sometimes. I have my own dialect, according to my name.

Tofugu: This name is just a combination of Tofu and Fugu. I chose it because it's easy to say and easy to remember. A lot of similar syllables and letters make for better audience memory.

**FL:** What is the general response to your vlogs?

**K:** I think my vlogs cater to a fairly specific audience. Once it is outside that audience my videos aren't received nearly as well. There's a lot of angry people out there on YouTube. I think my videos do okay amongst the Japanese audience, but they almost never comment so it's really hard to tell. I get a lot of nice emails, though.

**FL:** What do you hope to accomplish with these vlogs?

**K:** Koichiben: I hope to teach Japanese people about the aspects of American culture they wouldn't normally be able to see through television/books. I also want to entertain people while doing it, taking them to interesting places and talking about interesting things from a perspective they don't normally hear from. I also want to practice my Japanese to get ready for the proficiency test, which is coming up soon.

Tofugu: I created this channel to help people learn Japanese. There are so many people out there learning Japanese for all the wrong reasons (anime, mostly), though that is solely my opinion. Those kinds of people forget that there is much more to learning a language. There is culture, people, places ... I want everyone to know about those things and get outside their box. My ultimate goal is to "make learning Japanese cool again."

**FL:** Can you cite an example of how your vlog has had a positive impact on a viewer?

**K:** I get a lot of people thanking me for inspiring them to study harder (or study at all) ... though I don't know how long they've kept with it.

**FL:** Are you seeking fame through vlogging? If you become famous, is that a positive or negative outcome?

**K:** I've seen a lot of folks become famous and fall hard on YouTube—I'm not sure if I want that to happen. If I was to become famous, I would want it to be for the right reasons. I don't think I deserve to become famous. I'm really happy where I am now—I'm still able to respond to everyone's emails.

**FL:** Of all of your videos, which is your favorite?

**K:** I really like my Seattle Mariners Baseball series. I got to meet a lot of interesting people and have a lot of good memories. I'm a really shy person normally, but making a video for my vlog forced me to get out of my comfort zone. I enjoyed it a lot (only after it was all over, though).

**FL:** Do you have any favorite videos from other YouTube users?

**K:** I don't really know what's going on so much outside the "Japanese YouTubers" video realm, but my favorites are Moonkey4U, maxdesu, awadance, and van-awesome.

**FL:** Do you have a personal website?

**K:** koichiben.com & tofugu.com. The videos on YouTube are supposed to only supplement the blogs (i.e., I make the videos for articles in my blogs).

# Q&A

## James Kotecki, Emergency-Cheese

James Kotecki interviews Senator Ron Paul in his dorm room in his video titled, "Senator Ron Paul Visits My Dorm Room."

*According to* The Economist, *James Kotecki is "… probably the world's foremost expert on YouTube videos posted by Presidential candidates." A frequent commentator on CNN, Fox News, and NPR, Kotecki began posting vlogs from his dorm room at Georgetown University. His vlogs on U.S. politics and involvement in the YouTube debates has inspired a whole new generation of voters.*

**FL:** When did you start making videos? Why did you start posting?

**JK:** In late January 2007, I got a webcam for video chatting, and decided to post videos on YouTube because it seemed like everyone else was doing it, and I could do just as well as most of the people on the site.

I decided to talk about politics because it's my favorite subject, and after a couple of hopelessly lame commentaries, I noticed that some of the presidential candidates had uploaded their own YouTube videos. I hadn't heard anyone else talking about this subject. One of those official videos, from Senator Chris Dodd, encouraged viewers to upload a video response. I decided to take him up on that, and the rest is history.

**FL:** How did you come up with the name EmergencyCheese?

**JK:** The answers can be found in this video:

www.YouTube.com/watch?v=zrrtaOUO7Tw.

If you don't feel like watching that, I'll just tell you: In eleventh grade, we were brainstorming small-business ideas for a class project. I came up with the idea for "EmergencyCheese," a thermos-like container filled with different flavors of cheese that you could carry around with you all day. In stressful situations, you would shout "Emergency-Cheese!", open up your container, and enjoy immediate and stress-reducing sustenance.

Needless to say, I have no idea how to produce thermoses or cheese. I also realized that the name "EmergencyCheese" was the coolest thing about my imaginary product. So, I've used the name in a number of different ways ever since. At one point, I had a website that sold EmergencyCheese merchandise (t-shirts, not cheese), and had little cheese characters (All-American American, Party-Time Provolone) on it. When I started my YouTube account, there was only one clear choice for a screen name.

**FL:** What did you study in college?

**JK:** I graduated magna cum laude in the Class of 2007 with a Bachelor of Science in Foreign Service from Georgetown University's Edmund A. Walsh School of Foreign Service. My major was International Politics with a focus on International Security Studies.

**FL:** You've gone from political blogging, to dorm room interviews, to on-location reports. I'm most impressed with your dorm-room interviews. How on earth did you convince political candidates to let you interview them from your dorm room?

**JK:** I asked all the presidential candidates on YouTube to visit my dorm room for an interview. One of those candidates, Congressman Ron Paul, was kind enough to say yes and set a date. I know someone kind of close to the campaign, so that may have helped. After the Paul interview, it was a lot easier to convince other campaigns to do interviews with me.

# James Kotecki (continued)

**FL:** Of all the interviews you have done (in and out of the dorm), which has been your favorite?

**JK:** The interview I did with Congressman Ron Paul, for a few reasons:

1. It made history. This was the first time a presidential candidate had ever come to a college kid's dorm room for a webcam interview, and I give Paul and his staff a lot of credit for being willing to take the risk.

2. Ron Paul, along with Mike Gravel and Dennis Kucinich, are unconventional politicians both in the issues they fight for and in their personal style. That meant that in talking with them, I really didn't know what they were going to say. In Ron Paul's case, we got into a great discussion about the role of the Constitution in modern life. That's the kind of thing one rarely sees in a cable news interview.

**FL:** Do you think Channels like yours were the catalyst for the Democratic YouTube debates?

**JK:** I do think that the political activity that I and others have been a part of on YouTube certainly helped to convince the powers that be that a YouTube debate was a viable concept. But Steve Grove, the News and Politics editor at YouTube, is a very creative guy, so I imagine that this idea would've come about whether or not I personally was posting videos to YouTube.

**FL:** Do you believe that YouTube can actually influence the next presidential election? To what extent?

**JK:** Yes. At least for this election cycle, I don't think YouTube will replace any other media source, but it does fill in gaps with all the media that existed before it. For one thing, it has the potential to reach, though casual, personal, interesting videos (which politicians aren't necessarily producing) a group of younger voters who may have been turned off by glossy, PR-driven politics we've seen up to this point. It also allows for lesser-known candidates, like many of the ones I've interviewed, to get their message out without using a lot of resources.

There are also the obvious and occasional viral videos, like the macaca video (the infamous speech by Senator George Allen that was captured on video in which he unwittingly referred to a dark skinned man as "macaca," which is a French-Tunisian racial slur), that can actually bring down a candidate. Perhaps one day we'll see a viral video that puts a candidate over the top (although negative seems to work better). If a video gets enough attention, eventually the mainstream media will begin to talk about it.

So for all these reasons and many we probably haven't thought of yet, YouTube will have a significant impact on the 2008 election.

**FL:** What is your opinion of the candidate YouTube pages?

**JK:** Many of the candidates have tried some innovative things, but no one has the full package yet—the full package being a casual, ongoing conversation with voters combined with other fun, experimental, and moving videos that are made specifically for YouTube.

Dennis Kucinich, Tom Tancredo, and now Bill Richardson are the best in terms of the continual conversation. They each respond via video to individuals that ask them questions. Tom Tancredo has been especially good at being casual in his responses, which occasionally take place as he's driving his car.

I've also been impressed by Joe Biden, who actually responded to Rudy Giuliani's YouChoose Spotlight video with a video of his own, that calls out Giuliani by name.

Chris Dodd, in his YouChoose Spotlight video, actually encouraged people to go out and make YouTube videos asking their members of Congress about Iraq—that showed a great understanding of what YouTube is and what it's capable of.

Mike Huckabee has also been very good at posting casual clips that, like the image he presents to the world, are not overly produced.

I've been less impressed when candidates like Mitt Romney, Rudy Giuliani, and Barack

Obama fill their YouTube channels with clips from speeches or news clips instead of creating more unique YouTube content.

My opinion of Hillary Clinton's Channel is mixed—on the one hand, she suffers from a lack of casual YouTube videos, and her attempts to converse with the community have been overly produced. However, she has created a few very funny videos (also very produced) that have garnered national and even international media attention, which is probably a good way for her to shake her somewhat icy image.

James Kotecki vlogs about politics and the upcoming presidential election.

**FL:** What is your opinion on the candidate's ability to control and screen comments left on their pages?

**JK:** Many candidates are way too strict about censoring the comments they get. For example, a recent Rudy Giuliani video in the YouChoose Spotlight got hundreds of thousands of views, but only 100 comments, all positive. His team must have been doing some serious screening. I think that candidates who

do this look closed off from the YouTube community and send the message that they don't want an open dialog, only a one-way broadcast of their message. That's the opposite of what YouTube is all about.

A member of the Mike Huckabee campaign told me that the only comments they censor are those that are vulgar or those that are just advertisements for another candidate ("Vote for Ron Paul!"). Any other kind of dissenting voice, they leave up. I think that's a much better model, because it engages the community on its own interactive terms and is not an attempt to dictate to them.

**FL:** Who is on your wish-list for interview subjects?

**JK:** Every presidential candidate listed on the YouChoose page that I haven't interviewed yet. I'm gunning for all of them.

**FL:** How did you begin collaborating with David McMillan?

**JK:** David sent me a YouTube message saying something like, "I like your videos; check out mine." I get this type of message from a variety of people several times a week, but in David's case, I actually did check out his content. I was immediately impressed—having seen so much mediocre video blogging on YouTube, it was great to see someone so talented and funny.

I got back to David that day saying that we should find a way to work together using the collaborative power of YouTube. He agreed. We started our Kotecki and McMillan video series the next week.

**FL:** Talk a bit about community when it comes to YouTube and politics.

**JK:** YouTube is more than a repository of videos—it's a community where people can interact with and respond to each other. Most of that communication is done through video, but it also happens when members rate videos, comment on videos, or send each other private messages.

That interactive element makes it distinctly different than television, which has none of those interactive elements. Yes, both YouTube and television are primarily moving pictures with synchronized sounds, but they are distinct and different mediums.

Candidates who grasp this difference will interact with their YouTube audiences and upload unique content for YouTube that takes advantage of YouTube's interactive elements. All other things being equal, those candidates will have a richer presence on YouTube than a candidate who simply treats YouTube as a repository for television clips.

**FL:** What is your day job? What is your dream job?

**JK:** I work for a consulting firm in DC called The Cypress Group, which is online at www.cypressgroupdc.com. I do research to help hedge funds understand how political events might impact their investments. I've been working there since before I started making videos, and they've been very flexible in allowing me to build a schedule around my increasingly hectic video-blogging career.

## James Kotecki (continued)

> " ... On YouTube, the only person who can cancel your show is you."
>
> —James Kotecki

I'm working on several very interesting video-related projects right now that, if all goes well, should be able to sustain me going forward. Since they haven't done that yet, I'll have to hold off on telling you in case they don't pan out.

My dream job would be to host an interview show, like Larry King, that would be highly interactive both on television and on the Web. Most of my top videos are interviews, and I always have a really fun time doing them.

**FL:** Has YouTube provided you with opportunities to launch a career in political journalism?

**JK:** Yes. The first time I got paid to be a journalist was when Politico.com hired me to be a freelance video blogger at the Iowa Straw Poll. I even got a press pass. This was a direct result of Politico staff seeing my YouTube videos and offering me the opportunity.

**FL:** Of all of your videos, which is your favorite?

**JK:** Probably this one: www.YouTube.com/ watch?v=nl8w8u9Gr50.

**FL:** Do you have any favorite videos from other YouTube users?

**JK:** Yes. Not necessarily political ones, though. These users actually have a lot of great videos, so [go to] their Channels to see more:

http://YouTube.com/ watch?v=itbOQ6QLu60

www.YouTube.com/ watch?v=DKCKrCKQT_s

www.YouTube.com/ watch?v=5nKL4mbUleI

http://YouTube.com/ watch?v=0LZtSdM337Q

http://YouTube.com/ watch?v=11Camuw2cgI

http://YouTube.com/ watch?v=f45K8Jh14-k

**FL:** Do you have a personal website?

**JK:** Yes. www.JamesKotecki. com. This includes my EmergencyCheese videos, my Kotecki and McMillan videos, and a lot of personal information.

**FL:** Is there anything else you would like to add?

**JK:** I'm living proof that through persistence, anybody with something to say can become successful using YouTube. I'd highly encourage everyone who wants to get their message out to give it a try, and to keep trying— because on YouTube, the only person who can cancel your show is you.

# Q&A

## Cherry Lee, TheBathroom-Girl

TheBathroomGirl doing what she does best … singing in the bathroom!

*Cherry Lee is a British-born Chinese student living in London and studying Economics and Development Studies. She coined her moniker by singing and playing guitar in the bathroom where she claims the acoustics are better. Her music is a mix of originals and covers.*

**FL:** How long have you been singing, playing guitar, and writing music?

**CL:** Learnt my first chords from my mum when I was 9 … wrote my first song at 11 but only started really getting into songwriting when I was 15/16 … I have been through lots of phases!

**FL:** What brought you to YouTube?

**CL:** Last year my friend asked me to check out his idol dancer/choreographer. Before that, I had never even heard of YouTube and now I can't imagine my life without it! Ha ha.

**FL:** Why the interest in broadcasting yourself over the Internet?

**CL:** It was primarily just a bit of fun. I knew that it was open to the public but I thought it would basically be just friends and family that searched me and found me. It was a way of keeping in touch with friends, I guess; letting them know I'm still alive and singin'.

**FL:** How did you come up with your screen name?

**CL:** I'm a girl who sings in the bathroom!

**FL:** When did you start singing in the bathroom? Is it something you started to do just for YouTube as a gimmick?

**CL:** When I uploaded my first few videos in the bathroom, I never thought that I would be calling myself TheBathroomGirl, so it definitely wasn't a pre-planned gimmick.

I played in the bathroom that night because it was late at night, some of my family was sleeping already and others were occupying other rooms. It was the best place for me not to disturb anyone!

Now I just play there because I like the acoustics and it has good natural light for the videos.

**FL:** You say that you don't think you're good enough to go pro, but if a record exec scouted you on YouTube, would you be interested in pursuing this as a career?

**CL:** Hmm … a lot of people are curious about this. No matter what happens, I want to finish my degree and there are certain things that I really want to do in my life that are pretty much non-negotiable. But, you never know, I guess!

**FL:** Have you been scouted by industry professionals on YouTube? What did it lead to?

**CL:** People claim to be industry professionals all the time, but I've really been too busy working lately to follow up on these musical trails.

**FL:** Have you ever been recognized in the real world from YouTube? Was it weird? What happened?

**CL:** Ha ha. I have actually! I was out clubbing with friends in a club in Leicester Square (don't judge me; it wasn't my choice) and two girls came up to me and asked if I was TheBathroomGirl! I was so gobsmacked! They took pictures with me! Nathalie and Kiki … I'll never forget them!

Another time was after clubbing in London as well, we went to China Town at around 4 A.M. to satisfy the usual munchies, and the next day I got a random message on MySpace asking if "the bathroom girl was in 1997 [a restaurant] at around 4 A.M." It was totally bizarre!

## Cherry Lee, TheBathroomGirl (continued)

**FL:** Do you think YouTube is a good venue for new talent to be discovered?

**CL:** Most definitely! Terra Naomi is testament to that.

**FL:** Of all of your videos, which is your favorite?

**CL:** Erm … that's a tough one. I guess my favorites are "Chasing Cars" and "Take Care Baby." For the latter, especially, my emotions were so raw that I was practically crying during the song. I want the YouTube audience to know the real me, and I strongly believe that a person has to really "feel" a song in order to perform it faithfully.

**FL:** Do you have any favorite videos from other YouTube users?

**CL:** I adore Terra Naomi. Andy Mckee's "drifting" … some really funny clips. The usual shebang.

**FL:** Do you have a personal website?

**CL:** Not as of yet; just my MySpace page at www.myspace.com/thebathroomgirl.

**FL:** Is there anything else you would like to add?

**CL:** Would just like to thank all the people who've supported the Channel and I'm proud to be a member of the YouTube community! :)

# Q&A

## Ben Going, boh3m3

boh3m3 poses the question, "Why do You Tube?"

*Ben Going is a 23-year-old waiter living in Southern California. While the average diner may not recognize him, he's got a huge following on YouTube. His vlogs have close to 40,000 subscriptions.*

**FL:** Let's start with your screen name, boh3m3. What does it mean and how did you come up with it?

**BG:** "boh3m3" is a bastardization of bohemiabsinthe, which was a screen name that I came to adopt as my own when I started doing digital art. It's a reference to the Bohemian art movement in France in the late 1800s.

**FL:** One of your videos is called "Why do You Tube?" in which you ask people why they come to YouTube, watch and make videos, etc. So, I throw that question back to you, why do you tube?

**BG:** I tube, therefore I am. I started just to get the thoughts that were rumbling around in my head out in the open. I continued because I started to get more attention on my thoughts and personality than I had ever had before. Nowadays I tube out of habit and hope. Habit, because I've done at minimum one video a week for the last year, and hope because I have received some interesting work offers.

**FL:** What were some of the most interesting answers you received as video responses to this question?

**BG:** Well, to be honest, I lost interest in watching them all after about 50 videos, but I remember one user was just trying to impress his high school sweetheart. Kind of a cute idea, really. Devoting a whole Channel to impressing a girl.

**FL:** How did you get so popular on YouTube?

**BG:** That's a good question … I wish I knew the answer so I could capitalize on it. The only lead I have is the notion that there's a market for every kind of video or personality ... I just fell into a pretty good-sized one.

**FL:** Any secrets for those who want to use YouTube to get their 15 minutes of fame?

**BG:** Aye. The biggest secret is that those 15 minutes matter less than the time it takes to get there. If we can assume for a minute that I'm having (or have had) my 15, then I can tell you it was not what I expected.

**FL:** Another one of your videos is called "A Day in the Life of a YouTube Celebrity." How would you rate YouTube celebrities as compared to working actors and musicians? Reality stars?

**BG:** Err ... well, every time I've used the term "YouTube Celebrity" it's been more of a mockery of the term .... But I would rate YouTube celebs along the lines of the local crazy homeless man. People know who he is in the town, but there's really nowhere for him to go from there. Or, at least, that's how I look at it.

**FL:** You've addressed the topic of haters in many videos. Where do they come from and don't they have anything better to do with their time?

**BG:** We're all haters in one way or another. The only thing that varies is the bluntness of delivery, the topic of mockery, and the ferocity of anger. It's a blanket term that seems to describe everyone from people who disagree without tact to people who are simply rude to be rude.

**FL:** Have you ever been recognized in public from YouTube? Was that a positive or negative experience?

**BG:** Well, just recently I was at the mall and some young girl screamed, "Oh my god, is that boh3m3?!" I really had no clue what to do ... I felt exposed, like some lame spy whose only goal was to blend in with the world at large and be anonymous. I did smile a little bit, though.

**FL:** I saw in one of your blogs that a YouTube viewer bought you a camera. What prompted a complete stranger to do that for you? Have you gotten any other nice gifts?

**BG:** Well, the viewer in question wanted me to pursue making short films as well as wanting me to blog outside my room and the limitations of my webcam. Other than that, some people have sent money and companies have sent shirts and hats. Not a bad deal overall.

**FL:** Have you been able to make money from your vlogs? What's the secret?

**BG:** Yep. But there's no real secret. I've made it through being a partner with YouTube and through accepting PayPal donations.

**FL:** There's a great sense of community on YouTube. You have collaborated with several other YouTube vloggers. How do these collaborations generally come about?

**BG:** Collaborations are born out of boredom, location, or just

friendship. One person will start noodling over an idea and the other will add to it, snowballing the whole shebang into a collab by video made and sent online or in person. It's just the child of two or more people's passion for video and making entertaining content.

**FL:** You've done comedy, movie reviews, straight vlogging, etc. What's your favorite type of video to make?

**BG:** My favorite so far is the narrative, which I've only done two or three of. It's kind of neat to write out a good voice-over script and then illustrate the ideas on video. I hope to get enough free time to do more of those soon.

**FL:** Of all of your videos, which is your favorite?

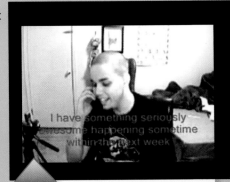

boh3m3 learns incredible news in his personal favorite video, "Exciting Mystery WOOOO."

**BG:** Honestly, it would have to be a video currently called "Exciting Mystery WOOOO," because it captures how I was

# Ben Going, boh3m3 (continued)

feeling at the time so well I can relive it any time I like. I had just found out I was being flown out to New York City to interview the owner of CBGBs before it closed … and I was as bouncy as Jenna Jameson in one of those inflatable bouncy rides you see at scary carnivals.

**FL:** Do you have any favorite videos from other YouTube users?

**BG:** It's too much for me to narrow it down, honestly. There is so much good content out there that I just couldn't in good conscience decide on one over any of the others.

**FL:** Do you have a personal website?

**BG:** Yes I do. It's www.boh3m3.net.

# Q&A
## Stevie Ryan

A shot from Stevie Ryan's silent short, "Comptine D'un Autre Ete."

*A Los Angeles–based actress who has landed bit parts in commercials and music videos, Stevie Ryan has found stardom on YouTube. She has several Channels designed for each of the characters she plays. They include Little Loca, TheRealParis, Ooolalaa, and others.*

**FL:** When did you start making videos?

**SR:** I started making videos when I was really young, like seven. I would steal my dad's camcorder and make commercials. I still have most of the footage and it's really funny to see myself doing the same thing as I am now. About a year and a half ago I bought my first laptop, and I saw this Windows Moviemaker editing program and read in it that I could hook my camera up to it with a little cord. At this time I was really obsessed with silent films and the old actors from them like Buster Keaton, Harold Lloyd, and Charlie Chaplin. I saw that I had this old movie effect that looked like these silents I was watching, so I started making my own. I would design my sets, get in an old costume, set my camera on a stack of books because I didn't have a tripod, and shoot the scene. I would then edit the piece together, throw some ragtime music in the background and make it look like a real silent film from the 1920s. I became instantly addicted to

producing my own short movies, and I'm still hooked.

**FL:** When did you first start posting on YouTube? Why?

**SR:** I started posting on YouTube in May 2006 under my stevieryan account. However, I was watching videos on the site long before I ever posted. I thought this little community of creative videomakers was really cool and I wanted to share my little videos, too. I didn't really think much of it, I just wanted to see if anyone liked what I was making. Before I knew it I had more people watching me than I had expected, and my creative juices starting flowing like never before. I couldn't stop making videos and characters. I mean, how could I? I had thousands of people to entertain.

**FL:** You've got several Channels: StevieRyan, LittleLoca, TheRealParis, OooLaLaa …. Why so many Channels? What distinguishes one from the other? Are there any I am missing?

**SR:** I felt like it was important to create separate worlds for each character to make it more believable for me and the audience.

Like Ooolalaa, I didn't just want to make videos as this character; I wanted her to have her own profile and YouTube channel, so that it's that much more real. She would have more colors on her profile than Loca, because she is an emotional character who involves lots of colors in her videos; whereas Loca has a black, white, and gray profile, because Loca has a very black and white attitude. TheRealParis is my "silly" account. I stick the funnier things on that channel. StevieRyan is the account that fits me as a person; that's who I am outside of YouTube. I've learned it's really hard to stay caught up on each account so I'm trying to limit myself to the four that I have. And to be honest, the Internet really isn't big enough for me and all my characters anyway.

**FL:** You're also behind Faye006, but those videos are only on LiveVideo.com. How come?

**SR:** It's a secret. ;) And, NO, they don't pay me.

**FL:** How does LiveVideo.com compare to YouTube? What other sites do you like?

**SR:** Well, they're basically the same thing. LiveVideo hasn't gone corporate yet so the community is smaller and the hater population is very low. A low hater population is always nice. I love MySpace, PerezHilton, and Digg. Stickam is addicting, but I love it.

**FL:** Talk to me about the haters. Until recently, rumors flew that LittleLoca wasn't real. Why did you come out of the closet about LittleLoca?

**SR:** I don't even really know who LittleLoca is. I mean, I do but I don't.

**FL:** Drake Bell has been featured in some of your videos. Rumors have abounded that the two of you were romantically involved. Was that true? Did he give you any pointers in making your videos?

**SR:** I dated Drake for a little while, but he had nothing to do with my videos. He thought I was crazy running around in costume with a camera all the time. He was my muse for a bit, but that's all.

**FL:** What's your day job when you're not making videos?

**SR:** Currently I have been filming a TV show, but when I'm not doing this I'm auditioning or shooting for something else, which is really cool. I have the best job in the world, now.

**FL:** Has YouTube helped move your career forward?

**SR:** I wouldn't say any site in general has "helped" me, but posting my videos on the Internet has definitely opened some doors for me. It's hard to make it in Hollywood, and people think that I just got it easy by sharing my videos, but I have definitely paid my dues. I've been auditioning and doing commercial work for years, before YouTube was ever around. I didn't have any

Stevie Ryan as LittleLoca.

intentions to be an Internet personality; it just happened. I just uploaded on the right site, at the right time.

**FL:** Can you give my readers some advice if they want to become the next YouTube star?

**SR:** Just have fun creating it, that's all that matters. As soon as it's not fun, it's not worth doing.

**FL:** Do you have any favorite videos from other YouTube users?

**SR:** I love BowieChick and all her videos. Also, Liam Sullivan is a really funny dude and [I like] his video "Shoes."

**FL:** Do you have a personal website?

**SR:** Yep! www.stevieryan.tv.

**FL:** Is there anything else you would like to add?

**SR:** Thanks for interviewing me. This is cool that my typing will be in a book. Oh, HI MOM!

# Q&A

## Michael Buckley, WhatTheBuck

Michael Buckley as his alter ego WhatTheBuck.

*Tabloid TV comes to YouTube each week when Michael Buckley's alter ego, WhatTheBuck, dishes the latest celebrity dirt. He's crass, funny, and extremely loveable. He also vlogs under his own persona at Peron75.*

**FL:** Which came first, the vlog or the "What The Buck" Show?

**MB:** The show came first. I never had any intentions of vlogging, but when my account got suspended, I had no choice but to reach out to the community that way. It worked out great for me and I found that people enjoyed seeing me at home and just being myself—not this horrible person who just said mean things about celebrities.

**FL:** How did the idea for the show come about?

**MB:** I do a local public access show and was hoping to get some good clips together to send out to agents, for castings, etc. My cousin who worked on the show put one of the clips on YouTube and things started to happen from there. "What the Buck" was meant to be a once-a-week thing, and it became so popular and enjoyable for me that now it is a four-to-five-times-a-week show.

**FL:** How much time goes into each episode?

**MB:** It is pretty much a 40-hour-a-week job for me on YouTube. I spend probably 12 to 16 hours a week writing, 3 hours shooting, and several hours editing and promoting.

**FL:** Do you write the scripts yourself or do you have help?

**MB:** I write the scripts myself. I do not have any help. I would love some joke writers!

**FL:** How much of the real Michael Buckley is in the character on "What the Buck?"

**MB:** It's an extreme version of me. I don't think I am that gay or that mean in real life—maybe I am. Many of the things I say, I do not believe; I just say them to be funny or offensive. Once I started vlogging it was hard to keep up the façade of being a bad guy. Sometimes it's hard to separate the two and I find when I talk to people, they want me to say bad things about Britney Spears and Beyonce and I really love them!

**FL:** Why did you create the show and start broadcasting on YouTube?

**MB:** I created the show just as a way of getting practice doing TV and broadcasting stuff. I knew I didn't want to do news but more of an *SNL, Best Week Ever* comedy recap-type show. And like I said, my cousin posted videos for me at first. I had no idea what YouTube was!

**FL:** How many of your viewers are gay versus straight?

**MB:** It seems pretty mixed! I would say 50/50. The gays love me—some hate me for being stereotypical gossip gay! The housewives who watch lots of TV love me! And I get lots of emails from straight guys saying they like me in a "non-gay way"!

**FL:** Given your large straight viewership, do you think you are helping to push the boundaries of tolerance and acceptance?

**MB:** Yes—very much so. I get a lot of hate mail, too, but it is mostly positive feedback. I think regardless of your sexual orientation or even if you hate gay people, most people appreciate the amount of time and work I put into the show.

**FL:** What does Perez Hilton have that you don't?

**MB:** 180+ pounds! No—he is easy to pick on but he is clearly a good businessman and he has totally developed his brand, which is what I am trying to do. I have a great respect for him and what he does. Good for him and his success!

**FL:** Have you gotten any response from the celebs you discuss on your show?

**MB:** No. Some of the reality "stars" but no real celebrities. Well, Shar Jackson—so again, no real celebrities.

**FL:** What happened with Dick Clark Productions that led to your temporary suspension on YouTube? Please share so other users don't make the same mistake.

**MB:** As I understand it, you have three strikes on YouTube before you get your account suspended. My account had two offenses, both of which were made very early on before I knew I would be posting so many videos, and before I really had any ideas of the rules. The first was [where] I had videotaped the TV with my camcorder and talked about it. It was a few seconds of MTV's *The Real World*. Viacom is one of the big companies that really monitors YouTube, and it got pulled. The second one was [where] I did a fake *American Idol* audition and spliced in some footage of the Idol judges—it was really funny but got pulled. I think it is fair use and parody, but I didn't fight it or even think about it. After this, I was very careful and never posted video that wasn't 100 percent mine.

In the spring of 2007, I did a video about *American Idol* and their Idol Gives Back program. Freemantle Media filed a claim against any video with the "Idol Gives Back" search tags and

that got my account suspended the first time. I felt my world collapse—all my 100 videos were gone. At this point I knew nobody at YouTube or any other YouTube users so I had no idea what to do. Luckily, the claim was lifted. It was a bogus claim. This is when I started vlogging. Then two months later, I did a review of *So You Think You Can Dance* and Dick Clark Productions filed a claim. I know they flagged lots of videos with those tags so I wasn't that worried, but I made a vlog about it, and one of my viewers called Dick Clark Productions and complained, and they said it was because I had used their logo. I talked to a lawyer and was ready to argue fair use as a "journalist" and a review of the show. I also wrote a heartfelt letter to them to explain how important it was to have the claim lifted. I never had to send it because the claim got lifted. Hundreds of people emailed them to complain on my behalf. It was amazing! It was at that point things really started to take off for me, too! It was some good YouTube drama! You really need to be careful and not post copyrighted music or video or you will get in trouble. And since I am high profile, I need to be extra careful. Some people post full episodes of TV show and never get caught.

**FL:** You mention that you film "What the Buck" in a studio. Where is the studio located, and is it expensive to work from there as opposed to shooting in your house?

**MB:** I have a public access show so I use the studio there. They are very nice to me and very happy for my success. I have two shows that air in town—"What the Buck" and a talk show with a co-host.

**FL:** Do you have a day job? What line of work are you in?

**MB:** I do have a day job. I don't like to talk about it because I work for a large company so I like to keep it separate. I work in an office nine to five. They know about the YouTube thing but don't really know how popular I am—neither does my family or friends for that matter! Ha ha!

**FL:** How was YouTube responsible for your opportunities with Leeza Gibbons and DirecTV?

**MB:** Everything that has happened has come out of me being seen on YouTube. I was contacted by the producers of *The Leeza Gibbons Show* to come on and now I have a weekly segment. Same with DirecTV—though the show I was on for them is not on that much anymore, I still contribute occasionally.

**FL:** Can YouTube help launch someone into celebrity?

**MB:** Of course! [Jessica Rose of] Lonelygirl15 got a series on ABC Family. There are some singers who have gotten recording deals! LisaNova got on *MadTV!* William Sledd has a deal with NBC. The list of success stories is growing! I think many more celebrities will continue to be discovered on the Web!

# Michael Buckley, WhatTheBuck (continued)

**FL:** Was that your goal—to launch a career via YouTube?

**MB:** Yes. I wanted to be seen and I wanted to develop a show for myself and establish an audience so I could pitch it. I have an agent now and having a show on YouTube is a great "demo" for me.

A more relaxed Michael Buckley vlogs on his personal Channel, peron75.

**FL:** Have you ever been recognized in the real world from YouTube? Was it weird? What happened?

**MB:** I often get recognized from YouTube, DirecTV, or my public access show. Mostly people just say, "WHAT THE BUCK!" or, "You're that guy." I love it but it always makes me a little nervous that they may hate me! I never know what to say; I just try to be gracious because I am. I always think it is disappointing to meet me because I am not that funny in person.

**FL:** Do you think YouTube is a good venue for new talent to be discovered?

**MB:** Yes, totally! Many producers, agents, and casting directors are there looking for new talent.

**FL:** Of all of your videos, which is your favorite?

**MB:** Wow! I have so many it is hard to pick which is my favorite! I love them all! But I think I would pick my "Beyonce Threatens to Kill Jennifer Hudson if She Wins an Oscar" video. This was the video that got me noticed and a lot of new fans. This video also showed me the value of having a good title and having good timing. The title was silly, making people want to click on it, and I posted it right around *Dreamgirls* previews, so many people were on YouTube looking for those videos. This was also when I stopped worrying about reporting on real things and just made stuff up!

**FL:** Do you have any favorite videos from other YouTube users?

**MB:** I really like LisaNova and Spricket24. They are very pretty and super funny! I like that in a girl! They are my two favorites!

**FL:** Do you have a personal website?

**MB:** www.buckhollywood.com.

**FL:** Is there anything else you would like to add?

**MB:** I love YouTube and it has been so good to me! Any success I have in the industry will be because of YouTube. I have also met many wonderful friends there as well. I pretty much live my life for all of YouTube to see. It is very personal and strange! I love it!

> **"I have an agent now and having a show on YouTube is a great 'demo' for me"**
> —Michael Buckley

# Q&A

## Charles Trippy

Charles Trippy in a typical video. See them first at www.charlestrippy.com.

*Charles Trippy may look like a slacker, but he's anything but. He was a contestant on the Web's first game show, "The Next Internet Millionaire." When he's not studying for finals or throwing a keg party, he's in front of his camera making videos.*

**FL:** When did you start making videos?

**CT:** I've been making videos since high school; however, I never really took them seriously until I noticed more people watching. It used to be so hard to get people to watch your videos online (if possible at all). You used to have to upload it and embed an ol' .mov in your page and have it load for 25 minutes. No one wanted to watch them. Then I started posting on You-Tube and ... well ... oh! I can use a cliché tagline ... here it is. The rest is history! Sweet, my life is complete!

**FL:** When did you first start posting on YouTube? Why?

**CT:** Um, I first started posting on YouTube in 2005. I have an old account floating around somewhere, but then I made another one so I could use my name as my username. Not sure why, but—I'm happy I did!

**FL:** One of the things I like most about your videos is the interactive nature of them and how they really work to foster community on YouTube. What made you choose this direction for your videos?

**CT:** Well, I saw all the cool little features that YouTube gave us to "make" a community—but no one was really using them. So I figured, why not? Plus, it's fun, right?

**FL:** How did you get involved with "The Next Internet Millionaire"? Why do you think you were chosen?

**CT:** Well, I saw the "ads" floating around YouTube and thought it would be funny to do one as a joke. I didn't realize that I would get in. I was totally shocked! I was thinking, "Woah, I didn't mean to do that ...." Ha ha.

**FL:** You really are quite entrepreneurial. Putting henna tattoos on your body to sponsor your trip to the YouTube gathering in New York City was genius. Were you able to pay for the entire trip that way?

**CT:** Hah, thanks! I figured it would be a good idea (though, in the back of my head I thought it wouldn't work). Being a college student, you can imagine having money is, well, not an option. Ha ha! It totally was worth the weird looks on the plane and in the city. The people at airport security didn't look happy to see me, jerks.

**FL:** I noticed that you even had sponsors on your official website. How did you line them up?

**CT:** Well, I love helping smaller companies out. A couple of the sponsors I have are clothing companies. I'm not sure how it happened, but somehow we just "merged" and struck a deal. It's actually kind of fun making a video and using a product—but not making the video a commercial. It's challenging and really fun!

**FL:** Is it possible for someone to make a living through viral video on the Internet? What advice can you give someone who wants to do just that?

**CT:** Hm, define make a living. Hah—currently, it's hard. You can make a side income, sure. But, if you have kids and a mortgage (I have neither), it's probably not possible. If you are a student, it's somewhat possible. The only advice I can think of is, be persistent. If you are having fun, keep doing it.

**FL:** What's your day job when you're not making videos?

**CT:** Well, I'm a student at the University of South Florida. I

## Charles Trippy (continued)

also work as a projectionist at a movie theater, so it's great for editing and thinking of ideas!

**FL:** Is it possible to find fame on YouTube?

**CT:** Well, yeah—it's possible. Hell, anything is possible. If you are talented enough (or even lucky enough), you can land a deal. I hope a majority of the "next gen" celebrities are from the Net. That'd be pretty sweet.

**FL:** Can you give my readers some advice if they want to become the next YouTube star?

**CT:** I can try. Do something good, or, er, do something stupid. Or cute … hmmm, that's hard. Just network your way through; it's almost like a business now. Network, network, network.

**FL:** Have you ever been recognized in public from YouTube? How do you react to fans?

**CT:** Yeah, it happens a lot (not to sound like a jerk). It usually happens on campus. I try to be nice and talk with people, but it's weird—even for me. Still ….

**108**FL: How do you react to on-line haters?

**CT:** Oh, I love them. They probably watch my videos more than my "fans," even though they claim to hate them. [It's] strange how they operate.

**FL:** Of all your videos, which is your favorite?

**CT:** I would have to say that the mini-keg stand was really fun to make and so was Appartifican Safari (which my friend Jeff Take-over starred in). However, Jeff and I have several new ones that should be out soon that I think blow those away (but I can't tell you because, well—it's a secret! Dun dun dunnn!

**FL:** Do you have any favorite videos from other YouTube users?

**CT:** I really enjoy watching videos by the YouTube users: Nalts, sxephil, mysteryguitarman, smpfilms, boh3m3, apauledtv, and so many more! As far as videos, I'm totally digging on that Dramatic Chipmunk video—I think I gave them 10,000 of their quad-ra-billion video views!

Charles Trippy attempts a keg stand in his video "Mini Beer — Keg Stand." See it first on www. charlestrippy.com.

**FL:** Do you have a personal website?

**CT:** Yeah, it's www.charlestrippy.com. I usually post my videos on that site a couple days in advance as sort of a "sneak peek" thing for people before they're posted anywhere else!

**FL:** Is there anything else you would like to add?

**CT:** I'm not wearing any pants right now. Oh, and I'm sort of thirsty. Wait, this isn't being printed, is it? Dammit!

"Just network your way through; it's almost like a business now. Network, network, network."

—Charles Trippy

# Q&A

## Luke Barats and Joe Bereta Baratsand-Bereta

Screen cap from "Barats and Bareta Theme Song."

*Luke Barats and Joe Bereta began collaborating in 2003 at Gonzaga University in Washington State where they were active in the theater department, broadcasting department, and led the school's improv comedy troupe. Later that year they began making short videos, which they posted to YouTube. Today they're one of the most popular comedy Channels on the site.*

**FL:** Let's start at the beginning. How did you guys meet?

**LB:** We met in 2003 at Gonzaga University through the school's improv troupe, GUTS (Gonzaga University Theater Sports). Soon after, we were in some university theater productions together, we both worked for Residence Life … we got to know one another very well in 2004 when we were elected to lead GUTS.

**JB:** That's pretty much the story. The two worlds we were both involved in, Residence Life and Improv, both had very tight-knit groups and kind of crossed into one another. As a result we became friends and we were also surrounded by a fun, creative group of friends.

**FL:** More importantly, how did you guys start working together?

**LB:** We enjoyed one another's comedy on the improv stage and decided to put some of it on tape. We made a couple of videos just for our college buddies, then we made a few more for a comedy show on the campus TV station. After a while we had a handful of videos lying around and decided to put them on the Internet so our folks could see what we were up to at school. After that we started doing stand-up together and wound up working at the same video production company after graduation. Being surrounded by video equipment for 40 hours a week has naturally led to [us making] videos ever since.

**JB:** I think we both retained a desire to try various avenues of entertainment, from improv and stand-up to theater and video production. The jump from one form to another is much easier when someone has your back supporting you. We liked each other's style enough to jump into some of these venues as a team.

**FL:** You easily could have been called Bereta and Barats. How did you decide whose name would go first?

**LB:** I'm not sure how or when "Barats and Bereta" actually got coined … I guess it stuck the way it did because "Bereta and Barats" rolls off the tongue the same way "Garfunkel and Simon" does.

**JB:** I fought for Bereta and Barats and it actually came down to an epic rock, paper, scissor match on the top of a mountain during a terrifying downpour where we were surrounded by thunder and lightning. My hand cramps whenever I attempt to throw rock or scissors, so paper is my only option … Barats knew that and the name has stuck ever since.

**FL:** What brought you to YouTube?

**LB:** In 2005 we were having technical difficulties with our personal website—we couldn't accurately count video plays, we couldn't embed video, no particular video format could please everyone … then lo and behold "Lazy Sunday" hit the Web and we were exposed to YouTube. The site was the answer to all our technical problems, so we started tossing our videos onto a YouTube account.

**JB:** We just woke up one day and surprise, there was this so-called YouTube. Like Luke said, we saw "Lazy Sunday," which was created by some former on-liners (The Lonely Island) that we

--:111

# Luke Barats and Joe Bereta, BaratsandBereta (continued)

really respected and figured we'd give it a shot. It turned out to be a simple way for our videos to be hosted online.

**FL:** Who comes up with this stuff? Do you co-create? Do you come up with the ideas separately?

**LB:** We definitely co-create. We toss sketch ideas back and forth all the time, and once a month or so an idea will strike us as particularly good. We collaborate through the entire production process, though Joe tends to take the reins in the edit bay and I tend to do the footwork on the scripts. Our improv background plays a big role, too … we certainly don't go into shoots overprepared. We like to change the dialogue on set and we like to have plenty of options in the edit bay. Few things in this world are as cheap as DV tape, so we waste a lot of it.

**JB:** The whole duo thing we've got going has worked out great for us. When we started, Luke tended to focus on writing and I wrote with the mouse and keyboard in the edit bay. In the last couple years, my writing ability has vastly improved from being around Luke, and his editing skills are on par with mine. The process is satisfying because we are both involved in creating the story from start to finish.

**FL:** How long does it take you to put together a YouTube video?

**LB:** I'd say a video takes us three weeks on average: one

week to conceptualize and write the script, another week to screw around and act like we're getting somewhere, and a third week to actually shoot the thing and edit it together.

**JB:** It's so sad that that is true. We are horrible at creating deadlines for ourselves. We could pump out a video a week if the whip was cracked on our backs. In the end, I believe in our methods because I think we tend to lean on quality as opposed to quantity.

**FL:** What are the challenges in working with a partner?

**LB:** Is it legal to equate the challenges we have as a comedy team to the challenges of a marriage? Let's just call it a comedic civil union, then. But in all seriousness, I'd say our partnership doesn't pose too many challenges—when we collaborate comedically, the result tends to be greater than the sum of our parts. To us, comedy is no place for drama.

**JB:** Wow … I really can't top that. Let's just say that if it doesn't work out, I get the kids … what? The only "challenge" might come from the fact that for whatever reason, people seem to mix us up and can't figure out who is who. I know, I don't get it either.

**FL:** Advantages?

**LB:** We've learned a lot from one another and I like to think we push one another to become better comedians.

Joe Bereta in a shot from their video "Suburbanites."

**JB:** We always have someone to bounce ideas off of. If we can make each other laugh, it seems to be the perfect humor indicator.

**FL:** Although it's the two of you in front of the camera, you work with a whole team to put these videos together. Who are the magical elves behind the scenes and how did you find them?

**LB:** Our "magical elves" are friends of ours, many from college, who help us out of the goodness of their hearts. Our webmaster is my roommate Paul Wildermuth—he was the first to post our videos on the Internet and has redesigned our website several times as it has evolved over the years. One of Joe's best friends, Tyler Jacobson, is responsible for our artwork—our logo, many of the graphics in our videos, and a good deal of artwork in our NBC pilot. Either Ben Mallahan or Andrew Weed runs the camera when Joe and I are on screen. A couple of our improv buddies, Caleb Strine and Michelle Philbin, lend their acting talents on a regular basis.

**JB:** I'll continue the name drops. We constantly borrow equipment from Corner Booth Productions in Spokane, WA. They've been awesome about letting us use quality equipment to keep this vid train going. We've enlisted the writing talents of our friend Dan McGivern, and my girlfriend, Heather Moxcey, has helped out on numerous shoots.

**LB:** Yes, and we're very glad they did. When Windward approached us, Joe and I were working as editors for a video production company. Ninety-five percent of our work there was on television commercials, so we were bracing ourselves for another advertising project and all the creative input that clients (for better or worse) tend to offer. To our surprise, Windward placed all their trust in us and simply let us make the video we wanted to make. The result was a win-win; we wound up with a video we consider one of our best, and Windward was exposed to a couple million folks for a fraction of the cost of a traditional TV spot.

**JB:** Windward Reports = best client ever.

**LB:** Whatever notoriety we've achieved on YouTube can be attributed to the fact that we've had a handful of our videos featured on the front page. "Mother's Day" was the first to be featured, and that's what really brought us out of YouTube obscurity. After the first video was featured, we had a series of really, really good emails—the first email was from [talent manager] Dan Farah, soon after came an email from [talent agency] CAA, and soon after came an email from NBC.

**JB:** That was a good couple of weeks. I think we might have thought that every email and phone call was part of an elaborate practical joke our friends were playing on us. Like Luke said, we are a product of the YouTube movement.

**LB:** We got an email from them one day saying they were interested in making a low-budget comedy series with us. We read the email at work, so we had to celebrate quietly and dance around discreetly. We had originally posted the videos on YouTube because it was very easy for our folks to watch the videos we were making while off at school, so the exposure on YouTube and the ensuing NBC deal were not things even on our radar of hopes and dreams. I would liken the feeling of opening that email from NBC to the feeling of winning the lottery.

**JB:** But it was like winning a lottery that you didn't buy a ticket for. NBC was looking to make low-budget programming and also wanted to dip into some alternative television. The You-Tube, user-generated trend was surging and they decided to try and tap into that world by giving us a shot. We were more than surprised by the offer, but as soon as we got over that, we were more than happy to try and make that leap from YouTube to the BoobTube.

**LB:** *This Is Culdesac* is a 30-minute comedy pilot we made for NBC. Basically, it takes place in the fictional suburb "Culdesac," a community populated by our characters. You've got mailmen, milkmen, construction workers, missionaries, interns … all played by Joe and me. The episodes are comprised of roughly 10 two-minute sketches (similar to the shorts we post online) with a theme carried throughout the episode as a whole. NBC lets us write, produce, direct, and play the principle roles, so it was a real trial by fire for us, considering we had never dreamt of using some of the equipment they let us mess around with.

**JB:** I like to call the format we created serial-sketch. *This Is Culdesac* was essentially a sketch show, but we created a fictional town for the characters of these sketches to live. As a result, the plan was to introduce new characters as needed, but we would also go back and revisit certain characters each episode. This would have allowed for story arcs of various lengths, from one episode arcs to series arcs. Eventually, characters from one sketch would interact with characters from other sketches.

## Luke Barats and Joe Bereta, BaratsandBereta (continued)

**FL:** I know the project got made, but I read somewhere that it wasn't picked up. How do you deal with the highs and lows of Hollywood?

**LB:** It did not get picked up, no ... and I guess I'd liken that particular feeling to the feeling of not winning the lottery. The fate of the pilot was certainly unfortunate for us, but all that is easily eclipsed by the fact that we had the good fortune to make the pilot in the first place. We like to think that our approach to Hollywood is more casual than most people's—Hollywood came to us, not vice versa, and when Hollywood spits us out, we'll be no worse off than when we started.

Luke Barats in a shot from their video "Auto Insurance."

**JB:** We made a friggin' television pilot! How sweet is that? Of course we were disappointed when we finally figured out that there wasn't much of a future for *Culdesac,* but we kinda knew

that was going to be the outcome from the start. A very small number of pilots ever get picked up and *This Is Culdesac* was an alternative sketch comedy made for a network hosting the Mecca of sketch comedy (*SNL*), so the chances were slim from the start. In the end, we made a professional television pilot that we are very proud of.

**FL:** What is next for you?

**LB:** The whole experience with NBC has exposed us to the entertainment industry to a degree, and so far we like what we've seen. No plans to move to L.A. just yet, but we've started to put our comedy into some scripts longer than two minutes (imagine!) and if the Hollywood gods keep smiling on us we might see some of those produced down the road. As for the Internet, we plan to keep on making videos until we grow weary of it.

**JB:** We just gotta keep doing what we feel works for us. That philosophy has worked out pretty well for us so far. We'll keep posting videos, we'll keep performing in improv groups, we'll keep on writing, and when another opportunity comes knocking, if it works for us, we'll take it on with full force.

**FL:** What advice can you offer that next comedy duo who wants to launch their career off of YouTube?

**LB:** Posting your work online leaves you very vulnerable—

expect a good deal of unwarranted criticism as well as unwarranted support. If you can stay honest with yourself you'll be able to filter both.

**JB:** Remember that it works as your resumé. Anyone and everyone will be able to see your work, so make sure you are proud of it and that it screams with your voice.

**FL:** Of all your videos, which is your favorite?

**LB:** It's like picking a favorite child ... I'll say "Theme Song" or "Suburbanites."

**JB:** "Robot," "Fast Food," "Windward Reports," and "Suburbanites."

**FL:** Do you have any favorite videos from other YouTube users?

**LB:** "George Washington"—Brad Neely, "Keyboard Kid"—Derrick Comedy, "Hyperactive"—Lasse Gjertsen, and "Just 2 Guyz"—The Lonely Island.

**JB:** "The Role Play Tournament"—Brad Neely, "Here it goes again"—OK GO, any "Ask a Ninja," any by Lasse Gjertsen, and "Ka-Blamo," "Stork Patrol," and any other music by The Lonely Island.

**FL:** Do you have a personal website?

**JB:** Yes: www.baratsandbereta.com.

# Q&A

## Tay Zonday

Tay Zonday belting out "Chocolate Rain," the song that put him on the YouTube map.

*Tay Zonday is a singer/songwriter with a uniquely deep voice that is frequently compared to James Earl Jones and Barry White. The 25-year-old lives in Minneapolis where he is a full-time student. Zonday rose to prominence on YouTube when his original song, "Chocolate Rain," became a breakout hit among users.*

**FL:** How long have you been writing and recording music?

**TZ:** I have written and recorded music as a hobby since I was about 13.

**FL:** It's my understanding that music has always been a hobby. You are actually a grad student. What are you studying?

**TZ:** I am a Ph.D. student in American Studies where I study the relationship between theater and social movements.

**FL:** With the success you've been having on YouTube lately, do you think about making music your career?

**TZ:** If I could stabilize food, shelter, healthcare, and safety while making a career out of music, I would. But I was taught growing up that art careers mostly lead to poverty. Sometimes doing what you love doesn't keep you alive.

**FL:** Let's talk about "Chocolate Rain." This song seems to have really put you on the map. What is the song about?

**TZ:** Why does a song need to be "about" something? We have become a sound-byte society in order to fit everything in before the next commercial break. But confusion is more transformative than dogma. For some, the lyrics are cryptic. They are not directions for putting together a table: "this leg goes in this groove."

**FL:** Why do you think the song resonates with so many people?

**TZ:** Many just find the song to be a catchy beat. They shake their body to it and it doesn't matter to them what the lyrics mean. Some experience it as a deeper social commentary. I don't force anybody to experience the song in a particular way.

**FL:** Are you overwhelmed by the song's popularity? It's gotten nearly 1,000 video responses, including cover versions, parodies, animations, etc. Which have been your favorite?

**TZ:** It is fantastic that so many people have been interested in my music. I respect artists. Period. I don't have a "favorite" anything. We have a cultural bias that life would be too boring if we didn't turn everything into a contest. You're asking me to place the video responses in an economy of scarcity in order to favor "the best." Why is your head producing that economy? There can be enough "best" to go around for everybody.

**FL:** Have you gotten any professional opportunities from your YouTube experience (agents, record deals, gigs, etc.)?

**TZ:** There are various opportunities in progress that I cannot discuss in detail. There's no point in making things public before they happen.

**FL:** Do you think someone with talents such as yourself could come to YouTube to launch their career?

**TZ:** I find it hard to use me as a template for other people. There aren't many other 25-year-old mulattos who look 15, sound like Barry White, and don't adhere to musical categories.

**FL:** What advice can you offer to users who want to have their song be a huge breakout YouTube hit like "Chocolate Rain"?

**TZ:** The popularity of "Chocolate Rain" was never in my control. The analysis of the Tay Zonday phenomenon might be better left to the critics. I just keep making music and deeply appreciate

## Tay Zonday (continued)

anyone who takes the time to enjoy my work.

**FL:** What is next for you?

**TZ:** I continue to grow as a musician and produce new songs.

I am also exploring voiceover work. Graduate school takes a significant chunk of my time.

**FL:** Do you have a personal website?

**TZ:** Yes. My website is www.tayzonday.com. I am also on YouTube at www.YouTube.com/tayzonday and MySpace at www.myspace.com/tayzonday.

# Q&A

## Ryan Divine of Maldroid

Maldroid's "He Said, She Said" video won the inaugural YouTube Underground Music Contest.

*Ryan Devine is the lead singer of Maldroid, a band that won the very first YouTube Underground Music Contest. This led them to their first record deal with Fuzz. Divine also directs the band's music videos.*

**FL:** Tell me a bit of the history of the band. How did you guys first come together?

**RD:** The band started off as just me making music and videos about two years ago. I wanted to start a project that was an outlet for all my creative interests, and a band seemed like the way to go. As the first music video ("He Said, She Said") was nearing completion, I decided it was time to put a full-on band together and began stealing members from my favorite bands around town.

**FL:** How did you come up with the name Maldroid?

**RD:** I believe that technology has already beaten us, and will ultimately destroy us. Not only are we dependent on technology for almost every little thing, but I believe we're essentially becoming robots ourselves. The individual is being lost in a consumer-driven group dynamic and I'm the Maldroid. I'm the malfunctioned robot ... not functioning properly because I yearn for originality and individualism.

**FL:** Is Ryan Divine your real name?

**RD:** Yes sir, it is.

**FL:** What brought you to YouTube and whose idea was it?

**RD:** I had always intended on breaking this band with music videos. When I'd started making the video, no one had heard of YouTube, but by the time I was wrapping it up, it'd rose to prominence. Being a video-centric band and music video director myself, I can't see how I could have avoided YouTube ... it's the new MTV.

**FL:** Which is more effective in promoting your band: posting videos and vlogs on YouTube or playing the club circuit?

**RD:** Well, I think it's a combination of both. Our success on YouTube has certainly earned us a national and international fanbase without having to leave our living rooms. That's something that would have been impossible to do even a couple years ago without hitting the pavement in the van. I think it's raised awareness, but you can't just be a digital project. You still have to go out there and play shows. Let people know you're something real.

**FL:** How did winning the best video award for the YouTube Underground Music Contest affect your career?

**RD:** It truly jump-started it. We had a plan we were working on. Phase one was promoting ourselves with cool videos (before playing any shows) to raise awareness of the band. That ended up working better than we possibly could have expected. Winning that contest forced us to move faster than we expected. Suddenly we were being written about, played on the radio, and talked to by record labels. It really forced us to solidify, put the pieces in place and get started.

**FL:** When did you get signed by Fuzz? Was this as a result of winning the contest? Exposure on YouTube?

**RD:** I don't think it hurt. Ha ha. Actually, the guy that signed us didn't know about the YouTube stuff when he first heard about us. He was driving around town and heard "He Said, She Said" on the radio and loved the song. He called the station, asked who we were, and did some research. I think the videos and YouTube success were the icing, but the music was the cake. At the root of this as in any band is good music.

**FL:** Ryan, you're not only the lead singer of the group, but also the director of all of the music videos. Was filmmaking something you were interested in prior to music?

**RD:** Actually ... no. I went to school for fine art (painting) and animation. While I was there I got more involved in music and bands. I eventually left school, but I never abandoned my art

roots. I started making videos as a means to integrate my artistic abilities with my music. I think you'll notice my style is a little more on the Michele Gondry tip, blending animation and live action rather than straight band-playing-their-instruments footage. I'm more interested in concept. If I could have my way, I'd never show the band.

**FL:** Your videos are really amazing. I love "He Said, She Said" and can't fathom how you made it for no money. Please share some of your secrets to low-budget filmmaking.

**RD:** Step one is a great concept. It's far more valuable than a big budget. If you've got a great idea and know how to pull it off, it will translate. Step two is knowing how to work with what you've got. I worked with this band called "Royalty" and they wanted to do this crazy horror piece where they kill all the competition. Great concept, but with only a couple hundred dollars, a bit out of reach. I flipped the idea to make it a more campy, B-movie, "Grindhouse"–looking thing. By playing to the fact that we could only make cheap special-effects instead of trying to make it look like we were a top-dollar production, we came out with a better product. Work within your means and use it to your advantage. Step three is doing anything to get a camera. I didn't own one until recently and literally begged, stole, and cheated to get my hands on one for the shoot. The rest ... hard work, man. Be creative!

Maldroid's "Heck No! (I'll Never Listen to Techno)" video was made using stop-motion animation and a Lite Brite set.

**FL:** "Heck No! (I'll Never Listen to Techno)" is another of my favorite videos. How long did it take you to make this film, given all the stop-motion animation and Lite Brite configurations?

**RD:** It took about six months of sore thumbs. In stop motion, you take a picture, move it slightly, and take another. The thing with a Lite Brite is you're pressing these color pegs into little holes on a backlit board. Moving slightly on a Lite Brite means taking each peg out and moving it one over. As if that wasn't tedious enough, every time you take a peg out, it leaves a hole in the construction paper that leaves a pinprick of light, so you have to also go back and cover each little hole with something ... for every single photo you take.

**FL:** I like the Maldroid Demo reel. Have other users taken you up on your ad and hired you to make a video for them?

## Ryan Divine of Maldroid (continued)

**RD:** I've completed two music videos for other bands so far, and I'm currently working on a third. Now that the band's signed, I get more time to focus on my own work, and believe me … I've got some awesome videos in store for you.

**FL:** I also like the episodes of MaldroidTV—it's a great way to get to know the band on a personal level. How have fans responded to this?

**RD:** Yah … I really gotta get back on those! Season 2. Ha ha. I think fans have responded well. YouTube opened us up to an international fan-base, but we can't get to all those places yet in person. It's mostly for them to get to know us, and I think there's something interesting about watching a band happen. We're still a young group and far from famous, but climbing quick. The cool thing about MaldroidTV is you get to be there from the start and watch what it's really like being in a band, without all the FAKE reality-TV re-shoots. This is made by us, on our home-video cameras. You really are getting a true experience.

**FL:** How much of your current success can be attributed to YouTube?

**RD:** A lot, I think. We've been so focused on finishing our record and touring that I think we've neglected it a bit of late, but it's been instrumental in our success. We've been able to get way more attention and build way more buzz without leaving our home base too much. It's rad to have fans in a foreign town before you've ever played there.

**FL:** What advice can you give other up-and-coming bands about using viral video to promote themselves?

**RD:** Make it good. Just like your music, you can't just put some crap up and expect people to respond. YouTube is not the end-all solution. It's a tool. Millions of videos go up every day, thousands from bands alone. Not every band that puts a video on YouTube gets a million-plus views. Ours do because we spent the time to make a quality product.

**FL:** What is next for you?

**RD:** World domination. We've just finished our debut record and we've got a crazy plan on how we're releasing it. We're not interested in doing anything the traditional way … that's why we signed with Fuzz. The traditional route to stardom is flawed. We're charting our own course.

**FL:** Do you think YouTube is a good venue for new talent to be discovered?

**RD:** Absolutely … if you know where to look.

**FL:** Of all of your videos, which is your favorite?

**RD:** Right now I really like the video I did for "Royalty." I think people were starting to think of me as the guy that does good animation-type stuff, but I wanted to show that I can do the live-action thing just as well. I also feel like this is one of the first videos that came out exactly as I envisioned it.

**FL:** Do you have any favorite videos from other YouTube users?

**RD:** I like that I can find old videos I haven't seen in a while on YouTube. I was way addicted to "Yacht Rock" (the101onDirecTV) and I dig "Snowmen Hunters." Mostly random tidbits I come across.

**FL:** Do you have a personal website?

**RD:** Yes we do. www.maldroid. com.

**FL:** Is there anything else you would like to add?

**RD:** Thanks so much for taking the time to write such good questions! I hope this has been informative. The greatest thing about the Internet and viral video is that you can now have your own television station. That said, think about how many crappy stations are on TV and try to make sure yours isn't one of those.

"…Think about how many crappy stations are on TV and try to make sure yours isn't one of those."
—Ryan Divine

# Millie Garfield, MyMomsBlog

Millie demonstrates the difficulty she has opening a coffee can in her video "I Can't Open It I."

*At 82 years old, Millie Garfield is one of YouTube's oldest vloggers. But just ask her how she feels. This self-proclaimed "Thoroughly Modern Millie" loves her newfound interest in video-making. With the help of her son, she posts new vlogs frequently.*

**FL:** Tell me about your background. Where are you from? What did you do before you retired?

**MG:** I was born in Chelsea, Massachusetts, and lived there until I got married. I worked as a bookkeeper for many years. When I was a stay-at-home mom, I sold Avon Products and then became an Avon Rep with my own salespeople. Volunteered at a daycare center, conducted a Yiddish class that was fun for me and the daycare people. Did some food-demonstration work at a supermarket. Active in Hadassah—did fundraising and was program chairman, treasurer, and chaired many events.

**FL:** It's really not that common to find someone your age making videos for the Internet. How did you get started?

**MG:** My son is very involved with blogging and video blogging. He got me involved in all of this. Just yesterday I started "Twitter" [a blogging and social networking site] with his encouragement.

**FL:** When did you first learn to use a computer?

**MG:** About five years ago.

**FL:** Who handles the technical aspects of your videos?

**MG:** My son Steve—offonatangent.blogspot.com.

**FL:** Where do you come up with ideas for your videos?

**MG:** It all started when I told my son I couldn't open a jar of coffee. We went to the market, he had his camera, and we "just did it." That was how it got started. Whenever he comes over to visit I always have some things that I can't open and that's what we do. People respond to these videos because they "can't open things either."

**FL:** How did the Yiddish lessons get started?

**MG:** My son knows that I speak a good Yiddish and I throw in a Yiddish word now and then, so he just thought it would be fun to do—I think the term is, "a long-tail." It's for a small percentage of people that would be interested in such a video.

**FL:** Who watches your videos? And what kind of response do you get from the people who watch them?

**MG:** People who read my blog watch them. They love them and want more of them. I get responses like, "I thought of you when I couldn't open the jar." And even husbands who don't read my blog say, "Millie can't open that, either." And they love my Yiddish blog, and want more of that, too.

**FL:** What do your friends think about your video-blogging career? Have they seen your videos?

**MG:** Good question. There are just a few of my friends that have computers; they rarely read my blog, and even when I tell them that I have a new great video, they just are not interested. I can't understand that! When they come across something in the newspaper about me, they get excited because they found it, but to go read my blog, they just don't do it!

**FL:** The latest video seems like a commercial for Heinz Ketchup. How did that come about?

**MG:** My son and I were in the supermarket and I stopped to pick up a bottle of ketchup. He

## Millie Garfield, MyMomsBlog (continued)

saw Heinz was having a contest for the best commercial so we just did it as a lark! He always has his camera with him.

**FL:** What advice can you offer people about making videos for YouTube?

**MG:** Be yourself and don't do anything outrageous.

**FL:** A lot of users post videos hoping to launch a career in show business. Is this a goal for you? Have you gotten any offers?

**MG:** It's not a career goal for me, [I] just do it for fun. The only offer I got was to be on *The Ellen DeGeneres Show* and I was not able to make it.

**FL:** Of all of your videos, which is your favorite?

**MG:** I like each one of them; they were all fun to do so I can't say I have a favorite. But I must say my favorite "Yiddish Lesson" one is the one where I tell a Yiddish joke! I laugh every time I see that one!

**FL:** Do you have any favorite videos from other YouTube users?

**MG:** The YouTube videos that I see—I truthfully don't care for any of them. They are just too far out for me. I have several videos that I enjoy that are not on You-Tube: "Carol and Steve Show" 05, 06, 07; Josh Leo.com/vlog; and "Jerry's Time."

**FL:** Do you have a personal web site?

**MG:** Yes, mymomsblog.blogspot. com. It will be four years this October. I am one of the Inter-net's oldest bloggers.

**FL:** Is there anything else you would like to add?

**MG:** Four years ago when I asked my son what blogging was, he told me and said, "Ma, why don't you do it?" Two weeks later I had my own website. I often think, at the Academy Awards the recipient thanks their parents for their support; I thank my son for introducing me to the World Wide Web and helping me be "Thoroughly Modern Millie."

# Q&A

## Clive Newstead, Nuodai

*This 16-year-old from the United Kingdom chose a screen name he knew no one would be able to pronounce. And while he appears to be a bit of a loner, he's any-thing but alone with almost 5,000 subscribers. Ever want to get inside the mind of your average teen? Check out Clive's Channel.*

**FL:** You're one of the younger vloggers that I've interviewed. How old are you and how old were you when you started mak-ing videos?

Clive Newstead, a.k.a. Nuodai, sits in front of his computer chatting about life in a typical vlog.

**CN:** I started making videos when I was 14, about a month before my fifteenth birthday, and I'm now 16.

**FL:** In one of your videos, you mentioned the fact that you ini-tially didn't tell your friends and schoolmates that you were post-ing videos online. How come?

**CN:** It wasn't so much the fact that I was making videos as it was the fact that I was making video blogs. Video blogging gen-erally includes sitting alone in a room, speaking to an inanimate object—a camera. Some would consider this extremely sad. For example, I, and other video blog-gers I know of, often get the odd message telling us we have too much free time or need to "get a life," but these days I just shrug them off! On top of that, I made videos with things that made me look like an idiot or that were plain embarrassing to watch, and I'd sooner have my friends find out than I would delete the videos, so I definitely didn't want my friends to find out because I knew I'd take the blow instead of actually deleting anything to save face.

**FL:** What was their response when they eventually found out?

**CN:** From what I understand, a group of them stumbled across my videos when they were at one of their houses. They sent me several comments, kindly (or not) informing me that I was a geek, and I even got a couple of threats. Of course, the threats were dry; they were just the sort of people who would send that kind of thing across the Internet when they found something they thought was funny. I haven't actually seen any of them since this happened, though, because it happened after school had broken up for the summer holidays.

**FL:** How did that response compare to their response when they found out you were gay?

**CN:** The response to finding my videos was actually worse than the response to finding out I was gay, but I was expecting it. Most people, except one or two, seemed to just accept the fact that I was gay and move on! Perhaps it is the same with my videos, but the fact that they won't

see me face to face makes them feel more free to send abuse over the Internet. They used my sexuality against me in some of their messages to me, but it was nothing that I haven't heard 1,000 times before and won't hear 1,000 times again.

**FL:** Is YouTube a place where you fit in? How does the site foster a community for the "weirdos" of the world? (By the way, I'm using your word—I don't think you're weird at all.)

**CN:** I don't think that YouTube fosters for anyone in particular, which is why absolutely anyone who uses it can (and does) fit in. It has its fair share of weirdos, among just about every other type of people in the world. I don't consider myself particularly weird, though some of my videos might suggest otherwise! For some people, YouTube may be a place where they can seek refuge away from the world, but for me at least, it's just a website which lets me enjoy making videos and entertaining people at the same time.

**FL:** How did you come up with your screen name? What does it mean?

**CN:** I chose "nuodai" the day I signed up to YouTube. Before then, I never really had any specific name; I'd either use my real name or a variant, or a completely random word. When it came to signing up to YouTube I thought I'd choose an alias, which I'd keep for most online things, and, for lack of better inspiration, and because I was

(and still am) learning Lithuanian, I hit the Lithuanian dictionary. I found a word which looked like it would be fun to use because no one would be able to pronounce it, but they'd still remember it, and there we have it! I didn't think to actually look at the meaning until a couple of days after—it means "poison," which doesn't reflect why I chose the name at all, let alone my videos! The advantage of it being such a strange word, at least to English speakers, is that no one else appears to use it, so I don't have to worry about username clashes. I think there are other people that use it, but they're mostly confined to Lithuanian websites, and websites with huge user bases like MySpace.

**FL:** You have made so many videos and they seem to cover everything from games and lip-syncing to comedy bits and straight vlogging. Is there one genre you most enjoy?

**CN:** I enjoy different genres depending on what mood I'm in, and I generally enjoy making all the videos I do. The blogs are good to get things off my chest, the idiotic and pointless videos enable me to let the inner idiot out, and the videos that I put more time and effort into often have satisfying end-products! Some people subscribe for different types of videos, so I tend to try and keep a regular variety going so that no one gets bored, including myself.

**FL:** Of course your most-viewed video is one you took of a

# Clive Newstead, Nuodai (continued)

woman milking a horse. What kind of statement does that make?

**CN:** People like seeing things which are bizarre to them. To your average person, if watching a horse be manually milked isn't bizarre, I don't know what is! On top of that, it seems that the horse being milked was an innuendo of something quite different for some of them ....

A shot from Nuodai's video "Mongolia Part V: Milking a horse (a mare [female], dammit!)."

**FL:** Is it a rule that everyone on YouTube must make their own Numa video? ;)

**CN:** Yes! Those who say that they haven't made one, or that they won't make one, aren't telling the truth.

**FL:** Of all of your videos, which is your favorite?

**CN:** I honestly can't answer that question. It would depend on which video I like the end-

product of best, which I enjoyed filming the most, which I put the most work into, or which blog I made the best point(s) in.

**FL:** Do you have any favorite videos from other YouTube users?

**CN:** Yes—lots, in fact! Again it would be difficult for me to name which video is my favorite of all because I like them for different reasons.

**FL:** In one of your videos you mention that your acting isn't very good, but if someone offered you a job as an actor, you wouldn't turn them down. LOL. Did you come to YouTube seeking fame? Do you think that's why some people post videos on the site?

**CN:** I didn't come to YouTube seeking anything except a new hobby. Over the last year a lot has changed in terms of my videos and YouTube, and I have got various things which can help make my videos better (e.g., a tripod and a greenscreen), but videomaking is still very much a hobby for me, rather than anything else. If good things come from it, that's great, but the most important thing is that I have fun. I think that some people do go to YouTube seeking fame, though, and if they find it, best of luck to them!

**FL:** What do you think of the success of those users who have found fame by posting on YouTube?

**CN:** Good for them! Most of the people who found new opportunities (and, indeed, fame) on YouTube deserved everything that they got.

**FL:** Your videos are quite popular as evidenced by the large number of subscribers you have. What do you think makes you so popular online?

**CN:** I don't consider myself very popular online. I do have a large number of subscribers, but I don't think that an amount of subscribers on a website can reflect a person's popularity, especially when it is the videos which are popular and not the person (and, at that, some videos more than others). I don't know how so many people came to find, and like, my videos, though; that question remains unanswered even for me.

**FL:** Any advice for users who want to start posting videos?

**CN:** I couldn't advise anything specific. Just don't be afraid of posting videos you consider to be crap—some people might actually like them, and there's always potential to improve. Also be prepared to take criticism, but don't take it to heart if someone insults you.

**FL:** Do you have a personal website?

**CN:** I have a website where I post my videos, among various other things: www.factoropinion. net.

# Q&A

## Remy Munasifi, GoRemy

Remy Munasifi as Habib.

*Remy Munasifi dropped out of law school so he could make videos. He's not that crazy! He saw others turning a profit, so he figured, why not him? While he may not be able to retire quite yet, his videos are getting noticed, especially after one ran on the CNN YouTube Presidential Debates.*

**FL:** What brought you to YouTube?

**RM:** I was going to law school when I was introduced to the site, and thought YouTube would be a great study break. Okay, maybe not so much of a "break" as a "distraction." Eventually, I came across this "Lonelygirl" and thought to myself, "Hey … I'm marginally entertaining, too." So I didn't go back to school, bought a camera, a PC, and gave it a shot.

**FL:** So let me clarify. You dropped out of law school to make videos?

**RM:** Ha ha, yeah. If it doesn't sound like the best idea, imagine how it sounds to parents! I remember seeing how big LonelyGirl15 was, and realizing it was possible to be self-sufficient from a website and thinking, "Well, if it's possible, I'm going to find a way to do it."

I don't make any money from the videos right now, but the interest in the videos has brought with it some other opportunities. Now I write and produce some commercials in the GoRemy style, and also do some live performances. So far, so good!

**FL:** Had you always been making up raps and skits, or did YouTube inspire you to start?

**RM:** I had never made videos before YouTube, so there was certainly a learning curve involved. I'm still learning as I go along, but it's getting better.

I remember being in fifth grade and trying to write funny songs and stories. I guess it started there. In college, I gave stand-up comedy a shot, and that was also fun.

**FL:** While you mostly rap, the few songs you've done are actually very good. Will we be seeing more of them in the future?

**RM:** Well, thank you for saying that. Yes, more to come. I really enjoy making them. Plus, it helps me justify buying a nice guitar.

**FL:** How did you come up with the character Habib? What are you trying to say with him?

**RM:** Habib came about when I was doing a stand-up show in college, and wanted an opening act. It was a lot of fun, so he stuck around.

There's a positive message behind the Habib character, and people seem to appreciate that. With all the coverage of the Middle East these days, you never see anything humorous. Habib seems to be a refreshing change in that respect.

**FL:** A lot of people use YouTube as a way to showcase their talent, hoping to catch the attention of Hollywood. Is this your intention?

**RM:** When I decided to give it a shot, my goal was to start a website and generate enough interest to make a living from that. I would be more than content with that. Then again, if Hollywood came calling, that would be icing on the cake!

Pardon me for the cake analogies. Thoughts of cake permeate my brain.

**FL:** You wound up catching the attention of Washington when your question was used in the very first CNN YouTube Debates. How did you feel when you found out it was going to be shown?

**RM:** The questions which were going to air were secrets kept by CNN, so nobody told me. So there I was sitting in the debate hall when, all of a sudden,

--:123

## Remy Munasifi, GoRemy (continued)

there I was prancing around my house in front of Presidential candidates. I really have to thank YouTube and CNN, because that was just a tremendously cool experience.

Remy was one of a handful of lucky users whose question was chosen and aired on the CNN YouTube Debates.

**FL:** Why do you think your question was chosen and you were selected by YouTube to attend the debates?

**RM:** I guess there weren't many questions which were also songs. That's my guess.

YouTube and Google were kind enough to send a bunch of us down to cover the event. I think they wanted a good mix of folks.

**FL:** Your question was about tax relief. Senator Biden's response was to take tax credits away from people who don't need them. What did you think of his answer?

**RM:** I certainly appreciate the fact he didn't dodge the question, but I would have liked to hear a different answer.

**FL:** Have you always been politically active, or were you just taking advantage of another way to showcase your talent?

**RM:** Being able to submit a question directly to the presidential candidates was an opportunity too great to pass up. I hope future debates ultimately begin to embrace the new format.

**FL:** Has this experience made you more politically aware?

**RM:** I think it has left me less jaded about the political process. There's a great deal of apathy in America when it comes to the political process. People sometimes feel helpless and without a voice. But it's encouraging to see all these candidates embracing YouTube and directly engaging citizens in political discourse. Hopefully that will get all sorts of people interested.

**FL:** What advice can you offer users to help them make their videos stand out on YouTube?

**RM:** I don't think you have to have professionally polished videos to stand out. Just go out, have fun, but keep it short.

**FL:** Do you think it's possible for someone to launch a career from YouTube?

**RM:** It's being done, no question. I guess it depends on the career you're looking for, though.

**FL:** Of all of your videos, which is your favorite?

**RM:** My favorite would probably be "Macaca Blues," a video about the 2006 Virginia Senate race. It was the first video I made, and I just remember being so happy that I figured out how to make a video.

**FL:** Do you have any favorite videos from other YouTube users?

**RM:** I like to follow the work of some of the other YouTubers I've gotten to know in person and by email. I'd have to say my favorite video on YouTube is a song called "Sometimes," by "Speak the Hungarian Rapper" (found at www.youtube.com/watch?v=--Vaz9jW054).

**FL:** Do you have a personal website?

**RM:** Yep! www.GoRemy.com.

**FL:** Is there anything else you would like to add?

**RM:** I think "viral" is an accident, but quality is not. I'd say go for quality, and maybe viral will come! And just have fun!

"I think 'viral' is an accident, but quality is not."
—Remy Munasifi

# Q&A

## David Colditz, Dave Days

Dave makes another video about LisaNova.

*Another 16-year-old vlogger, but he's not your average 16-year-old. Dave Colditz is funny and fearless. He puts himself out there, networking with the YouTube community better than most sales execs at a Las Vegas trade show. This Pennsylvania native has a bright future ahead of him.*

**FL:** How old are you? How old were you when you first started posting videos?

**DC:** I just turned 16 in August, but was 15 when I first started a few months before.

**FL:** Why did you start making videos and posting?

**DC:** I watched others' videos and it seemed like they were having fun, so I decided to start posting videos to see what others thought. And why not give it a try at being a YouTube celeb!

**FL:** Your sound design and editing skills are excellent. Where did you learn to do these things? What equipment do you use?

**DC:** I have always been into music and I started pretty young. Several years ago my dad bought a Tascam 2488 digital recorder for the band so I used that to learn how to record. Now I use my computer with Acoustica Mixcraft for editing and I use a crappy Fender 35-watt amp for recording guitar (sounds so great, though!) when I could be using a Marshall Halfstack. I record everything with a mini mixer board plugged into my PC. [The] bass just plugs into the mixer board and I use a condenser mic to record the guitar/vox. As for my videos, I started using windows moviemaker, which is so laggy and slow, but I got to learn how to edit on beat and just overall editing. Now I just started using Vegas and I love it! It's simple to use once you get the hang of it and there's a lot you can do with it!

**FL:** How long does it take you to make an average video?

**DC:** If it's a song/video it usually takes me like four or five hours for the song, then like two or three or maybe four for the video/editing! But a normal blog takes about like one to three hours filming/editing/uploading time, but I love every second of it!

**FL:** I think you may have discovered one of the secrets to success on YouTube. You make videos about other YouTube users. Why do you think they're so popular?

**DC:** I think my videos about others are so popular because people find it interesting to watch more about that person and also because usually that person likes the video being made about them, so sometimes they will favorite it/help you out. I think they are popular because they have been making unique and entertaining vids and communicating around the community a lot for a while. Most of the celebs have been around for over a year, and a lot of them started around the time YouTube was just getting popular, which meant not many celebs back then! Also, networking is a key to success on YouTube.

**FL:** So what's the beef between you and LisaNova?

**DC:** Well, she blocked me after I left like five comments in a row, so I made that song/video about her where I'm just making fun of her. She saw it and unblocked me, saying that [YouTube] auto-blocked me but ... I don't believe her. Ha ha. Then I made that song saying I liked her then she said, "Make up your mind!" I didn't like that! So I recorded me playing that hate song about her again. So yeah, me and her are over! But along the way she has helped me out by auto-playing several of my videos and favorite-ing just about half of them.

## David Colditz, Dave Days (continued)

**FL:** What's with your obsession with Dax Flame?

**DC:** Dax Flame is just hilarious! He's funny, awkward, and just acts plain … goofy! You can't help but laugh. His character is very interesting and unique and it really shows when you watch him!

**FL:** Have you ever met any of your fellow YouTube celebrities?

**DC:** No, but I would love to!

Dave vlogs with a furry friend.

**FL:** Do you consider yourself to be a YouTube celebrity?

**DC:** Not really, no. I think once you hit like 13,000 subscribers and become a partner and get the banners/auto-play, then you are a YouTube celeb.

**FL:** Do you think it's possible to use YouTube to launch a career in the entertainment business?

**DC:** I think it is possible if the right people see you. I would love to get into the entertainment business. Maybe YouTube will be my ticket there!

**FL:** What advice can you offer users to help them make their videos stand out on YouTube?

**DC:** Be unique and interesting! Also, networking [plays] a BIG part in getting popular!

**FL:** Of all of your videos, which is your favorite?

**DC:** Honestly, I have my ups and downs about all of them, but my favorite … is probably my You-Tube song/video. I just like the overall song and clips of me acting completely random yet going along with the song.

**FL:** Do you have any favorite videos from other YouTube users?

**DC:** I would have to say Dax-flame's "Cool Moves" videos. They are just so funny! I mean … is he serious?! ;-)

**FL:** Do you have a personal website?

**DC:** No. I have a MySpace and FaceBook, but YouTube is where it's at nowadays for me!

**FL:** Is there anything else you would like to add?

**DC:** Subscribe! :-)

"Be unique and interesting! Also, networking [plays] a BIG part in getting popular!"

—David Colditz

# Q&A

## Valentina, ValsArtDiary

Val talks about the inspiration behind her painting.

*This beautiful U.K.-based artist discovered the perfect balance of art, commerce, and technology. In her weekly vlog, she creates a new painting, then sells it on eBay to the highest bidder. Her virtual gallery is making art hip again.*

**FL:** When did you first get interested in art? How did you get started as an artist?

**VAD**: I have been painting since I was three years old and always knew I wanted to be a painter. Painting has been my focus throughout grade school, middle school, and high school, and it was only natural that I went to an art school after graduation.

**FL:** Your videos all show you working with paint. Are there other art forms you enjoy?

**VAD**: My focus is painting and my videos were originally meant to simply showcase my paintings. I do, however, enjoy the process of making the video itself and expressing myself through a combination of canvas and video. I have heard many people say that the video and the painting in my episodes complement each other and are strongest together. It's impossible to ignore feedback like that. I like the synergy of art and technology and I draw a lot of pleasure from experimenting and trying to find new ways of expression.

**FL:** Art is sometimes a thankless endeavor. In fact, many of the world's greatest artists weren't even recognized until well after they were dead. How has YouTube helped you get your artwork out to the mass public?

**VAD**: The main reason I started making videos was that I wanted to find an audience for my paintings. I think we live in the times when the traditional fine arts are often seen as snobby and elitist, and this perception often hurts artists who struggle to find an audience.

It is hard for a painter to make an average person interested in his or her work. The presentation of the artwork in galleries and museums often does not attempt to reach out and explain the intentions of the artist. That's why the proper artist's statement was always very important to me. I felt that people who take their time to look at my art have the right to know what my intentions were when creating it. But I'm not a good writer and was always horrible at making a cohesively written artist statement. That's why I thought, "Why not let myself ramble a bit on camera as I paint? Wouldn't that make it a truly ideal statement?" I believe there is something to it. I posted it on YouTube as an experiment. I was very curious to see how people respond to it. That's how "Val's Art Diary" was born.

My expectations were very low. I hoped few people would care enough to comment and give me feedback on my work, which, by the way, in itself would have made me very happy. Even at the time when I started my art diary, I thought about YouTube as a place for goofy videos of accidents, awkward moments, and sketches. I never really believed there was a big audience for more serious art-related content. But I hoped there were a few souls out there that would care about my work. I guess I didn't know YouTube well enough to know its power.

The response I got was a total surprise. My videos have been watched by over six million people since November. I would have never suspected that so many people cared about my art and the creative process. But what surprised me more than that number was the support and appreciation for art I found among the viewers who post comments under my videos. I post my videos every Sunday, and each Sunday I host a virtual party where I have a chance to respond to comments and

 --:127

## Valentina, ValsArtDiary (continued)

connect with the viewers and discuss the latest piece of art with them. It really feels like having a gallery show opening every Sunday. What more could an artist ask for? Making art can be a very lonely activity and YouTube made it rewarding by giving me a loyal audience. Beyond that, the exposure I gained through YouTube opened a lot of doors for me. I received tons of commission requests, job offers, people offered to help in organizing a real-world show, and so on.

Val paints ENVY.

**FL:** Have you been able to sell all of your paintings documented in your videos? What's the highest price one has sold for?

**VAD**: So far I have been lucky enough to see every single painting sold. The most expensive one was called "Energy," [which] sold for $1,025.

**FL:** I imagine users who see your work must contact you to commission paintings, as well. Have you been commissioned by any YouTube "celebrities"? What's

the most interesting job offer you've received as a result of YouTube?

**VAD**: I haven't been commissioned by any of the YouTube "celebrities" yet. The most interesting job offer had to be the offer to teach art to victims of domestic abuse somewhere on a distant Pacific island. It sounded extremely tempting.

**FL:** Your videos are so well produced. Do you have a background in filmmaking?

**VAD**: It's not easy making a living as an artist and I had been struggling for a while. I was open to any kind of art-related projects, and once I was asked to work as an art director on a small, independent film. I liked the experience. Later I did more films, and a couple of commercials. That's how I got involved with the film/video production community, learned how to edit video, and eventually started my own small production company. All this time I had to put painting on the side, as I was too busy doing things that would pay rent. I wasn't very happy and felt frustrated that I had so little time for painting. I was painting, of course, but not as much as I wanted, and the time didn't allow me to properly engage into the art scene. Little did I know that the video production and editing skills would eventually help me market my art.

**FL:** If YouTube is a canvas, does that make all your fellow vloggers artists?

**VAD**: The question of what constitutes art is a huge one and it seems that it is becoming harder to answer every year. After all, with the emergence of new technologies there are new ways to express yourself, and express your ideas. Vlogging is definitely a form of self-expression. There is no doubt about that.

**FL:** I love your art lottery. Each week, at the end of your video, a lucky subscriber is chosen randomly (by throwing a dart toward a list on the wall) and they win a free print of one of your paintings. Has this promotion helped increase subscriptions?

**VAD**: I'm sure it helped to some degree. My "d'Art Lottery," as I like to call it, is pretty popular but I like to believe it was not the only reason people subscribed to my Channel. I have seen many vloggers try to give out cash prizes to their subscribers since, and more often than not the potential of a prize alone is not enough to make people watch your videos. Actually, my main reason for the lottery was to express my gratitude to the existing subscribers. YouTube has changed my life and I realize that I owe it all to the viewers who tune in every Sunday. As cheesy as it sounds, without them there would be no "Val's Art Diary." The giving away of a painting every week is just my way of saying "thank you."

Val shows off her finished painting, ENVY.

**FL:** If you had to paint YouTube, what would it look like? Hmm-mm, that might be a fascinating idea for your next painting!

**VAD:** I did paint "YouTube"! I did it at about the same time when I started my d'Art Lottery, and the video documenting the process of creating it is called "throwing darts at people." My YouTube painting is a collage consisting of the names of the first 10,000 of my subscribers. The names are covered with a thin layer of paint in various colors and form the characteristic YouTube logo. The painting is currently hanging in the YouTube headquarters.

**FL:** Tell me about the Web 2.0 Art Project.

**VAD:** In the spirit of Web 2.0 this art project draws from the talents and experiences of people around the world in a spontaneous painting collaboration. I created a piece consisting of four canvases and explained the relationship between each canvas. Then I invited other artists to paint additional canvases, making sure there is some kind of relationship established with the neighboring works. What I'm hoping to achieve is a huge work of art that will combine the works of many people. Just like the now-famous websites YouTube or MySpace, the Web 2.0 art project is completely dependent on and controlled by the mass of people. "Web 2.0" is a piece that is a work in progress and by definition will always be "a work in progress." I am very curious to see what it will turn into.

**FL:** Do you consider yourself to be a YouTube "celebrity"?

**VAD:** Ha ha … I know I don't really embrace that label. Yes, I do happen to have thousands of subscribers, and frequent YouTube users likely know about me, but I am very far from calling myself a YouTube "celebrity." The way I see it, YouTube became so popular partly because people were seeking an alternative to the existing world of slick, Hollywood-produced entertainment. I think that people who are popular on YouTube right now are the direct opposite of what you would typically call a celebrity. Yes, we are familiar faces on YouTube, but calling us celebrities is somewhat misleading.

**FL:** Have you ever been recognized from your vlogs?

**VAD:** It did happen a couple of times. Every time they were teenagers. I have to admit it was flattering but somewhat awkward at the same time.

**FL:** What advice can you offer fellow artists about using YouTube to help launch their art career?

**VAD:** I believe that the future of art is in the synergy with technology and media. My advice is to not be afraid of alternative ways to connect with your audience and keep an open mind about not just YouTube, but all emerging technologies. I was very lucky to know quite a bit about video production and editing beforehand, and that definitely helped my videos, so my approach might not be for everyone. But there are new things happening every day and the new, unique idea and approach is waiting for you to discover [it].

**FL:** Of all of your videos, which is your favorite?

**VAD:** It would have to be "Night Out Secrets" (which can be seen at www.youtube.com/watch?v=F8DI8vrS7j8).

I spent more time working on this one and played with greenscreen in order to insert myself into the finished painting and interact with the characters within it. It was a lot of fun working on this video and I think it turned out well. I would love to do all my episodes this way, but greenscreen and all the editing takes way too much time, and I have to make a new video every Sunday. I will have episodes like this one again in the future, but at this point it would be impossible to make it into a regular thing.

## Valentina, ValsArtDiary (continued)

**FL:** Do you have any favorite videos from other YouTube users?

**VAD:** It would have to be the very first video I have ever seen on YouTube. In October of 2006 a friend of mine forwarded me a link to a funny video with animated pictures of a cat and a funny song that went something like "I'm a Kitty Cat. And I dance, dance, dance and I meow, meow, meow …" I loved it! I loved the simplicity of it and the feeling of joy that it immediately evoked. The song got stuck in my head and I was showing the video to everybody. I started clicking around and found a lot of more funny videos. This was the very first time I went on YouTube so it also has somewhat of a sentimental value. I know it's silly. What can I do?

**FL:** Do you have a personal website?

**VAD:** www.valsartdiary.com.

**FL:** Is there anything else you would like to add?

**VAD:** Just some facts in case you need them:

6.5 million total views since I started in November last year.

19,000 people subscribed to my Channel—they watch it on a regular basis. Nominated for BEST SERIES in the first annual YouTube Video Awards (there were 10 nominees). A new video every Sunday.

**FL:** Thanks so much. Best of luck with your artwork and videos.

**VAD:** Thank you! Best of luck with your book!

# Q&A

## Kevin Nalty, Nalts

Nalts vloggging to the webcam.

*By day, he's a consumer-marketing director for a Fortune-100 company. At night, he's making another video to keep up with his "new video a day" motto. I think he's a genius and at the forefront of the future of viral marketing.*

**FL:** I think you've posted more YouTube videos than any other user. Is this true? How do you find the time to make so many videos?

**KN:** I generally create my videos very quickly, except for the editing. So I typically get up at about 4:45 A.M. and do my editing in the morning before the kids wake up and before I head to work. Sometimes I stay up late to do my editing. It's taking maybe 30 to 40 hours per week, but it's an investment in what I hope to make a full-time job.

**FL:** Your videos have come a long way. From the early days of Scary Santa and Evil Hand where you were just playing around with your kids on camera, to your more politically charged commentaries that you do today, what do you think is the best use for viral video?

**KN:** I love the niche entertainment, and the fact that you can develop a loyal audience for different specific genres. I happen to be a strong believer in the prospect of online video and marketing. Marketers are desperately trying to explore this medium, and amateurs are often happy to create a promotional video for revenue. I think this is a great intersection. Creators need money, and marketers need exposure. I believe there will be a cottage industry that connects these forces in the coming years.

**FL:** There seems to be some anger in your videos toward YouTube. In your video, "Learning the Business Through Lemonade Stand," you say, "Why don't you do like YouTube and give it away for free?" What's the deal?

**KN:** I was initially frustrated by YouTube's popularity without a solid business model and because the company wasn't sharing advertising dollars with creators like Revver, Metacafe, and other sites. I believe content creators should participate in the advertising dollars, since it's their content that draws viewers. YouTube has now invited me into a partners program where I make a percentage of advertising revenue. And they're beginning to explore what may be a sustainable and profitable model. So some of that frustration has passed. I still regret that the program isn't more broadly accessible to emerging amateur artists.

**FL:** You also seem to have been an early supporter of Revver. com, a site that shares revenue with its content creators, but despite your problems with YouTube, you still continue to post and support the site. Why is that?

**KN:** I love Revver, and initially posted exclusively to Revver. However, Revver failed to attract a large-scale audience and find ways to keep them returning (subscriptions, community). Ultimately I realized that for the long haul I was better off finding a fan base on YouTube (fish where the fish are) with hopes that I could amortize that eventually. It's starting to pay off. I believe Revver is more creator-friendly and honors copyright laws more vigilantly. But I was having difficulty finding an audience via my Revver videos even when I created a website (using Revver) to solve that problem: cubebreak.com.

**FL:** What do you think of the YouTube partners program?

**KN:** I think the program is fair, even though I can't comment on the specifics of it. It's no secret that YouTube's banner model is not sufficient to sustain the company or pay creators. However, the embedded videos (Invid ads) is a much stronger way to create revenue. YouTube announced a $20 CPM (20 dollars per 1,000 videos), which is great for YouTube, creators, and brands. And I believe it's minimally intrusive for viewers since it's not requiring people to sit through an annoying "pre-roll" ad.

**FL:** Why is YouTube so huge compared to the other viral video sites? How did it become the leader among these sites?

**KN:** Like many online plays, the market tends to gravitate toward one predominant player. YouTube was providing a vehicle to mass-distribute and view copyrighted material, and that kick-started the company just like it did for Napster. YouTube then created vehicles for community, which ultimately bridged YouTube from a video-sharing site to a community like Facebook or MySpace.

Soon the name became synonymous with online viewing and the defacto destination for stolen and amateur content.

**FL:** Tell me a bit about your background and how you use viral video in your day job.

**KN:** My background is in video production, but I moved into marketing when I realized it was a tough place to make a living. I now work in the pharmaceutical industry and focus on innovative marketing. I've done viral video campaigns in my day job, so I have a view of the industry from a marketer's perspective as well as a content creator. Unfortunately the pharmaceutical industry is highly regulated, so it's been tough to exploit the full potential of viral video.

**FL:** I like the idea behind cubebreak.com, but as a business owner myself, I try to keep my employees away from sites like YouTube ... at least during business hours. How did most businesses respond to this concept? Was it a successful venture?

**KN:** CubeBreak was initially a way that I could attract viewers to see my content via Revver ads, as well as other good content on Revver. For a while it was one of the most popular sites, and easily found if you searched "online video" or "viral video." I soon got bored with populating it manually, and set up ways for it to automatically repopulate with good content. Unfortunately, the search engines began to see it as a stagnant site (since they

# Kevin Nalty, Nalts (continued)

don't know that the videos are rotating—they only see the stagnant content). Then the site dropped on the engines, and I ultimately abandoned it.

Some of Kevin's favorite videos are those that include his children.

**FL:** You've posted all sorts of videos online from comedy and pranks to social commentary and serialized drama. What is your favorite type of video to make? What would you like to be known for?

**KN:** I really like making videos with my family, and that represents about 25 percent of the 475 videos I've posted. But I also like short comedic sketch comedies and "candid-camera"-style videos. My most popular videos are the ones where I pit myself against real people in public locations. Unfortunately these are difficult to produce, and technically require me getting signed releases from the people that appear in the videos. That becomes unwieldy given that I don't have

a crew … most of my videos are done with me as the actor, cameraman, director, and editor. I do hope to create more candid-camera-style videos with help from other actors. If I get signed releases from the "victims" then I can monetize these in other ways. It's frustrating when I get requests from networks and television shows to use these videos and then I tell them I don't have releases on all of the people in the videos.

**FL:** You tend to collaborate with a lot of your fellow YouTube users. I particularly like the cameos in your video "YouTube Viral Broker," not to mention the message that you're disseminating. Please talk to me about the community aspects of YouTube.

**KN:** I began my YouTube uploads simply to distribute on a site that was more popular, and with hopes to draw them onto Revver or CubeBreak. Then I discovered the community aspect, and became intrigued. I liked that there was a way to respond to videos and message other creators. Soon I began collaborating with local amateurs, and that became very rewarding. I also discovered that viewers loved seeing other YouTubers in my video. It's like watching an episode of one television show and then seeing another actor from another show make a cameo. So I began to actively pursue opportunities to collaborate, and found those experiences highly gratifying. Generally I'd meet with a YouTuber with little idea

of what we'd do, and together we'd develop something that was far funnier than I could have conceived on my own. Almost all of my collaborations are spontaneous concepts rather than planned.

**FL:** You've made some extremely intelligent and thoughtful videos, yet it's your video entitled "Farting in Public" that is your most viewed to date. What does this say about YouTube users?

**KN:** I suppose farts are a good common denominator for humor. Universally funny even for a global audience that may not understand the spoken words in the video. I think people love to see real reactions from people, and we gave them a chance to participate in the prank. To date, most of the viral videos are somewhat moronic, short, and surprising bits. But that will evolve over time as people become intrigued with more intellectual concepts. But we're not ready for that yet. My "Viral Video Genius" involved a subtle satire and some word plays. It was largely misunderstood by people that discovered it on the homepage.

**FL:** Tell me a bit about the Goo-Tube Conspiracy videos. How did this concept come about? Have you received official feedback from the powers that be at YouTube?

**KN:** The GooTube Conspiracy was a fun experiment at creating a serialized story that was unplanned. I was getting feedback from creators and was literally making a video each day without knowing what would happen the next day. Soon others got involved and the concept got more sophisticated when a New York filmmaker and actor (Kyle Pierson) stepped in as the villain—Loquesto. He's been driving the plot, and he's a lot more deliberate about his production, so the videos have slowed down. At one point we had the YouTube founders considering entering the plot, and one of the YouTube editors was trying to help us. But the plotline involved Viacom, and YouTube is in the midst of legal battles with them. So they understandably declined.

**FL:** Your videos constantly seem to challenge YouTube, yet they allow them to stay up on their site. Has there ever been a case where they removed one of your videos from their site? In a world where censorship runs rampant, YouTube seems to be fairly open and cool about free speech, even if it doesn't always showcase them in a positive light.

**KN:** YouTube has never removed my videos. Recently I inadvertently used copyrighted music and I got a call within hours. So I took the video down instantly. But for the most part, YouTube accepts criticism from the community and often responds to it (especially if it involves technical issues with the site). It's a completely free-speech environment, and the only videos I know have been removed have involved copyright infringement, inap-

propriate content, or videos by minors.

**FL:** Of all of your videos, which is your favorite?

**KN:** Difficult question ... I love going back and watching my kid videos, and hate going back and watching video blogs where I'm talking about topical issues. I suppose my favorite is "Mall Pranks (Bored at the Mall)" because I love the reactions from people. And I get highly embarrassed making those videos, but I love editing and posting them. "Blackberry Crackberry" has been the most popular video beyond YouTube—I'm still getting requests for people to use that on television. But here's the reason I create a video per day. I'm usually wrong about what they'll like and what they won't. Some videos I think are poor, and viewers love. And quite often I create something I think is hysterical, but viewers don't. By throwing a lot of stuff against the wall I'm able to understand what people like and don't.

**FL:** Do you have any favorite videos from other YouTube users?

**KN:** I really like short comedy videos. ZackScott, Nutcheese, MarkDay ... I also love the stories that Lemonette tells. And the cute videos of Mugglesam's children. I'm not a fan of YouTube weblebrities that vlog for nine minutes at a time. Probably my favorite short comics are Barats and Bereta, and my favorite serialized content is iChannel (I appeared in one episode and was

amazed with the care they put into their videos).

**FL:** Do you have a personal website?

**KN:** I have my blog (willvideoforfood.com), but it's only now emerging into a website. Initially it was a blog about the industry, but as my fan base has grown I think people are looking for more. So I'm posting my videos, introducing a forum, and providing other vehicles to hopefully subsidize my obsessive hobby.

**FL:** Is there anything else you would like to add?

**KN:** Where's all this headed? I think the next year or so will be interesting as the pros step into online video. It's a significant threat to amateur creators, but I'm still hoping that online video (by virtue of its low barriers to entry) will provide a way that amateurs can get discovered and make a living ... without needing to live in New York and Los Angeles. And I'm fully confident that this is going to change the landscape of marketing as we know it. Interruption ads will give way to more creative content that harnesses the collective creativity of the masses.

# Matthew Lush, GayGod

Matthew Lush in a typical vlog.

*Matthew Lush calls himself GayGod, but he says the name is an inside joke that he doesn't care to share. His vlog may have begun like many others do, with silly lip-sync songs and random rants. But he soon started helping other gay kids with his videos on tolerance and coming out of the closet. I think he might have more to offer than just another pretty face.*

**FL:** Why did you start posting videos to YouTube?

**ML:** I got bored, saw Brookers lip sync, and I thought, "Hey! That looks fun!"

**FL:** Why do you think you've become so popular?

**ML:** I had a bit of help with my MySpace, and my huge fan base on there.

**FL:** Would you like to be able to turn this notoriety into a career?

**ML:** If I could somehow turn this into a career, that would make me really happy.

**FL:** What is your day job currently?

**ML:** That's personal.

**FL:** When you first started adding videos, you did mostly lip-sync videos to popular songs. Lately you've gotten into vlogs that are both personal and political. Why the change?

**ML:** Lip sync is fun and cool, but if you have that much edge in the LGBT community, why not use it for good, too?

**FL:** I really liked your iSupport campaign (a video discussing bi, gay, and confused people who don't think anyone supports them and eliciting users to make a 3-second video response saying "I support." It garnered over 350 video responses). What gave you the idea to do this? Were you surprised by the response?

**ML:** If you liked that, just wait till iSupport really gets going. I'm sure it will help so many people, and that makes me very happy.

I always wanted to help people, and thought this would be one of the best ways. The response was mostly good, so I'm glad it turned out a success.

**FL:** You have several blogs dedicated to various boys. Have you ever dated someone you met through YouTube?

**ML:** Ha ha, no. I haven't dated anyone through YouTube. Those boys are mostly "Internet crushes." I rarely date in real life. =/

**FL:** In one of your videos you talk about another of your videos being flagged and removed from YouTube. What was the content of the flagged video and why do you think YouTube removed it?

**ML:** I was in the shower with my boxers and shorts on, but I guess when I put the camera down, it only showed me [from the] belly button up, and to the ceiling. [It] wasn't what I expected. =/

**FL:** Why do haters exist? How do you deal with them?

**ML:** Haters exist because people fuel them with more hate, causing a cycle of never-ending hate. There needs to be a love revolution.

**FL:** You do a lot to promote Stickcam. Can you tell me a bit about this site and what you do there?

**ML:** I have the most popular webcam show at Stickam.com, and it reaches about 20,000 [users] in an hour. It's really fun, and I love talking to all my fans. In the future we will make it not just talking on the phone. =]

**FL:** Of all of your videos, which is your favorite?

**ML:** "Coming Out Straight Edition!" YEAYAAAAA I got so pumped. LOL.

**FL:** Do you have any favorite videos from other YouTube users?

**ML:** LisaNova's channel is fun to visit over and over.

**FL:** Do you have a personal website?

**ML:** MatthewLush.com has all my websites on it, and my merchandise. It will soon be remodeled.

**FL:** Is there anything else you would like to add?

**ML:** That I love everyone no matter what!

> "There needs to be a love revolution."
> —Matthew Lush

# Q&A

## Myles Dyer, Blade376

Myles vlogs in front of his webcam.

*Myles Dyer is studying psychology at a university in England. He's a living example of the new YouTube generation. Some of his vlogs are funny; others are thought provoking. He's looking for answers and using the Internet to make this world one small networked community and a better place to live in.*

**FL:** What brought you to YouTube? What made you start posting videos?

**MD:** I began using YouTube like many other people, who on the Internet would come across videos that were embedded from the website, the majority of which being funny clips. I then set up my own Channel so I could build up my own list of favorite videos, and then I began making my own content. That included random clips such as music videos of heavy-metal songs, where I subtitled funny lyrics that it sounded like the vocalists were singing (shouting). Then one day on the television was a news [story] about an elderly man, known as Geriatric1927, who had posted a vlog on the website. That was when vlogging first became very apparent to me, and it was actually when I saw video responses to his videos that I realized it may be something I'd enjoy doing. So I posted up a video response and I received comments from people saying they were interested with what I had to say. Now I've been on the website content-creating for over a year now, and so much has happened and changed since. It's incredible.

**FL:** It's funny. You asked me why, out of all the YouTube users, I wanted to include you in my book. But I want to ask that question back to you. What do you think makes you so interesting that over 5,500 people subscribe to your vlog?

**MD:** I'm always interested to hear from people why they watch my videos, because it allows me to get a sense of what impression I truly make, and what I'm doing "right." Over time it's painted a good picture, and for me, I think people who watch my videos do so because I'm real and genuine. There are a lot of people out there who are true on camera, but because they post videos which don't really show who they are deep within, people find it hard to relate. I don't hide anything, because I am comfortable with who I am, and it allows me to progress with self-discovery.

--: 135

# Myles Dyer, Blade376 (continued)

**FL:** You pose interesting questions to your viewers. I'd like to ask you some of the same ones. What makes a successful YouTuber?

**MD:** Success is purely subjective to the individual who is on YouTube, just like the question of what is success in life. But what do I believe it to be? I think success for me comes down to inspiring people, and I succeeded a long time ago when I first started. However, when you meet a goal, it's time to set a new one, and for me that is to increase my exposure so I can get through to more people.

**FL:** What makes a YouTube celebrity?

**MD:** For me celebrity is a status obtained when an individual has a very interested following. The way this tends to occur is by having an intangible presence. If someone vlogs and the only way to "contact" them is through watching and commenting on their videos, etc., they will get many more views and exposure on YouTube than someone who would give out their contact details like instant messenger, or go on live-chat websites such as Stickam. Although I do have a very tangible presence, which results in me in not having the views of some others, I appear to be very well known across the main community of YouTube. How can I be so sure? When I went over to New York for the YouTube 7/7/07 gathering, from 11 A.M. when it started until I left at 4 P.M., I was approached nonstop by people who said they watched my videos. It was truly surreal, and confirmed for me I do have a presence in the eyes of so many people worldwide. People would ask me about my life and videos; it was just so surreal.

**FL:** Do you think it's possible to launch a career from YouTube?

**MD:** I think anything in life that has demand is an opportunity, which if gone about in the right way can lead to a career. There are examples of this already with some of the most subscribed being taken on by agents and companies who will then pay them to promote a product, or something along those lines. Is it a career, though? Well if you look at anything in the media, people's "careers" can come and go very suddenly.

**FL:** What advice can you offer users to help them make their videos stand out on YouTube?

**MD:** If people want to stand out, be controversial; that's how the media works when it comes to standing out and obtaining many views, because people love drama, whether they like to admit it or not. For me obtaining views isn't a priority, or else by now I would have made much more controversial videos, but that wouldn't be "me." Everyone has a goal when they get the opportunity to broadcast themselves across the world, and I think that goes back to the question of what makes a successful YouTuber.

**FL:** You often talk about haters. Why do they exist? How do you deal with them?

**MD:** Haters are a common occurrence on the Internet, because there are so many people out there who are bored, and will spend time tapping away on the keys, safe behind the cyber screen, making harsh comments. This can be due to anything from general boredom and immaturity (although that is a subjective statement) and even jealousy. I say jealousy because the majority of "haters" are users who do not actually make their own videos, and perhaps seeing others succeed with such things as a fan base causes them to feel a need to counteract that. But like anything, names for groups of people lead to vast assumptions to be made, where now people may claim someone to be a hater, when in fact they were actually just making constructive criticism. As long as people keep giving a reaction to these people, they will continue to do what they do. I for one react at times, because haters can lead to more comments on videos and views; so there is a plus side! (I'm such an optimist.) I can appreciate for some people, they find it hard to deal with haters, and especially when it results to extreme measures of death threats, etc., but unfortunately that is the harsh realm of the Internet where people can get away with it, and perhaps if you are not strong enough to deal with it, then vlogging on the Internet is not for you. When people go into vlogging, they should know how mentally strong they are to deal with criticism, and use that as a basis to decide on how much they expose themselves on the Internet to potential threats.

**FL:** Speaking of haters, you've let it be known that you're not a big fan of William Sledd. How come you make fun of him so much?

**MD:** Oh really! I'm not much of a fan, but I wouldn't say I hate him, or anyone for that matter. When I started vlogging, he and I were neck and neck on exposure and subscribers, and there is a competitive element on YouTube (for some, and I'd admit I'm one of them). When I feel there's an opportunity to make a parody of something then I will, but I tend not to do it so much now. I leave that for my alter-ego "Peter File," but that's a whole other interview. I can say though that William at first thought I was making a personal attack with the "Ask a Gay Man: British Edition" video I made, but we spoke and he realized I was just doing a parody, with no intention of causing major offense. It all comes down to integrity on YouTube, but you learn with the Internet and vlogging that integrity is one of the hardest things to judge.

**FL:** Maybe you're a lover, not a hater. You've spoken about meeting a few ladies online. Don't tell me you have trouble meeting girls in person?

**MD:** The whole concept behind me and girls is a complex one, like it is for so many others, and

for that I talk openly about it on the Internet to help others in similar situations. I see so many people rush into relationships, especially at a young age, and end up getting hurt. All my life I have dealt with a lot of friends, and people in general who have issues. Many of them were girls who had been mistreated, etc. This painted the perfect picture of what is not desirable in a relationship, and I apply that to situations where I have a chance of starting one with someone. I do have opportunities, but I just choose not to take them. If there is someone you like, and they like you, I say ask yourself the question, "Can you see yourself being with them forever?" and if you can't feel your heart saying "Yes," then it's not worth it, because you've already found there to be a potential existence of heartbreak in the near future. Maybe I play it too safe, but who knows, with relationships it comes down to trial and error; I'd rather go down the spectrum from too safe to too ruthless than the other way around, like so many people do.

**FL:** What's your take on computer dating?

**MD:** I think it's the evolution of meeting new people, like it is on a friendship basis, too. Going out to a nightclub and chatting with new people is just the same as doing so online. In both instances you may meet someone who is not who they say they are, and in both cases you could have bad experiences. The Internet widens the volume of people

you can meet, and for me that suggests there are more chances of meeting people who would suit the individual more than if you just went to local areas in the real world. If you find someone, and truly feel there is something there, you would go out of your way for them, but unfortunately some people don't take the Internet seriously enough, and are more than happy to say they have an interest in someone when they actually don't really mean it; and when that happens one way, it can lead to heartbreak. The Internet is a realm of mainly fantasy, but I think with new developments in technology such as real-time video chat, more and more people are using the Internet as a way for being real, in the hope of finding other real people.

**FL:** Are you afraid a girl might want to be with you because you are a YouTube celebrity?

**MD:** I was thinking about the issue of girls going out with celebrities the other day, and if their heart was in the person, or in what they stand for. It's an interesting concept, but for me, if someone wanted to be with me because of my YouTube videos, then I guess that would be okay, because technically my videos are about who I am and my life, so to have an interest in the videos would be to have an interest in me. I'd have to meet the girl first!

**FL:** Many YouTube musicians have successfully utilized the site to showcase their music. How

# Myles Dyer, Blade376 (continued)

come you rarely post videos of your band, Doppelganger?

**MD:** My Channel provides a cross-section of my life, and there are so many elements to it. I try not to post too many videos, and therefore I have to select elements of things I do to put into the vlogging world. If something worth videoing occurs, then I will. I think the next time I'll do a Doppelganger video is when we go into the studio again, as when I usually record gigs, the volume overpowers the camera's microphone, and the quality isn't that great. If we had lots of footage, then a "Doppelganger" Channel would be a more likely possibility.

Blade376 meets fellow U.K. YouTuber charlieissocoollike.

**FL:** You were very excited when YouTube began making specific sites for different countries, like the U.K. Why do you think it's important for each country to have their own YouTube site?

**MD:** I was excited, and now I'm not so sure if it was a good thing. There are pros and cons with anything, and in terms of localized YouTube websites, I think the pros and cons are very balanced. It's a good thing because it allows more exposure for people outside the U.S., and adds a community feel for people who live in different areas of the world. I for one have found a lot more British vloggers since YouTube U.K. came along. However, pages such as the feature page just don't have the same rewarding effect as it did before when there was only one front page, which was to be seen by the whole world. Also, some people would rather YouTube stayed as one big community. I'm still undecided if I like it, but I doubt YouTube would ever revert it back now.

**FL:** You mention in one of your vlogs that YouTube changed your life forever. How so?

**MD:** Oh, it has very much so. A lot of people laugh, but that's usually because they are ignorant to what I've been through and how real it can get when you go beyond just posting videos up. I go out there into the real world and meet up with people from the website; I've been on a U.S. tour where I stayed with people in Los Angeles, San Francisco, and New York who I only knew through the website. Things like this I look back on and go "Wow! I really did that?" I still shock myself up to today, and I've found this site has given me a platform that's allowed me to exercise my confidence to a level where I'm no longer afraid to show people who I truly am. Sure, I get people who will criticize and make fun of me, but when I'm out there in the real world, people who looked down on me before seem to have a lot more respect; either openly, or they now leave me alone. As I said in one of my videos, people's attitudes around you will never change once something has been said or done, but your own can. If someone makes fun of you, that's happened, and the only thing that can change now is whether or not you crumble in confidence or bounce back

"I've found this site has given me a platform that's allowed me to exercise my confidence to a level where I'm no longer afraid to show people who I truly am."

—Myles Dyer

without giving a reaction satisfying those who don't show respect. And that's a philosophy I've learnt over the past year, and with that, I have become a much better person who will forevermore stand for what I believe to be right.

**FL:** Of all of your videos, which is your favorite?

**MD:** That's a very tough one ... "My 365 Days on YouTube ..." was probably my favorite, because it was a montage that displayed a good cross-section of what I had done over the first year of my vlogging experience, and it just blew me away how far the videos had changed, and how much I had evolved as a person.

**FL:** Do you have any favorite videos from other YouTube users?

**MD:** Of course, too many in fact! I feel it would be unfair to put any particular ones under the spotlight, because there are just too many who would deserve a mention.

**FL:** Do you have a personal website?

**MD:** I used to have one, but it became too difficult for me to run alongside all my other projects; but if you go to www.blade376.com you'll go straight to my MySpace.

# So You Think You Can Tube ...

You've seen the videos. You've read this far. You think you're ready to take video blogging to the next level. So you think you can tube?

I did it. I made my first vlog, posted it online, and waited for subscribers. No one came. So I got a little creative. And you know what? It worked!

Below I will share my strategy for making a great video. I'll tell you how to get noticed, how to stand out, and how to attract subscribers. Before long, you'll have your very own fan base. Maybe you'll even be able to springboard your newfound hobby into a rewarding and profitable career.

## How to Stand Out

With so many videos out there in cyberspace, it's a wonder how some get seen at all. If you want your video to become the next viral sensation, you've got to make it a cut above the rest. It has to stand out and create buzz so that people talk about it the next day at the water cooler and a combination of word of mouth and curiosity spur it into viral legend.

First and foremost, your video has to be unique and different from everything else like it on the

Net. Maybe it's a fresh take on an old idea. Perhaps it's something we've truly never seen before. Whatever the case may be, it needs to have that special factor that makes people sit up and take notice.

Someone who usually notices those unique videos are the YouTube editors who choose those videos that are featured on the site. Having a video featured on YouTube is like putting a full-page ad on the front cover of *Daily* variety. Everyone sees it. Most everyone watches it. And many people who enjoy it subscribe to your Channel. Because there is no formula to getting featured, and the whole process is truly subjective, my only advice is to keep making great product. Sooner or later, YouTube will take notice.

Video responses are a great way to network with the YouTube community and spread the word about your own Channel. Don't make a video response if you've got nothing to add to the conversation. But if you can add something of substance, there's a good chance that those users who subscribe to the initial Channel will at least glance at your video. If you captivate them by your comments, you may find some new subscribers.

My second vlog was a video response to boh3m3's vlog titled, "Film School?" In Ben's video, he asked if users thought it was necessary to attend film school if you want to be a direc-

tor. Because I not only work in the industry, but also teach at the USC School of Cinematic Arts, I made a video response sharing my thoughts. A lot of the people who read his vlog and others who were interested in the subject wound up subscribing to my Channel in anticipation of similarly themed videos. As a result of my little experiment, my subscribers quadrupled.

Another tactic that works very well is making collaborative videos—videos with appearances by more than one YouTube user. If one or more of those users happens to be a YouTube celebrity, even better. As Nalts mentioned earlier, collaborations are like TV shows where a character from one show crosses over to an episode of another show. You remember when Arnold and Willis from *Diff'rent Strokes* visited the girls from *The Facts of Life*,

or when someone disappears on *Without a Trace* and winds up dead on *CSI*. Crossover episodes and vlogs are a great way to cross-promote your videos.

Another type of video that seems to be very popular on YouTube is videos about the YouTube community. From Renetto's "'Tube It': The Unofficial YouTube Anthem" to Matt Chin's "RMCS—the Guide on How to Become Big on YouTube," users of the site love the self-referential shorts, and can't seem to get enough of them.

If all else fails, remember the old adage, "I'll rub your back, if you rub mine." Everyone wants subscribers. So if you start subscribing to other people's Channels, they may be more inclined to subscribe to yours. Try it out—it certainly can't hurt. You may discover some hidden gems; and they just may discover you.

## What Not to Do

Don't make long, rambling vlogs that are uninteresting and boring. Sure, you have 10 minutes to talk, but do you really have 10 minutes' worth of material to discuss?

Don't choose topics that interest only you or a small circle of friends. The broader the topic, the more interest you'll attract

from likeminded users. Hit on popular subjects and your videos will spread.

Don't use too many handheld camera shots. If every video looks like *The Blair Witch Project*, your viewers will get nauseous and unsubscribe. Even on location, use a tripod whenever possible.

Don't be a hater. You not only have to be careful when commenting on other users' videos, but you have to be equally careful when making your own video. Tolerance and acceptance go a long way. Be sensitive to others.

In the same token, be careful what you say. Once you upload

your video, it may be copied and emailed hundreds of times before you have second thoughts and take it down. Don't say anything you couldn't say to anyone you know, including your own mother. So don't say anything stupid, and think before you speak!

# 15:01

Are the stars of YouTube here to stay, or is their 15 minutes of fame already over? That's the real question we all want to know. But it has only been a couple years—even less for some. And only time will tell if they'll become the next Tom Cruise and Celine Dion, or the next Erin Moran and Gary Coleman.

If viral clips like "Numa Numa" and "Peanut Butter Jelly Time" can last for years and work their way into the mainstream consciousness, I think there's hope for the stars of the Net. These videos are as potent today as they were when they were first posted because their entertainment value is timeless. As long as our Internet stars continue to produce great content, they, too, can last forever.

To me, the question isn't whether they will get more than their 15 minutes of fame, but rather, where will this fame take them and where does the Internet fit in with their career? Will the Web be quickly shunned in favor of mainstream media, or will it be a loyal ally that continues to play a pivotal role in an accelerating career? Or will the very strength of the talent that the Internet has born help propel this technology to be the future destination of all media?

One thing that's for sure is that new "weblebrities" are breaking through each day. With very few barriers, anyone has an open invitation to join in on the fun. If you're itching to see if you've got what it takes, then give me your best "Numa Numa" and hit "record" on your digital camcorder.

One thing that's for sure is that new "weblebrities" are breaking through each day.

What the Buck?!

Godzilla Here

# chapter 8

# A Hollywood Perspective

It's funny. When I first began my career in feature film development and production, I was one of the pioneers of using the Internet as a tool to find new, undiscovered writers. I scoured websites reviewing loglines, hoping to find that next great screenplay from a young writer in Middle America with no ties to Hollywood. And I was very successful at finding these gems.

Another online sensation that captured my interest was early websites that featured well-produced short films. I'd spend hours watching shorts on iFilm and AtomFilms, once again hoping to discover that next great director. I even wrote a book called *Short Films 101*, telling readers how they could make a short film and upload it online to launch their filmmaking careers.

Cut to years later, I'm still working in Hollywood, and while I still produce films, I also manage talent: actors, writers, and directors. I had visited YouTube and similar sites over the past couple years, mainly when a friend sent me a link to a clip that amused him. Occasionally I'd run a search for a classic television episode, or check out the work of an actor I was meeting with. But for some reason, it never dawned on me to search YouTube for raw, undiscovered talent.

Writing this book has been a real treat. I discovered that the World Wide Web is filled with talented individuals making and spreading quality viral video. I've gotten to meet and interview some amazing people from all over the world. And I'm actually working with a couple new clients whom I discovered because of this project after having watched their videos.

Like the early online screenplay boom, I truly believe that Hollywood will come running to scour the Net for up-and-coming talent. In writing this book, I realized that I'm not the only one who has this idea. At the same time, I was somewhat stumped that more of my colleagues weren't taking advantage of what's out there. I went looking for water and struck oil. I think we'll see a lot more mainstream success coming from our viral stars in the not-so-distant future.

## Legal

But Hollywood is divided about their ties to viral video. While a major studio might sign a fresh new voice to a three-picture deal based on the video he or she had posted online, the very next day that same company might send a cease-and-desist letter to another user for posting copyrighted material online. It's an ongoing dilemma that needs to be resolved.

No one is saying that the system is perfect. When Google closed the deal to acquire YouTube, they set aside as much as $200 million for potential copyright litigation. Why would they do this if they weren't concerned about pissing off Hollywood?

Would you believe that major media companies actually have people on staff whose job it is to search the Net to find illegally posted copyrighted content? *The New York Times* reported that NBC Universal has three employees whose job it is to patrol YouTube every day looking for company-owned material. They send YouTube over 1,000 requests per month asking them to take down the video clips.

Earlier, in Chapter 3, we discussed lawsuits that had come forth due to copyright infringement. We also acknowledged that most of these cases were resolved, and partnerships and official licensing deals were born out of the backlash. But the threat still exists and media companies are wary. In fact, just as I was finishing this book, Prince announced that he was suing YouTube for copyright infringement of his music and videos.

The entertainment industry unions are exploring the rights of their constituents, which include actors, writers, and directors, when it comes to digital content. Michael Apted, president of the Directors Guild of America (DGA) told *The New York Times*, "We will aggressively protect our members' creative and economic rights."

If sites like YouTube had to pay an actor, writer, and director every time a user viewed their video, would they ever be able to make money from their site? At the same time, why shouldn't these artists be compensated for the continual enjoyment of their work, just as they are with residuals from film and television?

With the proliferation of content partners and the proactive approach by many media companies to create their own video-sharing sites, we push forward to find an adequate solution that pacifies both sides. As well, YouTube and other viral sites are developing stronger filters to spot and remove copyrighted clips that are uploaded illegally. Until that technology is perfected, the websites will have to use best efforts to police their content and take responsibility to prevent illegal activity.

# Marketing

For every corporate attorney sending off angry letters to YouTube, there are three more executives looking into potential partnership opportunities. Chad Hurley told *The Hollywood Reporter,* "There's been a few examples of marketing departments uploading content directly to the site, while on the other side of the company their attorney is demanding we remove the content."

Admittedly, studios and networks are happy to have some of their material online. In fact, they even supply it directly to sites like YouTube. Marc Schmuger, chairman of Universal Pictures, told *The New York Times* that for each new film the studio

releases, Universal sends out a digital "tool kit" containing video clips and music videos to viral video sites. "I think that the marketing side of our company and the copyright-protection side have contradictory impulses," Schmuger said. "But there is a huge appetite for content, and we are well advised to recognize that appetite and find constructive ways to feed it."

What better way to generate buzz than by launching a viral campaign? Isn't that how *The Blair Witch Project* became so successful? A viral campaign stirred the controversy: is it real or is it fake? Finally, marketers revealed that the hype was set up to promote a film. And it worked. The film was released on 27 screens (a very limited release), but earned over $1.5 million at the box office that first weekend.

While some people were upset when they found out that it was a hoax, others viewed it as a brilliant marketing campaign. If you look at a viral show online today, like LonelyGirl15, there's an inherent marketing plan built into the show. And while viewers might have been a bit more disturbed when they discovered that Bree wasn't real than they were with *The Blair Witch Project*, it certainly didn't cause the webisodes to lose viewers. If anything, the buzz surrounding the reveal drew an even wider audience to the Net.

In that same *New York Times* piece, Schmuger also said that Universal needs to embrace sites such as YouTube because they are the future of movie marketing. Ian Schafer, CEO of Deep Focus, an advertising agency with many film-related clients, told *The Hollywood Reporter*, "The more people who see [a] film's trailer, the more people we feel will get excited about [a] film." And it's already clear that an online trailer posted to a viral video site will get more play for less cost than more traditional means at the same rate.

So while the various departments within each media conglomerate continue to debate their involvement online, the excitement of what's happening continues to grow. Whether it's a studio marketing a film, a Web series marketing a product as LonelyGirl15 did by tying a character to a product (in this case Neutrogena), or using a vlog to promote your own book (see my vlog—LOL), we will continue to see marketers dream up creative ways to use the Net and viral video to spread the word on their products.

> "It's already clear that an online trailer posted to a viral video site will get more play for less cost."
>
> —Ian Schafer, CEO of Deep Focus

# Scouting Talent

Another way Hollywood utilizes viral video websites is by scouring them in search of new talent. Call it a lark? I don't think so. Esmee Denters, Terra Naomi, Mia Rose, Lisa Donovan, Barats and Beretta, and Blame Society Productions, among others, are just some initial proof that Hollywood is actively watching.

I was curious about this, because before starting this book, I myself hadn't spent much time scouting talent online. I wondered if my colleagues had been a few steps ahead of me in this game. So I spoke to about a dozen high-profile agents, managers, and casting directors to uncover their relationship and viewing habits with viral video. To my surprise, most of them were in the same boat that I was in.

The consensus seemed to be that all these industry professionals were familiar with YouTube and similar sites. Most of them used the sites to look up something specific, or to see a funny video that a friend had linked them to. But they said that they didn't spend much time exploring the site looking for that next big thing. Yet I knew there must be someone out there who's using YouTube to find the next big star.

## Who's Looking for Online Talent?

So who is scouting the Net searching for talent? I asked the talent who had been signed from YouTube, and sure enough, a small handful of forward-thinking industry professionals had found this goldmine of talent and kept it on the down-low. From network execs and A&R representatives to high-profile agents and entertainment attorneys, they may have remained under the radar, but they were indeed looking.

One expert who's definitely ahead of the game, Matt Sugarman, entertainment attorney with Weissmann Wolff Bergman Coleman Grodin & Evall LLP, agreed to talk with me about what he looks for in surfing the Net for undiscovered talent.

As for the talent who's hoping to be scouted and discovered, just remember, you can't force it. It has to happen organically. Certainly put yourself out there if you think you've got what it takes. Do something unique and different and better than what is already being done. Then build your subscribers to show us that you're marketable and that you can attract a large audience. If you've truly got the talent, we will find you.

Do something unique and different and better than what is already being done. Then build your subscribers to show us that you're marketable and that you can attract a large audience. If you've truly got the talent, we will find you.

# Q&A

## Interview with Matt Sugarman

**FL:** Do you ever look for new talent on sites like YouTube?

**MS:** Occasionally, although I did more in the past than I do now.

**FL:** Please tell me about some of the talent you discovered.

**MS:** I came across LisaNova (Donovan) and was then introduced to her by another client for whom her boyfriend had worked in the past.

**FL:** Once you signed Lisa Donovan, how did she go from YouTube celebrity to starring on *MadTV*?

**MS:** Actually, she had a number of competing offers when I met her that we held off on accepting because they were for little or no money (even though they were enticing offers from big names). After I introduced Lisa to Todd Christopher at Gersh, [casting director] Nicole Garcia at *MadTV* actually approached Lisa and asked her to try out for the show.

**FL:** Do you think YouTube stars can have longevity in mainstream entertainment, or are they like reality TV stars who only get 15 minutes of fame?

**MS:** I think it has yet to be seen what their long-term success will be. Just as in any other media, you'll probably end up seeing one or two individuals who do very well and go on to long careers. However, the vast majority will fade away. Usually to make it in TV or movies these people don't just show up and say "I want to be an actor"; they've had years of training. While the freshness of the untrained individual can be refreshing at first, in order to translate to long-term success they need training and time.

I think the biggest problem the Internet creates for these people is that you can go from a zero to a big-shot overnight, and the people who do that then get a false/unrealistic expectation that the rest of their career in Hollywood will happen that same way, but it doesn't. It takes years of growing and honing your talent to be successful over the long run. Big egos with little to back it up can kill a career in Hollywood before it starts. People have to realize that there are 500,000 people in this town looking for an agent and manager, and if you get a good one at a good agency, you're very lucky. But even with all that good representation, things take time to develop and grow.

**FL:** What are your favorite online video-sharing sites?

**MS:** Funny or Die and YouTube.

**FL:** Can you share some success stories where you used an online video site to launch or further a client's career?

**MS:** We had a client in a comedy troupe in Amsterdam and we had him post his reel on YouTube along with some funny videos that he did with the troupe. We were able to get the client looked at by a casting director from a network show by giving her the link, and based off of that, they had the client fly to the U.S. for an audition, which he killed and got the spot on the show.

**FL:** What advice can you offer people who want to get started in show business about utilizing sites like YouTube to launch their careers?

**MS:** It's great as a training ground. To see what grabs people, make as many videos as you can, make them as good as you can, and just keep doing it to gain experience.

# **Promoting** Talent

A handful of popular entertainers from film, television, and music have their own YouTube Channels and they're reaching out to a whole new fan base.

By now we've seen how YouTube celebrities use the website to promote themselves. But did you know that Hollywood hotshots are following suit? A handful of popular entertainers from film, television, and music have their own YouTube Channels and they're reaching out to a whole new fan base. "Weird Al" Yankovic, Tommy Chong, and Paris Hilton are just a few of the celebrities taking advantage of the viral video promotion machine.

Talent agent Bernie Spektor knows they're being smart. He urges his own comic clients to post clips of their comedy routines or sketches they've appeared in on sites like YouTube. It helps him do his job when he's booking an up-and-coming act at a comedy club where they may not yet know his comic by name. But tell them it's the guy from YouTube with over 500,000 views, and suddenly the club owners pay attention.

"It's a great opportunity for exposure and to broaden their brand," says Spektor. "With a lot of the upcoming comics, and especially with the tightening of the belts in the feature business, they are delayed until they get a chance to develop a voice. On YouTube and other sites that pay, they not only get a chance to develop their humor but they also make money, where that rarely happens at that stage of a young comic's career."

We're seeing the effectiveness of YouTube as a marketing tool on a daily basis. Any given YouTube celebrity posts a new Vlog and instantly it's viewed by thousands of users who subscribe to their Channel. What makes this so exciting is that talented people are able to promote themselves outside of the traditional film-industry production and distribution system. And if talent no longer needs the mighty studio to market and distribute their product, the power shifts back to the talent. It's a fascinating paradigm and only time will tell if this is truly the wave of the future.

According to *Business Week*, indie filmmaker Jeff Macpherson has received plenty of attention from Hollywood executives for his Internet show "Tiki Bar." But instead of jumping on the bandwagon to parlay his success into the mainstream media, Macpherson opted to raise money to create a series of similar shows for broadcast on the Web. He says, "This is the beginning of something big." As people spend more and more time online, some would-be movie moguls may begin to view the Internet as an end in and of itself. Some are even able to make money at it.

# My YouTube Experience

I'll admit it. I wasn't expecting much. In my mind, I placed the stars of viral video one step above the stars of reality television. And to be honest, I still consider many of them to be at that level.

What I wasn't expecting, however, was to find talent from viral stars that exceeded even my highest expectations. But I did. And I continue to be amazed at what's going on out there on the World Wide Web.

I called my agent the other day to let her know that I was finishing up this project and to tell her that I had actually signed a client from watching his videos on YouTube. What's more, I had my eye on a few others who I was actively tracking and considering as potential clients. I even helped place one of my existing clients as a new character on LonelyGirl15!

I saw videos from some users who I would have signed instantly— but they already had representation. Some of their reps found them on YouTube. Others found them in more traditional ways.

It's too soon to tell you whether my YouTube stars will translate to success in mainstream media. You'll have to check my vlog on my personal YouTube Channel to find out. But I predict that in time, they will succeed in mainstream media.

YouTube is a distribution outlet where anyone anywhere can share his or her videos about anything. I do believe those with true talent will rise to the top. If your videos are entertaining, unique, and different, and if your personality is engaging, you can use YouTube and viral video to launch your show-business career.

That's not to say that everyone who has what it takes will want to launch a career in the entertainment industry. Even some of the YouTube celebrities that I interviewed preferred to remain anonymous to the public than give away too much personal information. I respect that.

Even after I turn this book in to my editor, I plan to continue scouring the Net for the next big viral star, be it filmmaker, musician, or personality. And since I've started my own vlog, who knows? Maybe someone will scout me!

> If your videos are entertaining, unique, and different, and if your personality is engaging, you can use YouTube and viral video to launch your show-business career.

--:149

# chapter 9

# Competition

YouTube may be the number-one destination for viewing and uploading viral video, but it's certainly not the only choice available. In fact, so many competing sites have popped up within the last year that it's difficult to keep up with them all. Some have come and gone quicker than a Dax Flame rant. Still other brand-new ones are bound to appear, even after publication of this book is complete.

In this chapter, I plan to introduce you to some of the more popular video-sharing websites that are alternatives to YouTube. In addition, I'll include some specialty sites, and even a few sites that are a bit more obscure. I'll outline what I like and dislike about each site as it compares to YouTube.

When you're ready to leave behind what you now know and venture into the World Wide Unknown, use this chapter as a guide to test the waters. You may find something special, or you may come running back to the comforts of YouTube. In any case, you'll see that there is no lack of options when it comes to viewing and uploading viral content online.

## America's Internet

Democracy runs rampant on the Internet today. Someone has a great idea and nothing is in place to stop someone else from copying that idea and presumably making it better. This is especially the case when a chink is found in the armor.

The chinks in YouTube's armor may be its initial unwillingness to share revenue with content creators and the slow implementation and mysteries surrounding its partner program. YouTube partners range from large media conglomerates such as Universal Music Group and National Geographic to popular YouTube content creators such as Blame Society Productions and Emmalina. But not everyone can become a partner. You must be invited to join the program.

[T]here is no lack of options when it comes to viewing and uploading viral content online.

## Nalts Makes Partner

One of the most prolific content creators on You-Tube, Nalts, was not very happy. YouTube had started their partner program, and for some reason he was not invited to join. With almost 19,000 subscribers and 500 videos, Nalts was certainly one of the most prolific contributors to the site.

On June 1, 2007, Nalts made a new video titled "NAPPY," which stood for Nalts Advocates for Partnership Placement on YouTube. In this video he pled his case to YouTube and the viral video community, asking his fellow content creators to add video responses to his vlog offering up their support for Nalts's invitation to the partner program. Viewer response to this video was tremendous, garnering Nalts close to 600 response videos.

Almost one week later, Nalts posted another video, called "NAPPY Update." In the video, he revealed that the outpouring of support had helped his cause. He had received a call from George, a YouTube official, inviting him to become a YouTube partner.

Nalts appeals to the YouTube community in his NAPPY video, asking for their support in convincing YouTube to make him a partner.

Nalts is elated after hearing from YouTube's George, who told him that he would now be part of the partner program.

Even once you become a YouTube partner, there's little known about the benefits one might receive. Like most revenue-sharing video content sites, I imagine that users receive a portion of ad revenue based on the number of hits and clicks on the content they upload. What percentage they receive is anyone's guess. In fact, it wouldn't surprise me if certain partners had better profit-sharing terms than others. As a result, a slew of competitors began hitting the World Wide Web, all based on up-front revenue-sharing models.

A slew of competitors began hitting the World Wide Web, all based on up-front revenue-sharing models.

# I Knew I Could Make
## Money at This, Ma

One of the biggest complaints from content providers on YouTube had been their inability to profit from their creative contributions to the site. With the partner program, this concern should be less of an issue. However, because participant invitations are highly selective, there's no guarantee you will be chosen to join the program.

Several video-sharing sites have been created to combat this bourgeois issue. Many have begun to successfully lure content providers away from YouTube with the potential to cash in if their videos perform well. It is a bit ironic that in a World Wide Web filled with sites dedicated to social networking, a structured class system could potentially be a great downfall to YouTube.

It will be interesting to see, as the competition grows fiercer, if YouTube will open their partners program and incentives to all users who upload original content to the site. Only time will tell. But if you're anxious to make some cash off your videos right away, check out the following sites.

## Revver

Revver founder and CEO Steven Starr told a vlogger at the Sundance Film Festival, "Revver pioneered the idea that creators deserve to get paid. What we do is we sell advertising, and we affix a very small piece of ad insertion software onto the end of the video; and every time the video is watched, it's saying, 'Hey, Revver, I need an ad,' and what that means is, as a creator, you can take your video, and you can process it through Revver, take it back, and push it out to all your friends on websites that you have relationships with, and everywhere it's being watched [where] you're getting paid half the ad revenue that's generated by these videos. That's our current model."

Of course, this is a great model for several reasons. First off, YouTube just doesn't have very much advertising on its site. If YouTube were to offer this type of incentive, would it mean we'd have to sit through ads before or after we watch random videos? Would the YouTube homepage be crawling with banner ads asking us to click through to the next big ad? At the same time, do content creators

CEO & Founder
Revver.com

Steven Starr, Founder and CEO of Revver. Copyright Sandie Black/memechannel.com.

on Revver have to be careful, almost censoring themselves to a certain degree, to make sure that their creative product is advertiser-friendly? If Chad Vader had a milk allergy, would that kill that show's producers from being able to get a dairy sponsor on Revver?

The site itself seems fairly easy to navigate. But it doesn't have a lot of the same bells and whistles that YouTube has. It also doesn't seem to have the abundance of material one can get from YouTube. Nor does it have the same social networking capabilities, and as a result, it really lacks a sense of community.

--: 153

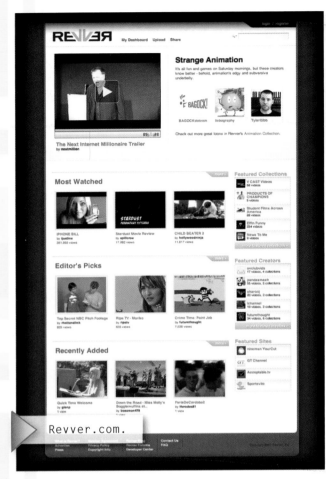

Revver.com.

VuMe homepage.

# VuMe

VuMe (pronounced "view me") actually began as another website called eefoof (pronounced ... actually, I'm not sure how that was pronounced). Kevin Flynn, the site's founder, started off with the philosophy that "It should pay to be creative." And one more revenue-sharing video-sharing site was born.

Flynn may be best known as the creator of the original video "Peanut Butter Jelly Time." When he posted that video online back in 2003, it quickly became one of the most-viewed viral videos of all time (see the interview in Chapter 1). But he never saw a dime from his efforts, which is why Flynn

created VuMe.com. He wanted to make sure that other content creators could profit from their hard work.

By adding banner ads to your video pages and an unobtrusive ad to the end of your video, VuMe enables you to get paid every time someone looks at your creative content. The interface is clean and easy to navigate. In addition to sharing video, the site is also deigned to help you share photos and audio podcasts.

I spoke with Kevin Flynn about VuMe, and here's what he had to say about the site.

# Q&A

## Interview with Kevin Flynn

**FL:** Tell me how you came up with the idea for VuMe. Please talk about eefoof and how it evolved into this new site.

**KF:** Well, it was due to me not making a cent off my movie. Actually, what happened is I heard that the guy that runs ebaumsworld.com (a site famous for stealing other people's content online) was clearing a couple hundred thousand dollars every month. One of the things he stole was, of course, "Peanut Butter Jelly Time." I always thought that was a really screwed-up business model—the only people making money off content were crooks. So I made a place where people could share in the money

being made, and stupidly named it the first available domain that I randomly punched in: eefoof. About a week after our launch, we were all over the news. Once we got some funding, the first order of business was to change that awful name to something a bit easier to spell. Hence, VuMe.

**FL:** How does VuMe compare to YouTube? Why should someone post on VuMe versus YouTube? Why should someone browse on VuMe vs. YouTube?

**KF:** The main issue with YouTube is their lack of oversight. They are basically the Napster of today … they built a $1.6 billion empire off of stolen content and copyrighted material. The difference between them and ebaumsWorld is that they didn't go out and actively steal content. However, the end result is the same. The people that actually made the content—whether it be *Saturday Night Live* or some 16-year-old kid that made a funny movie—are getting shafted for the most part.

We try to oversee things pretty well on VuMe … and that's just because of my own personal background. I think the obvious reason that someone should post on VuMe is that, of course, we pay you. It really doesn't matter where you post something as long as you can promote it a bit and get it out there. As for browsing … well, you know that every piece of media you see on VuMe is helping the author out.

**FL:** What are your favorite videos on VuMe?

**KF:** I'm not really sure if I have any favorites. What I do like is when people go out and promote their own stuff in creative ways. We have a few people on the site that are making a couple thousand every month just by promoting the heck out of themselves; it's pretty neat to see.

# Panjea

Panjea puts you in the driver's seat. Imagine that you are a network programming executive whose job it is to decide what goes on the air. You not only select which shows will premiere, but you also decide how they fit into the programming schedule. Panjea enables you to program your own network by selecting your favorite videos (or shows) and putting them in the order you want them shown.

Another way to think about Panjea is to envision that you are putting together a mixed tape. Mixed tapes consist of your favorite songs, thematically linked (usually love) that are sent to someone special. Panjea lets you make a mixed tape with video that you can send to friends anywhere.

Like Revver and VuMe, Panjea is another site that enables its content creators to generate revenue from the videos they make. Panjea's revenue structure is a bit different from the others. Content creators are able to set the pricing for their videos, and then keep 80 percent of the profit.

Whether users will pay for homegrown, original content is another matter. Not only does Panjea allow their users to upload and sell original content on their site, but they also utilize search engines that scout videos on other viral sites such as YouTube and Google Video.

## Veoh

Veoh is another site that lets content creators charge money to users who want to watch their videos. But revenue-sharing isn't really Veoh's hook. Their hook is viewing quality.

While users can easily screen videos online at veoh.com, this site has a second option for viewing full-screen, high-resolution video. By downloading the Veoh player, users can watch full-length, television-quality programs on their viewer, or even on their TV at home.

Veoh also acts as your very own DVR. The site searches multiple content providers for videos that you can watch instantly, or download to your computer for viewing at your leisure.

Metacafe homepage.

## Metacafe

At first glance, Metacafe looks peculiarly like YouTube. With tabs at the top of its homepage hovering over various featured videos, at first I thought I had gone to the wrong spot. But there are differences.

The revenue structure is based on a CPM (cost per thousand impressions) system. It kicks in once a user's video has generated 20,000 views. That user then receives $5 CPM (so when it kicks in, the user automatically receives $100). Some users have earned in excess of $20,000 since this program was implemented.

Given the number of hits documented on your average featured YouTube video, it's amazing that more content creators haven't made the move to Metacafe. But maybe that's because only 10 percent of videos uploaded to this site are accepted.

Apparently, there's a three-prong system for screening content. The first step is to eliminate duplicates, though most sites attempt to do this. Second, Metacafe has 100,000 reviewers who filter the material seeking not only inappropriate videos, but also those that they deem uninteresting. Finally, they've come up with a "Viewer Rank" system that translates viewer interaction with the videos into

mathematical algorithms that ultimately determine how the videos are featured on their website.

I spoke with Kip Kay about the videos he's posted on Metacafe, and here's what he had to say about the site.

## Interview with Kip Kay

Screencap from Kip Kay's highest-earning video "Laser Flashlight Hack!"

**FL:** While everyone and their brother is posting their videos to YouTube, you've posted yours on MetaCafe. How come?

**KK:** I did post some on YouTube years ago for fun. When I found out about the Producer Rewards program at Metacafe, that was what interested me the most and motivated me to produce and upload to Metacafe.

**FL:** To date, how much money have you made from your videos on MetaCafe?

**KK:** As of this writing, my total is $54,423. I have already received about $43,000.

**FL:** How long did it take you to start earning money from the time you posted your first video on MetaCafe?

**KK:** My first video, "Mystic Cube," was submitted in October of 2006. My first payment was in November for $470.

**FL:** Why would you recommend MetaCafe to other content creators?

**KK:** The Producer Rewards program has been a real blessing to me and hundreds of other producers. It's a great additional income, and the ideas are unlimited as to what you can produce. You never know for sure what the Metacafe audience will like until you try it. Metacafe is truly unique when it comes to making money with video on the Internet.

**FL:** Aside from monetary rewards, have any other opportunities been presented to you from posting videos on MetaCafe?

**KK:** I've been quoted in a magazine or two, been featured on ABCNews.com, and have been contacted about the possibility of a television show.

**FL:** You're a regular MacGyver. How do you think of all of the topics for your videos?

**KK:** Well, they are not all my original ideas. There is really nothing new under the sun, just redone for video. I've been around a while and know some unusual things, plus the Internet is a great source for ideas.

**FL:** Which video is your favorite?

**KK:** One of my latest videos, "Laser Flashlight Hack," is fast becoming my most-watched, highest-rated video. It has been all over the Internet. My second would be the classic "How to Chill a Coke" because that features my cats and was fun to make.

**FL:** What is your day job?

**KK:** I am a computer-repair tech and also part-time media director at our local church.

## Blip.tv

First of all, don't confuse this site with BlipTV.com, yet another short-form video content site that specializes in content for delivery to mobile phones. Blip.tv is thinking about a much bigger picture.

Dina Kaplan, COO of the site, says that the online video-sharing market can be broken down into three segments. She classifies the first segment as true viral video, where anybody can post anything, such as on Youtube. Next, there's the personal segment, where video is posted on personal websites so users can share it with their family and friends. Blip.tv focuses on the third segment of the market: TV shows and video blogs.

Blip.tv truly considers itself to be a network, along the lines of ABC or HBO, but for the Internet. They provide the hosting platform, the advertising, and the means of distribution. All that the content creators have to focus on is creating their content. Anyone familiar with the inner workings of a television network knows this is how it's done. Although in Hollywood, the networks often participate in the development of the content as well. Rarely is a producer left alone to just deliver the show sight unseen.

Ad revenue is split 50/50. And Blip.tv has a dedicated team that seeks out advertising opportunities. They're also a great source of syndication, distributing their content to sites such as Yahoo! Video, MySpace, and Facebook.

> [S]everal sites dedicated to professional-level content are popping up all over the Web.

# Quality, Not Quantity

We've talked about various issues as they relate to viewing quality. Let's face it, viral video isn't generally shot in high definition. Some might even find the grainy nature of webcam video somewhat nostalgic and charming.

But in this section, we'll refer to quality in relation to the content itself. There's something to be said about a site like YouTube that allows anyone to upload anything, regardless of content quality (and as long as the content doesn't violate the Terms of Service agreement). But there's also something to be said for sites that focus strictly on quality entertainment.

Most of the major television networks are already streaming their programming for free on their eponymous websites. Now several sites dedicated to professional-level content are popping up all over the Web. It may take the "viral" out of the video, but here are a few sites worth checking out.

## Babelgum

This site made major headlines when they announced that they would be the exclusive online destination for Spike Lee documentaries and shorts. And they've quickly been adding similarly impressive content partners to bring top-quality programming to the monitors of Internet viewers. They've also gotten innovative, striking up deals with companies such as the Rushes Soho Shorts Film Festival, screening the finalists of the festival, past winners, and exclusive coverage of the event.

The only major downfall at the moment is that Babelgum is only available to PC users. For a Mac addict like me, I'll have to wait for Babelgum to release a new platform. Hopefully that will soon be on the horizon.

## Joost

Joost will work with PCs and Macs—but only Macs with Intel processors. But if you keep up with the technology, then you're in for a treat. Most Viacom product (MTV, VH-1, BET, Paramount Pictures, and so on) is available online exclusively at Joost.

Whereas YouTube and similar sites specialize in short-form content and video clips, Joost is going for the market who wants to watch entire television episodes or movies on their computer. Naysayers who think viewers would rather watch this on their television may not be 100 percent correct—just look at all the iTunes downloads of similar content in recent history.

And Joost isn't relying on content from Viacom alone. They've actually signed a deal with Creative Artists Agency, one of the largest talent agencies in Hollywood, to scout out programs for their site.

Joost homepage.

## Super Deluxe

In-N-Out does Burgers. Dominoes does pizza. And Super Deluxe does comedy. And they do it well. The site features exclusive comedic content from some of the best in the business. Bob Odenkirk, Maria Bamford, and Richard Belzer are just some of the hilarious comics providing exclusive content to this site. And while I've listed the site under quality, the fact that it's all comedy, all the time, could really classify it with the next group of websites—each going after a specific niche of the marketplace.

SuperDeluxe.com homepage.

## Media Companies Are Tubing, Too

Viacom is not the only large media company getting into the online video game. The others are taking note and following suit.

News Corp., the major corporation that owns Twentieth Century Fox and Fox TV, made headlines when they acquired social-networking site MySpace. Now they're entering the online video wars with the addition of MySpaceTV. They've already begun distributing what they're calling "minisodes" (an entire television episode cut together in a five-minute clip) of classic TV shows such as *The Facts of Life* and *Silver Spoons*. Surely more content from the Fox entities will follow.

In addition, News Corp. has partnered with NBC to launch "the largest Internet video distribution network ever assembled with the most sought-after content from television and film." Here you can watch the best shows from NBC and Fox including *Prison Break* and *The Office.* Check out the site at Hulu.com.

Sony Entertainment purchased a popular video-sharing site called Grouper. Although they gave it a complete overhaul and name change (see "Crackle," following), they've come up with an innovative way to compete in this crowded market and utilize the various products and divisions of Sony Entertainment.

Time Warner was the first major media conglomerate to get their feet wet in the online world with the acquisition of AOL. Their strategy seems to be buying up various smaller video-sharing sites, and combining them into an AOL portal they're calling uncutvideoo.com.

# You Gotta Have a Gimmick ...

As you're beginning to discover, there are so many sites out there on the World Wide Web. So how do you distinguish one from the next? A whole new crop of sites are blooming all over the Internet, and like Super Deluxe, each one is targeting a specific niche.

If you just want to find comedy content, prepare to be funny, or die! Want to see what it's like for TV producers in the cutthroat world of Hollywood? Pitch a show to Channel 101. Or maybe you'd like to pitch an idea to executives at Sony Pictures Entertainment? There's a website just for you.

And these are just a few that exist. More and more are being created as you read this book! If you don't find your niche on the following sites, the right one can't be too far away.

## FunnyOrDie

The concept is simple. Anyone can upload original comedy content to the site. All viewers get to vote on whether they think it's funny. They have two choices: funny or die. If users think the clip is funny, it will stay online. If they don't, it will die and be sent to "the crypt." How's that for democracy?

This site made a huge splash when Will Ferrel, one of the partners in this venture, uploaded a short video called "The Landlord." In the video, Will Ferrel is late on his rent and the landlord comes to collect. They have a very funny argument about the rent, fueled by the fact that the landlord is a two-year-old girl. It's absolutely hysterical.

## Channel 101

Channel 101 simulates a real TV network. Users are invited to make pilots that are no longer than five minutes. They may then submit them for consideration on a miniDV tape (submissions are not digitally uploaded online). Once a month, a screening party is held in Los Angeles. Those in attendance vote to determine which shows make the "prime-time lineup."

FunnyOrDie.com homepage.

Channel 101 homepage.

Crackle.com homepage.

If your show is chosen to "air," it will be uploaded to Channel 101 and you will be asked to make a subsequent episode. This episode will then be screened at the next screening party to determine if the show should stay on the air. You may continue to make new episodes that will air on Channel 101 until your show is "cancelled" at a screening party sometime in the future.

Don't worry—there's still a place for cancelled shows on Channel101.com, as there is also a section for select failed pilots. And, hey, if your series gets cancelled, you can always post it to YouTube. Also, you don't have to live in L.A. to submit a show—that just makes it more convenient to attend the parties.

# Crackle

It started out as a site called Grouper—an extremely popular UGV (user-generated video) site, similar to YouTube. Then Sony bought it because they wanted to be in the online video game. The next thing you know, they change the name to Crackle, drop 90 percent of the UGV, and replace it with higher-quality professional clips and shows with the intent to syndicate. What were they thinking?

Apparently they were thinking of a great way to differentiate themselves in an overcrowded marketplace. In its first month, the site received over 25 million unique visitors. And it's growing stronger every day.

The best feature about Crackle is that it offers a slew of contests where amateur content creators have the ability to get their material in the hands of Sony Pictures executives and partners like the Improv comedy clubs. Are you an amateur filmmaker? Win a pitch meeting with a creative exec at Columbia Pictures. Forget open-mic night. Upload your comedy routine to Crackle, and before you know it, you could be playing the world-famous Improv.

# **Media**Scrape

How about one website with up-to-the-minute, round-the-globe video of breaking news? How 'bout MediaScrape? Whether you want news from the States, Europe, or even the Middle East, this site has it all.

It's like having CNN at your fingertips. Of course, CNN has its own video news site. And if you don't mind sitting through the advertisements, it's not bad at all. But with MediaScrape, you not only get top stories and what's popular, but you can also search by category, like politics, entertainment, sports, business, and so on. Not only that, but through integration of Google Earth software, you can pinpoint exactly, on a map, where the story is based.

MediaScrape.com homepage.

# **Pornotube & Xtube**

Well, really … what can I say about these sites? Their names really speak for themselves. Now don't get all coy with me. Pornography is one of the largest and fastest-growing sects on the Internet. I said "sects," not "sex!" So somebody reading this book must be enjoying it online!

If you want your porn categorized and sorted, then you may want to visit these websites. And, dare I suggest, if you create your own porno videos, then these are the sites for you. XTube even has a revenue-sharing program for amateur filmmakers. Anyone game?

XTube homepage.

# **Searching for** the Best

Simply put, Dabble is a search engine to find all video content on the Internet. It searches for content on over 200 websites including YouTube,

Metacafe, Veoh, and Blip.tv. But it doesn't do it alone—it enlists the assistance of all of its users.

Dabble.com homepage.

MrQuack homepage.

When you see video content on the net that you like, use your Dabble bookmark tool and hit "Add it to Dabble." Choose a thumbnail image, add some tags, and the clip is ready to be found when other users search for the tags you entered.

While Dabble is my favorite, there are a few other search engines that specialize in video content. Be sure to check out digg.com and videobomb.com as alternative choices. There are also several small sites that exist to simply categorize content—other users doing the dirty work for you by putting together lists and links of the best video content on the Web. One of my favorites you should check out is MrQuack.com.

# And the Rest ...

As they say in the theme song to *Gilligan's Island,* "... and the rest." Of course, there were only two castaways remaining, which is probably why they later changed the song to include them. However, there are many more than two video-sharing sites left to touch upon. In fact, I could probably write a whole book devoting a chapter to each of the sites out there.

But as that probably won't happen, here's a list of additional sites to check out. Send me a video on my YouTube account to let me know which sites are your favorites. Even better, let me know if you discover a brand-new one that's worth investigating. Although, between you and me, I think we can hold off on any more porn sites.

## Additional Sites for Video Viewing and Sharing

BiggyTV.com is a multi-channel entertainment network providing both professional and semi-professional content that also allows users to buy and sell products through their innovative video shopping network.

Dailymotion.com is the US version of the popular French website that brought video sharing to France long before YouTube went international with fr.youtube.com.

Facebook.com is a social networking site, like MySpace, that allows its users to share videos on the site.

GoFish.com is a video-sharing site that focuses on "directed" content (i.e., telling users what kinds of videos to make rather than simply allowing users to upload whatever they wish).

Googlevideo.com. Why Google still has its own video site even after acquiring YouTube, I'll never understand.

Heavy.com is a site that mainly produces comic programming and online flash games.

MySpaceTV.com is the popular social networking site's attempt to compete with YouTube.

Uncutvideo.com. Like Facebook and MySpace, AOL had to get into the game with their own personal video portal.

Vimeo.com is a video-sharing site that prides itself on carrying only user-generated videos that the whole family can watch.

Yahoovideo.com began as a video search engine, but later blossomed into a full-service video-sharing site.

# chapter 10

# The Future

It has been called a revolution. Just when media began to feel steady, audiences called for a change. YouTube and sites like it responded. People want their pop culture short, mobile, free, downloadable, and—most important—under their own control. It is no longer enough to have the American dream of fame and fortune ephemerally available to everyone—people want it on their desktops and on their cell phones. The demand of the new user generation and the technology of viral video have changed media culture indefinitely, but the revolution is far from over.

Remember drive-in movies, audio cassettes, laserdiscs, and BetaMax videotapes? What facets of current pop culture are soon to become outmoded and obsolete by the viral video craze? Where is the next generation of stars going to come from?

Will audiences remain the guardians of their own culture or will the studios take control of this new wave of technology?

In the previous chapters, I discussed how YouTube has already begun to address these concerns, but what of the future? Lev Grossman of *Time* magazine writes, "It's about the cosmic compendium of knowledge Wikipedia and the million-channel people's network YouTube and the online metropolis MySpace. It's about the many wresting power from the few, and helping one another for nothing, and how that will not only change the world, but also change the way the world changes." As the mass of YouTubers continue to demand and control change in media and pop culture, the revolution rages on.

It is no longer enough to have the American dream of fame and fortune ephemerally available to everyone—people want it on their desktops and on their cell phones.

# **Where** We Watch

As YouTube and viral video continue to pave the way, the computer and the Internet are more than ever the vessels of global media. Box-office statistics show a general trend moving away from theaters to the laptop. According to Nielsen EDI, between 2005 and 2006, the same year that saw the birth and boom of YouTube, box-office gross receipts fell 4.1 percent, from $9.21 billion to $8.83 billion, a trend that is continuing. Sites such as al-lUC.org and tv-links.co.uk will link any user, free of charge, to counterfeit films and television shows wherever they are posted on the Internet, be it in 10-minute segments on YouTube or in longer clips on dailymotion.com or veoh.com. In a time where a movie ticket costs $10 and a DVD rental costs $4, unless audiences have a nostalgic draw to big screens and buttery popcorn, sites like YouTube are the future platform of film and television viewing.

So are we going to start seeing more television sets in dumpsters and boarded-up Cineplexes? Some, like Jennifer Maderazo of PBS, think not. She writes, "I don't enjoy watching television online—it's just not comfortable. Lazing on the couch with a remote control is much more enjoyable than hunching over a desk and maneuvering a mouse to make things happen." However, fewer and fewer viewers are spending their watching time in the vicinity of a La-Z-Boy. In January 2007, 37 percent of Internet video viewing took place during weekday work hours. Even within the home, alternatives to the television are growing in popularity. According to a study done by NBC, 68 percent of households with a video iPod used the iPod for viewing within the home. The release in 2007 of the Apple iPhone and its partnership with YouTube enables viewers to watch video on the move without having to pay a monthly fee. For audiences of non-channel flippers, viewers interested in specific material, and those of the YouTube phenomenon, television sets and movie theaters are becoming a thing of the past.

This transition has sped up with the rise of television online. More and more network and cable channels are streaming shows on their Web pages, trying to assuage the needs of fans while carefully attempting to ward off copyright infringement. As I discussed in the first section of this book, many television networks are striking deals with viral video sites such as YouTube to promote their online and broadcast material. Warner Music is working with YouTube to post every music video from their label on the site. The weekly soap opera and crime drama are rapidly becoming moot as viewers watch shows on their own time online. Even devices such as TiVo, services such as On Demand, and television on DVD, which all seemed so fresh five years ago, are slowly phasing out.

[T]he spirit of the user generation that YouTube embodies has changed more than viewing statistics and streaming technology—it has changed pop culture from the bottom up

The Internet archive of television and film may be growing, but the user generation demands material as soon as it hits the airwaves. Live television broadcast streaming sites are popping up all over the Net. Apple TV is one of the many attempts at consumer devices linking Internet and television that have been introduced in the past few years. As quickly as customers of the local video store have switched to DVD mail-order services, they now find themselves watching their media online for free as soon as it is available. Netflix, one of the most popular of these mail-order movie services, has started streaming films and television shows on its website for download as well, in order to keep up with the culture. As Frank Patterson, better known as popular YouTube blogger DigitalSoul, says in an interview with cNet News, "I think YouTube is the next television. I don't watch TV that much. I think people will find a lot of raw unknown talent on YouTube." Viral video as a medium has changed the when, where, and how of global media, but the spirit of the user generation that YouTube embodies has changed more than viewing statistics and streaming technology—it has changed pop culture from the bottom up.

# All-Stars

YouTube has brought an unparalleled level of democracy to popular culture. As studios and networks learn the ropes of what their consumers have created, a question for the future is posed: will the grassroots atmosphere of viral video continue to be the new frontier for fresh talent and fame and fortune, or will Hollywood find a way to sink their teeth in? YouTube has put pop culture in the hands of its citizens. "One could imagine a next-generation version of *Saturday Night Live* that's created entirely by the viewers," said Michael Hirschorn, creator of VH-1's viral video show "Web Junk 20" and VH-1's executive vice-president of original programming. "It might even be better."

In Chapter 6 we heard from the next generation of YouTube stars. It will not be long before these new faces are strutting their stuff in *U.S. Weekly*, like the generation of reality television stars before them. Brian Graden, president of entertainment at MTV Networks, said about viral video, "You can almost see a continuum with reality TV. Fame has become an overblown aphrodisiac in our culture, and now here you go: put your video you made on iFilm and maybe you'll be on TV next week."

YouTube has put pop culture in the hands of its citizens.

The stars, producers, directors, and performers of the future can make it big from their bedrooms and basements, from every corner of the globe simultaneously.

By the week after that, however, you may plummet back into obscurity. As clips become shorter, so do the life spans of stars. Viral video stars are more akin to the National Guard—called to duty from the ranks of the average citizen, then sent back to their everyday lives—rather than the elite tier of celebrity we associate with Hollywood royalty. Though this may mean that viral stars see their 15 minutes shrinking, at the same time, it leaves space for more to rise. As John Gappers argues in an article for *Financial Times*, we are seeing a shift away from the social distinction between professionals and amateurs, and instead seeing a revolution of "Pro-Ams"—people, like the stars of viral video, who take amateur activities to a professional status. "For Pro-Ams, leisure is not passive consumerism, but active and participatory." This shift toward shorter, yet more democratic, spurts of fame fits viral video, which has always been based more on community than image.

Already the stars of YouTube are gathering together, meeting at annual exclusive parties. In February 2007, YouTube's "As One" event brought together viral stars such as Ben Going (Boh3m3), a waiter from Alabama with a 26,000-person online following; Frank Patterson (DigitalSoul), a stay-at-home father from Pittsburgh; and Caitlin Hill (TheHill88), who flew all the way in from Australia for the event. Fans and groupies even approached the rising stars for autographs. Like television and movie theaters—tangible devices of the past—Hollywood is becoming a function of cyberspace. The stars, producers, directors, and performers of the future can make it big from their bedrooms and basements, from every corner of the globe simultaneously.

But can the masses realistically retain this leveled playing field? Brad Stone of *Newsweek* writes, "Amateurish home movies will not necessarily be shunted aside but will surely be overshadowed by the professionally produced fare of network and cable TV. Soon, Internet video will be all about the nightly news, the sitcom, live concerts, and the newest music video." Networks are already testing the waters. In 2007, NBC produced an anonymous viral video, "The Easter Bunny Hates You," and released it on YouTube as an experiment to see how successful it could be with viral video audiences. The short gained five million hits in the span of two weeks. Networks are promoting new viral video shows, like VH-1's "Web Junk 20" and "The Net with Carson Daly," in the works at NBC. As audiences and consumers have designated viral video as the platform of media's future, studios are looking for ways to assert control.

However, unlike past advances in media—films and television—the technology of viral video is not a gift descended upon us from above; it is an organic creation of the masses themselves. "People want to believe these were completely homemade expressions, that they were discovered out in the universe and were brought to air," says Graden. "If they look like slickly produced television I don't think people would buy into the utter randomness that is that show." There is a difference between the technology of viral video and the culture of viral video—one can, and most likely will, be used and abused by studios and networks; the other, the world where Ben Going, the waiter from Alabama, is a superstar, is going to remain in the hands of the people.

# Show Me the Money

The main reason studios have not capitalized on the viral video craze is that so far it is an industry driven by passion, not gross profit. A large part of YouTube's charm and success is that it does not force advertising on its viewers. The stars and producers of viral video do it for the love of doing it, while studios remain frustrated by lack of a better revenue model. Melissa Grego, managing editor of *TV Week,* told CNN, "If some inspired people on the Internet find something that they really connect with and want to share it with other people, the TV networks need to realize that these are likely to be the people they really want to reach, and that this is the kind of endorsement you couldn't pay enough for." The potential of the platform is endless, but so far there has been no viable solution to arresting copyright infringement and making profit off of viral videos. But that does not mean big business isn't trying.

New technologies and advertising strategies are in the works. This past summer, YouTube and media conglomerates Time Warner Inc. and Walt Disney Co. have started testing a new "video fingerprinting" technology that will be able to identify copyrighted videos when posted, letting owners decide whether or not to allow the clips to remain open to the public for free. As this technology is fine-tuned, it will be made available for use by all copyright owners—a goal YouTube hopes to achieve by the

end of the year. YouTube will sell advertising alongside those clips, splitting revenues with the proprietary companies. Once copyright infringement is abated, networks and studios will have a much greater handle on the viral video market.

Advertising itself is discovering new ways of functioning in the world of viral video. In June 2007, YouTube series LonelyGirl15 signed a sponsorship agreement with Neutrogena. The cosmetics company now promotes the popular Web series by streaming episodes on its site, and, in exchange, a new character was introduced into the storyline—a Neutrogena scientist who helps the main characters defeat an evil organization. "Our collaboration was inspired by the creators' inventive approach to integrating our brand into the storyline or the series in a manner that their fans will appreciate," says Neutrogena group product director Laurent Combredet. Michael Eisner's popular viral series, "Prom Queen," signed an exclusive contract with Amazon.com in July 2007, allowing episodes to be downloaded to both computer and television through Amazon's digital download service, Unbox, and its deal with TiVo.

YouTube itself is trying to balance its sensitivity to its audience's disdain for forced ad viewing with the pressure to generate profit. After Google announced that YouTube would, in fact, be running ad clips before its videos, YouTube spokeswoman

Julie Supan said, "We're taking our time. The model we bring forward is going to be a new model because this is a new market." Viral culture and YouTube's roots were founded in a non-ad environment, making the transition to revenue-seeking difficult for viewers and site owners alike. "That is the ironic nature of all of this," says online journalist David Poland in an interview with PBS reporter Mark Glaser. "If it is given structure, it is no longer viral. If it is viral, it can't be monetized very well (aside from banners on YouTube pages)."

Some advertisers are just as wary as audiences. On one hand, viral video provides an incredible platform for advertisers to reach wide audiences. YouTube in particular enables advertisers to reach a rare but highly desirable target audience of 18- to 34-year-old males. However, not all advertisers want their products to be associated with the sometimes-crass content of user-generated videos. "The problem is, advertisers want it both ways," says Karl Heberger, advertising director of ebaumsworld.com, one of YouTube's top competitors. "They want to be in front of that 18 to 34, but they don't want to be associated with much of what that demographic finds entertaining." In the future, sites like YouTube might have to establish censored areas where high-reputation advertisers can promote products. But any advertising that disrupts the organic flow of viral video culture is just another infraction on audiences, and the jury is still out on determining how these annoyances will affect viewership.

While many YouTube users may balk at the inevitable shift toward alliances with larger studios and corporations, other users seem to welcome it as a career opportunity. Many viral video stars are signing with agents in the footsteps of Hollywood. Talent agencies such as United Talent Agency,

which specializes in representing viral talent, are making it easier for viral stars and series to get recognition and contracts that generate income as well as viewers. UTA-repped creator Kent Nichols ("Ask a Ninja") says, "The key thing that UTA gets is that new media is just show business, but without the distributor. But show biz is show biz. It's just contracts and negotiations. That's what they know, that's what they do. The technology doesn't change that—what it does change is the need to go through a distributor. Now two people and a laptop can reach as big an audience as a lot of shows on cable. That is the shift." Some viral video sites, like Daily Reel, created by Jeff Stern and Jamie Patricof, try to separate themselves from the hodgepodge nature of YouTube by featuring videos of higher, more marketable caliber. Money will inevitably enter the equation, and as it does, some users will use it to their advantage while others will fight against it for the sake of the culture.

Like most pop-culture phenomena that are created from the bottom up, eventually the "powers that be" will find a way to sink their teeth in. Audiences and fans will split between the original culture of viral video, driven underground in attempts to remain independent, and store-bought viral video, slickly produced by studios and networks that cherry-pick the best talents from the independent artists. Like movies and music, the independent culture will have more low-budget crap, but also the more progressive, innovative, risk-taking artists, while the studio viral videos will have high-budget, high-concept gold, balanced by a fair share of sugar-coated, action-packed schmaltz. As advertising and entertainment companies evolve with the technology, viral video culture will divide.

# Authorities in Viral Video

As viral video becomes a primary mode of communication across the globe, governments and laws concerning censorship will have to evolve, as will large industries like journalism and publishing. Currently, the YouTube community censors its own material, but will that continue? Some, like Professor Robert Thompson, director of the Center for the Study of Popular Television at Syracuse University, think it is actually the future of how news culture will change. When footage of Saddam Hussein's execution was released, most network news stations did not show the entire clip, conforming to long-standing "appropriate viewing" standards, but the clip became viral on the Internet almost immediately. To catch up with viral video sites, news networks began streaming the full clip on their own sites, enabling viewers to make the conscious choice to watch it or not. "My guess, though," says Thompson, "is that in two or three years we're going to see it completely change. It's a quick step to go from saying, 'We can't show it because it's against our standards, but here's a link to it' to, 'If everyone can see it, including kids, what's the difference? Why not show it?'" As network news continues to feel more and more contrived, the shock and awe of viral video news, its organic flow from the people, and its self-censorship seem to be where traditional news media is headed.

In certain segments of the world, however, when it comes to viral video, unchecked freedom of speech may be in jeopardy. In countries such as Turkey and Thailand, governments have already put up bans on YouTube for allowing videos to be posted that speak against government officials. In Turkey, a posted video that ridiculed former leader Mustafa Kemal Ataturk inspired a "virtual war" between Greeks and Turks, with each side making subsequent videos attacking the other until YouTube was banned entirely from the country. That ban resulted in Turkey being further chastised by the European Union—which Turkey is trying to join—for not allowing freedom of speech. In Thailand, YouTube had to agree to take down any material the government did not approve of, in order to have the ban lifted. Of course, YouTube makes sure that users outside of Thailand can still see the content. You might think that America, the country that birthed YouTube, would be immune to this sort of interference, but with the controversial Patriot Act cropping up new stories of the violation of privacy rights of average citizens, how long before controversial YouTube posters are tracked down through their usernames and monitored by our own government? Though YouTube has not been held responsible for censorship problems, its users might have to be more cautious as their videos become viral.

YouTube does not specifically support any particular material posted to its site, making it the neutral middleman in viral material disputes, but authorities are beginning to keep a keener eye on Internet videos. A video posted on YouTube in December 2007, after a concert in Hamilton, Canada, showed the murder of a man in the parking lot as the show let out. After the video became viral, gathering over 30,000 viewers, the murderer, clearly identified from the video, turned himself in. Links to the video were actually posted on a number of websites by Detective Sergeant Jorge Lasso in order to identify the suspect, a tactic that is being employed by a growing number of police departments. In Mexico, police are monitoring YouTube pages set up by two sides of a drug war, who have each been posting videos featuring murders of members from the other side, many of them suggesting that organized crime was utilizing viral video. Though YouTube does not solicit footage of "sick or illegal acts," the clips were not taken down because YouTube users did not flag them. Here, viral video aided authorities by posting a violent video; however, when the video of three Melborne teenagers assaulting a girl was posted by the assailants themselves, 1,600 government-controlled schools banned YouTube for students, claiming that the content of the site supported "cyber-bullying." The push and pull that seems to accompany viral video policy has seen YouTube as an ally in the fight against crime, and at the same time, a bad influence for distributing material that some believe should be censored.

For all the threats of censorship, authorities are using viral video as more than just a tracking tool. The U.S. Office of National Drug Control (ONDC) maintains its own YouTube Channel, posting public-service videos to keep kids off drugs, and press conferences given by officials in the ONDC.

As of September 2007, 241 videos had been viewed on the ONDC Channel almost 45,000 times. A number of government agencies have been posting videos on an audience-controlled viral video site, FeedRoom.com, set up by the U.S. Government to promote educational shorts about the different agencies. The General Services Administration, Health and Human Services Department, the Pentagon, the State Department, and military branches have all participated in the viral site. The U.S. Navy posted a video educating audiences about its marine mammal program called "Sentinels of the Sea." Just as corporations have begun to adapt as their consumers transitioned to viral video, as governments and authorities become as well versed in the medium as their citizens and constituents, viral video could become one of the foremost means of communication both locally and internationally.

# **Culture** Shock

The question remains: how will viral video continue to change global culture? The average worldwide attention span seems to be rapidly diminishing, and usernames are taking the place of old-fashioned, face-to-face human interaction. "[Viral videos] are ground zero for popular culture," says Brian Graden. "It's no longer the moment on the Jon Stewart show; it's 'Did you watch the viral video of the moment on the Jon Stewart show?'" Even the nightly news references news events by video clips. For example, Senator John McCain's POW interrogation video clip, or even "Battle at Kruger," a safari video, were mentioned by Brian Williams in the cultural segment of the *NBC Nightly News* in August 2007. Despite these milestones, viral video, its technology and culture, is connecting people more than ever.

More than a new technology, viral video, and YouTube in particular, is a community of people. They are fairly self-sufficient, guardians of their own culture, and they take care of their own, providing each other with audiences, critics, and censorship. Perhaps it is because viewers can see the faces behind the usernames, or because the charm and pizzazz of homemade videos sparks relationships more than carbon-copy profiles on MySpace, but YouTube is not only the most popular video-sharing site, it is also one of the best for online networking. Living one's life virtually makes me a little nervous—you can never tell when your "friend" on YouTube will turn out to be the next Jessica Rose fakeout—but in terms of online relationships and communities, YouTube and viral video is the closest to face-to-face interaction there is. Part of being human is gravitating and searching out people you feel a connection to, and, virtually, viral video provides this human need for free on an international scale.

Viral video and popular sites like YouTube enable producers and artists to reach both more selective and wider audiences. "Now that our country is more culturally divided than ever," says Ruth Caruso, head of development at Carson Daly Productions, "we see networks struggling to find shows that have broad appeal. By tapping into the country's talent pool, we hope to cross these gaps." Viral videos are not limited geographically—the amazing and inane things caught on camera phones in Taiwan can be just as easily viewed in Paris as Birmingham, Alabama. Lev Grossman of *Time* magazine writes, "You can learn more about how Americans live just by looking at the backgrounds of YouTube videos—those rumpled bedrooms and toy-strewn basement rec rooms—than you could from 1000 hours of network television." He says it is about bringing together the efforts of the many to contribute something to culture that matters and is not factory produced by networks or studios.

By not relying on traditional media channels that have a mandate to find wide distribution for their product, viral video can support local pockets of culture. In June 2007, YouTube announced the launching of nine local channels in the U.K., France, Ireland, Spain, Poland, the Netherlands, Italy, Brazil, and Japan. "We want to create a YouTube experience that is a local experience," remarks Steven Chen. "Local sites that not only promote their communities but also speak their language." Both users and revenue-seekers among the local broadcasting channels are looking toward the future of localized viral video.

Again, one might think back to Gappers' "Pro-Am" generation in a more cultural context. Not only are amateurs professionalizing their activities through the Internet, but less corporately dominant cultures can now enter the lives of mainstream world citizens. By uniting under the banner of interconnection and viral life, smaller pockets of culture can be sustained by finding mutual support, unfettered by conformity to dominant global media.

So where does that leave us? It's really anyone's guess. What I do know is that there's never been a more exciting time to jump onboard the YouTube revolution. You can choose to be a part of it and make history. Become the next viral star or just be a silent observer. Either way, the online world will be watching.

# Glossary

**blogs** Online written journals that users update periodically for their friends or anyone else to read. Sometimes they feature photos, viral video, and even hyperlinks to other pages.

**Channel** An individual YouTube user's homepage is called a Channel.

**hyperlink** Hyperlinks are used to connect to different Web pages on the Internet. Simply click on the hyperlinked text or object, often notated by an alternative color, and a new Web page will appear. In this book, hyperlinks will be indicated by underlined text.

**pan** A pan is a horizontal camera move from right to left, or left to right.

**playlist** Users may create playlists to arrange their videos in a specific order or to share them easily with other users.

**podcast** Audio broadcast delivered to users over the World Wide Web. Think of it as radio for your computer.

**subscriptions** To ensure that you don't miss certain videos, you can subscribe to various Channels, user favorites, or tags. When a new item that matches your subscription list is uploaded to YouTube, it will appear in your Subscription center.

**tags** Words used to classify, and later, identify videos.

**tilt** A tilt is a vertical camera move up or down.

**viral video** Video content that gains popularity through email sharing, blogs, and other Internet websites.

**vlogs** Video blogs add a camera into the blogging equation. Journals are now visual and users speak their thoughts into the lens for their friends or anyone else to view.

**webisodes** Episodes of an entertainment program produced primarily for distribution on the Internet.

**zoom** A zoom is a rapid movement either toward or away from the subject being photographed. This affect can be achieved by either using a zoom lens or moving the camera on a dolly.

# Selected Bibliography

"About Terra." www.terranaomi.com/about.php.

"About Us." *PayPal, Inc.,* July 26, 2007.

Adegoke, Yinka. "YouTube Signs Broad Licensing Pact with EMI." *Reuters.com*, March 31, 2007.

Ahonen, Tomi T., and Alan Moore. "Viral Video and the Death of the Broadcast Casino." *Communities Dominate Brands: Business and Marketing Challenges for the 21st Century.* June 1, 2006.

Alexander, Andrew. "Ways to Connect Your Camcorder to Your Computer." camcorderinfo.com, September 26, 2001.

Allison, Kevin. "YouTube hopes video will make site the next big thing." *FT.com,* April 10, 2006.

Andreeva, Nellie, and Andrew Wallenstein. "Sanchez's Web Dare: FunnyOrDie." *The Hollywood Reporter*, April 17, 2007.

Arrington, Michael. "Confirmed: TV Networks Launch New Company to Counter Perceived Google/YouTube Threat." *techcrunch.com*, March 22, 2007.

Barnes, Brook. "Big TV's Broadband Blitz." *Wall Street Journal Online*, August 1, 2006.

Bartash, Jeffry. "Verizon, YouTube see a future for mobile phone." *Marketwatch.com*, November 28, 2006.

*BBCNews.com.* "Blair Launches YouTube Channel." April 7, 2007.

*BBC News Online.* "Google Buys YouTube for $1.65 Bn." October 10, 2006.

———. "YouTube Facing Football Lawsuit." May 4, 2007.

*Bigmouthmedia.com.* "YouTube Could Be in for a 'Happy' Wrist Slapping." October 2006.

Blodget, Henry. "Viacom's Joost Deal May Create Real YouTube Competition." *internet. seekingalpha.com*, February 20, 2007.

Boutin, Paul. "A Grand Unified Theory of YouTube and MySpace." *Slate,* April 28, 2006.

"Box Office and Admissions Continue Decline." *Mov-*

Broache, Anne. "SNL Cult Hit Yanked from Video-Sharing Site." *C/NetNews.com*, February 17, 2006.

"Brooke the Platypus!" *YouTube—Broadcast Yourself.* September 13, 2007.

Bryant, Steve. "NBC and Viacom Support Tur in YouTube Lawsuit." *Googlewatch*, May 7, 2007.

"Camcorders." ConsumerReports.org, 2007.

Carter, Bill. "Thanks to YouTube Fans, 'Nobody's Watching' May Return from the Dead." *The New York Times Online,* July 3, 2006.

Cashmore, Pete. "Google Buys YouTube." *Mashable. com*, October 9, 2006.

———. "YouTube Is World's Fastest-Growing Website." *Mashable Social Networking News*, July 22, 2006.

*Cherry Lane.com*, www.cherrylane.com/clpub/html/ body_newsdtl.cfm?fSYSID=85&fNewsDetail=Tru.

Childs, Craig. "Cyber Bullies Get YouTube Banned in Aussie Schools." Tech Blorge, March 4, 2007.

Cloud, John. "The Gurus of YouTube." *Time*, December 16, 2006, 4–7.

*CNN.com.* "Questions, Not Answers, Highlight Debate." July 24, 2007.

———. "The YouTubeification of Politics." July 18, 2007.

Connor, Erinn. "Networks Tuning into Concept of Online TV Shows." *The Daily Orange,* August 29, 2007.

"Cops Using YouTube to Catch Criminals." Fox News, March 4, 2007.

Crane, Dan. "Cubicle Dwellers' Funniest Home Video." *The New York Times,* March 26, 2006.

"Dabble Searches YouTube, MySpace Video, Metacafe, and More." web2.0stores.com, July 24, 2006.

Davis, Wendy. "YouTube Traffic Quadruples in First Half of '06." *MediaPostPublications,* July 24, 2006.

Delaney, Kevin J. "YouTube Finds Signing Rights Deals Complex, Frustrating." *The Wall Street Jour-*

Dreier, Troy. "The iPhone and the Future of Mobile Video." *Wi-Fi Planet,* June 22, 2007.

Eagan, Matt. "Condolences, Via YouTube." *Courant. com*, April 20, 2007.

"Esmée." www.myspace.com/esmeedenters.

*EW.com.* "EW's Entertainers of the Year." December 21, 2006.

Farber, Dan. "YouTube Going from Personal to Professional." *Between the Lines,* March 14, 2006.

*FinancialTimes.com.* "Interview Transcript: Chad Hurley, CEO of YouTube." October 8, 2006.

Finnegan, Michael and Matea Gold. "Average Citizen Is Star of Debate." *LATimes.com,* July 25, 2007.

Francia, Rubin. "YouTube: Who Will Benefit the Most?" *Techblorge.com*, March 2, 2007.

Frater, Patrick. "Thailand Lifts YouTube Ban." *Variety Asia,* September 3, 2007.

"French Soccer League, Tennis Association Join EPL Lawsuit Against YouTube." *Ars Technica*, June 6, 2007.

*Gameshout.* "YouTube Legal Issues Increase as NBC Joins the Fray." May 7, 2007.

Geist, Michael. "The Rise of Clip Culture Online." *BBC-News.com*, March 20, 2006.

Gillette, Felix. "Lorne Michaels: *SNL* Misses Its Dicks in a Box." *The New York Observer*, 2007.

Glaser, Mark. "Talent Agencies Evolve to Show Clients the Digital Money." *PBS: Mediashift,* January 31, 2007.

"Glossary for Video Formats." bhphotovideo.com.

Goo, Sara Kehaulani. "Five Months After Its Debut, YouTube Is a Star." *WashingtonPost.com,* May 1, 2006.

——. "Videos on Web Widen the Lens on the Conflict." *Washingtonpost.com,* July 25, 2006.

*Google Press Center, Press Release.* "Google to Acquire YouTube for $1.65 Billion in Stock." October 9, 2006.

Graser, Marc. "Amazon Crowns 'Queen.'" *Variety,* July 2, 2007: 3.

——. "Web's New Ad Fan." *Variety,* June 20, 2007: 1+.

Green, Heather. "Is the Web the New Hollywood?" *Business Week*, January 23, 2006.

——. "YouTube: Way Beyond Home Videos." *Business Week,* April 10, 2006, 2.

Grossman, Lev. "Creating a Cute Cat Frenzy." *Time,* July 12, 2007.

——. "Time's Person of the Year." *Time*, December 13, 2006.

Gupta, Shankar. "YouTube Supplants Google, Microsoft, Others in Video Search." *Media Post Publications,* May 25, 2006.

Hansell, Saul. "YouTube's Video Poker." *The New York Times Online*, September 30, 2006.

Hardy, Ian. "The Viral Video Online Revolution." *BBC News*, May 26, 2006, 1.

Hardy, Michael. "The Self-Made Star." *The Boston Globe,* June 27, 2007.

Helft, Miguel. "It Pays to Have Pals in Silicon Valley." *The New York Times*, October 17, 2006, 1–4.

——. "With YouTube, Student Hits Jackpot Again." *The New York Times*, October 12, 2006, 2–3.

Helm, Burt. "Viral Video Wins Top Honor at Cannes." *Business Week*, June 23, 2007.

Holson, Laura M. "Hollywood Asks YouTube: Friend or Foe?" *The New York Times*, January 15, 2007.

Hopkins, Jim. "Surprise! There's a Third YouTube Co-founder." *USA Today*, October 11, 2006, July 11, 2007, 1.

Hurley, Chad. "Interview with Brian L. Clark." *Tuning Fork 396 Views*. April 10, 2006.

——. Interview with Dennis Kneale. *Intellectual Property,* "YouTube Scores $3.5 Million." *Red Herring*, November 8, 2005.

——. "YouToo." *Forbes*, May 2005.

"Internet Phenomenon Esmee Denters Signs with Tennamen Records." *EsmeeWorld,* June 5, 2007.

Jaafar, Ali. "YouTube Sets International Channels." *Variety,* June 20, 2007, 1+.

"Joost Signs Creative Artists to Scout Out Programs." *Reuters*, May 22, 2007.

Jurgenson, John. "Movies Online: Clips." *The Wall Street Journal Online,* April 29, 2006.

——. "Television: Viral." *The Wall Street Journal*, April 1, 2006.

Karim, Jawed. "Commencement Address." University of Illinois at Champaign-Urbana, Illinois. May 13, 2007.

Kaufman, Gil. "Saddam Execution Spotlights How Viral Video Is Changing TV Standards." MTV, January 5, 2007.

Kelley, Rob. "YouTube vs. the Boob Tube." *CNN Money,* March 9, 2006.

Kuhnhenn, Jim. "YouTube to give politicians video boost." *USAToday.com,* March 3, 2007.

Kumar, Vishesh. "Candidates Prove YouTube's Clout." *TheStreet.com,* April 16, 2007.

———. "YouTube Is Still Standing Tal." *TheStreet.com,* March 1, 2007.

La Monica, Paul R. "Google to buy YouTube for $1.65 billion." *CNNMoney.com,* October 9, 2006.

———. "Time to kiss and make up with YouTube." *CNNMoney.com,* February 28, 2007.

Lashinsky, Adam. "Turning viral videos into a net brand." *Fortune,* May 11, 2006.

Lauria, Peter. "Ford Bets Models' Home Videos Are Runway Hits." *NewYorkPost.com,* July 12, 2007.

Lee, Ellen. "Online Video Sites Blend the Bizarre with the Mundane to Reshape Visual Entertainment." *San Francisco Chronicle,* March 23, 2006.

———. "YouTube's Video Boom 'a Social Phenomenon.'" *SFGate.com,* October 10, 2006.

Li, Kenneth. "Google Takes Swipe at Viacom, Talks Social Network." *Reuters Online.*

Li, Kenneth, and Eric Auchard. "YouTube to Test Video ID." *Reuters,* June 13, 2007.

Littleton, Cynthia. "Sony Flips for Clips, Conglom Hopes Crackle Pops with Vids." *Variety,* July 16, 2007.

Lombardi, Candace. "YouTube Cuts Three Content Deals." *C/NetNews.com,* October 9, 2006.

MacManus, Richard. "YouTube Nearly Doubles Traffic in May." *Read/WriteWeb,* June 27, 2006.

Maderazo, Jennifer W. "Is the Future of Television Online? Not Yet." *PBS: Mediashift,* August 10, 2007.

Maney, Kevin. "Evolution of YouTube could mark beginning of age of personal media." *USAToday.com,* June 13, 2006.

Matheson, Whitney. "Carson Daly Killed the YouTube Star." *USAToday,* June 14, 2006.

McIntyre, Douglas. "YouTube Growth Not Abating." *Blogging Stocks,* June 27, 2007.

"Mexican Drug War Finds Battle Ground on YouTube." *Reuters,* February 13, 2007.

Montopoli, Brian. "The Military Embraces YouTube." *Public Eye,* March 27, 2007.

Morrissey, Brian. "YouTube Shuns Pre-Roll Video Advertising." *Adweek,* August 22, 2006.

*Multichannel News Online.* "YouTube and the Sundance Kid." January 18, 2007.

Naim, Moises. "The YouTube Effect." *Foreign Policy,* January/February 2007.

Netherby, Jennifer. "NBC Tries Viral for Future." Video Business, July 23, 2006.

*NetRatings.* The Nielsen Company, New York, NY, July 27, 2007.

Noon, Chris. "YouTube Featuring MTV Videos." *Forbes.com,* March 3, 2006.

Petrecca, Laura. "Marketers Are into YouTube." *USA Today Online,* April 17, 2006.

*Podcasting News.* "YouTube Growth Spikes After Google Acquisition." June 18, 2007.

Prescott, LeeAnn. "The Year in Consumer Generated Content." *imediaconnection.com,* January 11, 2006.

Price, Emily. "Top 5 Video Editing Software Programs." *About.com,* 2007.

"Primetime U.S. Video Streaming Activity Occurs on Weekdays Between 5–8 P.M." *comScore.com.*

Raby, Mark. "Spike Lee Enters YouTube Competition Game." *tgdaily.com,* May 10, 2007.

Ratliff, Ben. "A New Trove of Music Video in the Web's Wild World." *The New York Times Online,* February 3, 2006.

Regan, Keith. "YouTube Scores Licensing Deal with NBA." *Technewsworld.com,* February 27, 2007.

*Reuters.com.* "Big Media Videos Play Small Role on YouTube: Study." April 4, 2007.

*Reuters Online.* "Google Takes Swipe at Viacom, Talks Social Network."

Sandoval, Greg. "French Sports Groups Join Suit Against YouTube." *C/NetNews.com,* June 5, 2007.

———. "Top YouTube Videographers Descend on San Francisco." *C/Net News,* February 17, 2007.

———. "Video of Teacher Rant Gets Students in Trouble." *C/NetNews.com,* November 24, 2006.

———. "YouTube Offers Mobile Upload Service." *C/NetNews.com,* May 10, 2006.

———. "YouTube: Too Rough for Advertisers?" *C/Net News,* April 21, 2006.

Schonfeld, Erick. "The Next Net 25." *CNN Money,* March 3, 2006.

*Scotsman.com.* "It's Likely Happy Slapping Will Run Its Course." February 7, 2007.

Seelye, Katherine Q. "Petition Urges Republicans to Take Part in YouTube Debate." *The New York Times,* July 27, 2007.

Shields, Mike. "YouTube Rocks Out with Chop Shop." *Adweek,* September 20, 2006.

Siklos, Richard, and Bill Carter. "Popularity of YouTube Brings Out the Competition." *International Herald Tribune*, December 18, 2006.

Sorkin, Andrew Ross. "Sealing the Deal, from the Handshake to the Tee-Hee." *The New York Times*, October 15, 2006.

Stafford, Alan. "The 100 Best Products of 2006." *PC-World,* May 31, 2006.

Stone, Brad. "Internet Film Feast." *Newsweek,* December 21, 2005.

———. "Is YouTube the Napster of Video?" *Newsweek*, March 7, 2006, 23, 1.

———. "The Battle over YouTube." *Newsweek msnbc. com*, October 9, 2006.

———. "Video Napster?" *Newsweek*, March 7, 2006.

Steinberg, Jacques. "Censored 'SNL' Sketch Jumps Bleepless onto the Internet." *The New York Times Online*, December 21, 2006.

"The History of Viral Video." *Tusk Magazine*, July 6, 2007.

"The Office of National Drug Control Policy." *You-Tube—Broadcast Yourself*. www.youtube.com/ondcp

*Thinkandask.com.* "YouTube Pulls Pornography, Bans Children." March 2006.

"Veoh? Vimeo Is Real YouTube Competition." *random-culture.com*, April 21, 2006.

"Viral video." *Webster's New Millennium Dictionary of English, Preview Edition (v 0.9.7)*, Lexico Publishing Group, LLC.

Wallenstein, Andrew. "Biz Not Sure How to Treat Up-start YouTube." *The Hollywood Reporter*, March 21, 2006.

———. "How YouTube Helped LisaNova Start Her Career." *The New York Times*, April 29, 2007.

Walsh, Trudy. "Feds Feed the Web." *GCN Insider*, August 6, 2007.

"Warner Music Group and YouTube Announce Landmark Video Distribution and Revenue Partnership." YouTube, 2006

"Webcams." *ConsumerSearch.com,* June 2007.

Whitney, Daisy. "YouTube Launches Sketch Comedy Contest." *TVWeek.com*, May 21, 2007.

*Wikinews.org.* "New Zealand School Children Put Fight Videos on YouTube." October 27, 2006.

Wood, Daniel, B. "Lawsuit over YouTube Video: It's What Everyone's Watching." *The Christian Science Monitor,* March 23, 2007.

Woolley, Scott. "Video Fixation." *Forbes.com*, October 16, 2006.

*Writer's Guild of America*. "Creative Rights Booklet." "YouTube Signs Licensing Pact with Hearst-Argyle TV," June 3, 2007.

*Yahoo!Finance.com.* http://finance.yahoo.com/q/bc?s=GOOG&t=2y.

"YouTube Access Banned in Turkey." *BBC News*, March 7, 2007.

*YouTube.com, Press Release.* "Warner Music Group and YouTube Announce Landmark Video Distribution and Revenue Partnership," September 18, 2006.

*YouTube.com, Press Release.* "YouTube and the Weinstein Company Premier First Eight Minutes of Lucky Number Slevin to Promote New Film," April 21, 2006.

"YouTube Opens Internet Video to the Masses." YouTube Press Release, December 15, 2007.

"YouTube Star 'LisaNova' Picked Up by Fox's MADtv." *The Daily Reel,* 2007.

*Zeller, Tom.* "A Slippery Slope of Censorship at YouTube." *The New York Times Online*, October 9, 2006.

# Index